Stephen Annett first came upon the spiritual growth movement when he was studying psychology at the University of Nottingham. He attended a Buddhist summer school, and later visited the United States and India on behalf of a meditation movement. A reporter for the Kentish Times group of newspapers, Mr Annett is married and lives in Bromley.

Edited by Stephen Annett

THE MANY WAYS OF BEING

ABACUS edition first published in 1976
by Sphere Books Ltd
30/32 Gray's Inn Road, London WC1X 8JL

Published simultaneously by Turnstone Books Ltd
37 Upper Addison Gardens, London W14 8AJ
Copyright © Stephen Annett 1976
Abacus ISBN 0 349 10071 3
Turnstone Books ISBN 0 85500049 X

Set in Linotype Times Roman
*Printed in Great Britain by Hazell Watson & Viney Ltd
Aylesbury, Bucks*

Contents

Introduction

The problems being faced by modern man in his technological wonder-world are not, as many seem to think, new. Certainly, the external trappings of the age are unique, and perhaps more complex than ever before. But fundamentally our situation is the same as our forefathers down the ages – we are struggling to come to terms with our environment, each other, and most of all with ourselves.

Foreigners seem to find the British a tolerant people who jealously guard their privacy. Few are aware of the variety of groups and societies dedicated to personal growth and evolution in Britain. Indeed most of the groups have also been content not to know about the other groups struggling for self-knowledge. This situation is rapidly changing, and behind their hedgerows and curtained windows, the British are beginning to make contact with each other in a way we have not for centuries.

To the newcomer to, for want of a better term, the 'field of human development', the groups discussed in this book must inevitably seem strange and far-out in their ideas and activities. Many of them did to me! Each offers its own particular solution to man's search for a meaningful understanding of life, often to the exclusion of others, and there is a bewildering number of possible approaches. Unfortunately it is all too easy either to be intimidated and frightened off by the language and concepts employed by them, or alternatively to dismiss the whole thing as 'cranky'.

But once one has overcome the initial language barrier, the 'New Age movement' offers a wealth of wisdom, understanding and experience to the individual who takes the time off to search for it. Each of us is unique, and consequently what we seek from life and the way we go about looking for it differs from person to person. Some strive for nothing short of God while others would be quite content with a bit of peace of mind. Some want to surrender their whole lives to the spiritual search, while others can only spare the odd weekend. This diversity of human make-up is mirrored by the groups presented in this book, and their variety of approaches and attitudes are a tribute to the richness of human experience. Together, they make a colourful tapestry of endeavour.

Britain has in its time given birth to some of the most important philosophical and social experiments. Modern examples of these can be found in each of the seven sections of this book. 'The Many Ways of Being' has two purposes: to give a broad picture of the extraordinary ferment that makes up the non-establishment spiritual state of Britain; and to help people make contact with groups that they might find sympathetic.

I would not be so foolish as to suggest that I have been entirely objective in compiling 'The Many Ways of Being', but I have at least been as fair to all the groups as I am able. I have tried to restrict myself to facts without being colourless, and I apologise in advance to anyone who feels that my prejudices and feelings have succeeded in creeping into the text in any particular cases.

My sincere gratitude goes to the members of the groups and organisations included for their kind co-operation in answering questions, providing literature and generally making the book possible. I hope they will let me have their comments, and that any groups I have overlooked will make themselves known to me so that any future editions of the book can be improved. If any other readers would like to let me know of their experiences in the New Age movement I will be glad to hear from them. Fundamentally I believe man's struggle to realise his potential is a noble one. In the words of the now famous phrase, 'if you are not part of the solution you must be part of the problem'.

My thanks to Alan Denman who did the research for the astrological and healing sections, and to Douglas Hetherington for work on the Buddhist groups and other contributions. Spencer Bright compiled and prepared the information for the development groups, and Mark Ackerman also assisted with the research. My special thanks to my wife, Kate, who provided tea and sympathy during what was often a daunting task.

Stephen Annett

Part One
The Established Societies

1 Christian Groups

There is probably no single individual who has more profoundly affected the world than Jesus the Nazarene. Born around 6 B.C. in Galilee, Jesus began his ministry at the age of thirty – only three years later he was dead. Yet his death, and reported resurrection, formed the basis for one of the world's greatest and most influential religious movements.

Virtually nothing is known of Jesus's early life. He himself never put pen to paper, and virtually all that is known about him is culled from a set of writings produced many years after his death by a number of hands. Concerning these writings, which we know as the 'New Testament', there is unabated controversy, which has dogged Christianity down the centuries. Between the third and seventh centuries controversies about the relationship of Jesus to God and to man caused a number of schisms in the Eastern Church.

In the eleventh century came the 'Great Schism' between Western and Eastern Christendom, with the Roman Church on one side and the Greek on the other. Today in the West, this legacy of a divided church is reflected in the seemingly endless number of sects and divisions which still flourish. Protestants and Presbyterians, Methodists and Modernists, Catholics and Calvinists – there is no one religion which is splintered into so many pieces.

In Britain we have seen in recent years a dwindling of the influence which the Church once held in people's lives. A majority of people in this country rarely set foot inside a church or chapel, and any moral or spiritual influence that the Church might have had is fast shrinking. The Church is seen by many as little more than a vast, institutionalised, monolithic structure, lacking all credibility. Priests and ministers are regarded as social workers and community welfare officers rather than spiritual guides.

It is against this background that we examine some of those groups of Christians who exist on the 'fringe' of orthodox religion, or perhaps it is more accurate to say offer an alternative to the accepted code of institutionalised Christianity. This is not to suggest that the institutionalised Church is entirely unaware of its precarious position. On an 'official' level, the move towards ecumenical Church unity is progressing, albeit slowly, and within the Church many individual priests and ministers are working

11

to bring about a re-instatement of the Church as an effective spiritual force.

Discussing the influence of both Eastern mysticism and the youth underground culture on society, the Rev. Ken Leech, who is an admirable example of such a campaigner, pleads in his book, *Youthquake*, for a Church which fulfils people's spiritual needs:

> 'If the Church is to recover credibility with modern man, it needs to become more, not less, theological. The priest in each parish needs to see himself as a theologian, one who points to the mystery of God ... The priest's primary function is to point men to God.'

The so-called 'Jesus Revolution', which began in America during the 1970s, was a direct result of this upsurge of spiritual interest among the young. There will not be any attempt here to analyse the phenomena which gave birth to the phrase 'Jesus Freaks' – there are many thorough accounts which do this job admirably. Suffice to say that by the time the movement spread to Britain, it had already begun to change its face. Some of the groups discussed in this section, who had their birth in the Jesus Revolution, have already moved towards the establishment position. Yet they still represent the feeling many Christians share that the time has come to look beyond the traditional orthodox Church with its rigid social rules and lack of living spiritual commitment. Alternative movements within Christianity are not new phenomena, and some older and more established alternatives to orthodox Christianity will also be mentioned. These alternatives, like the Jesus freak movements, differ a great deal among themselves. And yet they all share one dream in common – to get back to the original way in which Jesus meant us to live.

These groups represent the promise of something more than is offered in the local parish church. They offer commitment, regeneration of the spirit and renewal in one form or another. They offer a living experience of Christ, even though their philosophy and 'theology' may be at variance.

Children of God

Without a doubt, the most controversial group to grow out of the 'Jesus Revolution' is the *Children of God*, the movement which, through the vast amount of publicity it has received, represents for many what the Jesus Revolution is all about.

Founded in 1968 in California by David Berg, from the very beginning C.O.G. adopted a strict communal life-style. Its members were required, if they had not done so already, to drop out of society and join the community on a full-time basis. After setting up centres in major cities throughout America, some of the Children made their way to London, where they came into contact with a wealthy property developer who decided to support the group. In view of this, combined with increasing hostility being met by the Children in the States, C.O.G. moved its international headquarters to London in September 1971, using donated properties in south London.

The history of C.O.G. since has been an eventful one. In 1972 things came to a head – C.O.G.'s wealthy sponsor, who for a long time had doubts about the methods and organisation of C.O.G., decided finally to withdraw his support from the group. He even went as far as producing a pamphlet entitled 'Beware of the Children of God', which accuses David Berg of heresy, and attacks the movement's treatment of parents and its rejection of the system. As a spin-off from this, the media were quick to take up the attack, and press and television were soon carrying stories of the 'shocking' activities of C.O.G. Questions were asked in the House of Commons, but at no time was sufficiently documented evidence produced to show that the organisation had broken the law in any way. A demand to the Home Office for the deportation of C.O.G.'s leaders was rejected.

In the face of internationally bad publicity, the movement has continued to spread, and now operates a total of 185 colonies in sixty different countries. C.O.G. remains today as firmly opposed to the established Church as ever it was, a factor which has undoubtedly added to its opposition. It regards itself as fundamentally unorthodox and revolutionary, basically differing from the Church in its totally committed life-style.

The C.O.G. communities, or 'colonies' as they are known, form the foundation of its activities. The vast majority of C.O.G. members live in the colonies, with their wives and children where appropriate, and submit themselves to a rigorous and demanding communal life. Total commitment is required of each member, and on joining a colony one changes one's former name for a biblical one, to underline the complete transformation which accompanies becoming a member of the Children.

Emphasis within the colonies is upon sharing everything in common and surviving together, and members are expected to give up their personal possessions in accordance with Jesus's instructions. Colonies are generally kept at around twenty members, each of whom serves in a certain role and must have a trade, although each works entirely within the C.O.G. community and is not allowed to have outside jobs. Life in the colony is regulated by a schedule: breakfast is usually followed by a morning devoted to Bible study, learning and teaching, mixed with housework. The afternoons are generally spent in one of C.O.G.'s most important activities, street witnessing and the distribution of literature. Any interested people they meet are brought back to the colony in the evening, and following supper there is a period of fellowship, which includes singing, testimonies and the study of letters from David Berg, known as Moses David or more simply 'Mo'.

13

C.O.G. claims that its colonies are organised independently, each with its own shepherd who is chosen by colony members. Rules and schedules are decided upon by colony members, and each week there is a meeting of the 'colony council'. The question of who runs C.O.G. is one, however, which has caused much criticism. Many people have accused C.O.G. of having nondemocratic means of decision making. It has been stated that a strong control of the colonies is exercised by the London headquarters, who receive detailed reports of colony activities from the various shepherds. Power, it is said, rests primarily in the hands of the Berg family. All major decisions are first checked by telephone with Mo; his daughters Faith and Deborah act as roving ambassadors, staying in various colonies for short periods, and his son Hosea spends most of his time in London co-ordinating C.O.G.'s activities. But whatever the internal politics of the group, those who join it are made aware of what is expected of them, and join the group on an entirely voluntary basis.

The theology of C.O.G. is basically a Christian evangelical one which puts great emphasis on living the life of a totally dedicated Christian. Mike Nygaard explained: 'We believe that Jesus is the Son of God, and that He is the answer to all our problems. This is why we preach the gospel and sing on the streets. Our main motive is to live for Jesus. . . . Jesus was not a sweet blonde-haired pacifist, but a revolutionary, leading a band of revolutionaries.'

Another facet of C.O.G.'s activities which sets it well apart from other Christian groups, is the stress it lays on the MO letters sent around the world by Moses David, and regarded by the Children as on a par with scripture. In the same way that the letters of Paul explained the scriptures to the early Christians, so the Children claim the MO letters help them understand the Bible. They are, in other words, the modern-day epistles. The letters, often extraordinary in their style, are numerous and cover every topic under the sun, from politics to sex, sometimes in the form of poetry or a description of Mo's dreams.

Printed in the form of graphically illustrated leaflets, they come under such colourful titles as 'I am a toilet – are you?', 'Money explodes – Green pig blows bank to bits' and 'Revolutionary Sex'. These letters, avidly read and distributed by the Children, are yet another bone of contention with critics of C.O.G. Many people are outraged by both their style and content, and accusations of 'pornography' have been made of those which include explicit sexual material. The Children, however, have learnt to take such criticism in their stride, and regard both their leader and the letters he sends them with affection and regard.

The letters are often concerned with worldly matters such as politics, sociology and sex, but C.O.G. members point out that 'God is interested in everyday affairs'. Mike Nygaard describes C.O.G.'s politics. 'We do not believe that any country is righteous, but there are varying degrees, and some are better than others.

'We think that capitalism and communism are both wrong, and point as an alternative to a form of "godly socialism".

'America is the most to blame for spreading materialism, while communism too is a totally materialistic philosophy.

'The alternative of godly socialism will mean that the rising third world countries will rule the world. Capitalism and communism will both destroy each other, because neither of them have God.'

A further important belief, central to the C.O.G. philosophy, is that we are now living in the 'last days'. They believe the signs of the Second Coming are clear, and are involved in preparing themselves for the onslaught of the anti-Christ. The system, which is regarded as part of the anti-Christ, is doomed to destruction, and the collapse of America in particular is prophesied.

Overall, the Children of God are one of the most controversial groups in operation, but nonetheless, they are very open to anybody who wishes to know more about them. Accusations of brainwashing and coercion are hotly denied by members of C.O.G. 'We do not go in for high pressure sales stuff,' said Mike Nygaard. 'In the past we have had over-zealous individuals, but we have taken action over this and try our best not to pressure people.' Literature, including MO letters, will be sent on request, and interested parties are welcome to visit their nearest colony, talk to the Children, and even live in the colony for a short time if they so wish. Communications should be addressed to the London headquarters of C.O.G.

Lonesome Stone

Another group which was part of the Jesus Revolution's movement from America to Europe was first known here as the Jesus Family, later as 'Outreach for Jesus', and now calls itself *Lonesome Stone*. Founded in Milwaukee in 1971, according to one observer it has its origins 'less in a hippy background than in a somewhat more pronounced Pentecostal context'. It began as a commune, founded by Jim Polosaari, which gathered together a rock group known as 'The Sheep'. From an original group of seven, the commune grew to 120 within eighteen months, and in the summer of 1972 the decision was taken to split into four separate groups, each going its own way. Jim Polosaari decided to tour Europe with one of the smaller groups, and they visited Finland, Sweden, Germany and the Netherlands. The group failed to have any great impact, however, and it was in November 1972 that they came to England. Since then they have operated with heavy financial sponsorship from the Deo Gloria Trust, an organisation which had once given monetary support to the Children of God.

Since settling in England, the group has grown from the original thirty (which included The Sheep), to some eighty members, and contains a mixture of Americans, British and some Scandinavians. Lonesome Stone operates from two London communes, one in Bromley and the other in Norwood, and its efforts are now almost entirely centred around a rock opera, from which the group gets its latest name. The opera tells the story of a hippie who goes to California, becomes hardened by the 'scene' there, and is eventually converted to Christ, bringing his friends with him after much witnessing. Rock music is provided by The Sheep, and each show ends with the distribution of bible tracts and witnessing among members of the audience. Jim Polosaari explained the philosophy behind Lonesome Stone:

> We are dedicated to communicating to our generation, to taking our church to the people in a way they can understand through *Lonesome Stone*. We want people to enjoy life, even if they are not converted, and we realise that you have to love people where you find them. This is not a hard sell. If people are not open to responding to us then there is nothing we can do about it.

Lonesome Stone is based upon a community life-style, and, like other groups, models itself on the first-century Church, with elders, deacons and deaconesses in the community. Although life for members of the group is disciplined, there is no sort of schedule setting out times for prayer, etc. The community meets together regularly once a week, but its main concern is not to get trapped into becoming an institution.

After the show the audience are invited to stay behind and talk to members of the cast. A special room is normally set aside where coffee is served, and the cast mingle and witness to those who have stayed. The aim is to convert, but the cast have specific instructions never to be pushy. Although not part of the Church, Lonesome Stone does work with denominations in the local community which it feels are 'doing a good job'. Advance groups are sent to towns where the show is to be played, and they have the job of finding an auditorium, organising publicity, and contacting local schools, Christian groups, etc.

Those interested in the work of Lonesome Stone are always welcome to call round to one of its communes, although it is stressed that the group is not going out to recruit members. If a person feels he would like to join the group, and he is acceptable to its members, he can join either the cast or just the community. The community and the show are regarded as independent of each other, and although one may join either, the community is regarded as the more permanent of the two. Young people are welcome to call round, write for literature, or visit the show and talk to the cast.

Lonesome Stone remains, at least in its own eyes, primarily a revolutionary Christian group. 'The church is so organised that I believe it leads to death,' said Jim Polosaari.

16

Jesus Liberation Front

A Christian group which walks the somewhat precarious dividing line between the traditional Church and the Jesus movement is the *Jesus Liberation Front*. It was born from the Sunnyhill Fellowship, a non-denominational church in Hemel Hempstead, to the north of London, and was the result of an increasing response to its street evangelism. It was founded in summer 1971 by Geoff Bone and Chris Boxall, who built up a community by asking those they met in the streets of Hemel Hempstead back to their home, adjoining the Sunnyhill Hall. Eventually, more than forty young people were meeting regularly, and it was from this initial group that the J.L.F. sprang. An advertisement placed in *Buzz*, the Christian youth magazine, asked others in the country who shared the views of the J.L.F. to write, and more than six hundred replies came flooding in.

From this initial attempt to link up those of similar beliefs, an organisation claiming a membership of more than three thousand has gradually developed over the past four years. One of the J.L.F.'s biggest impacts came from its organisers' desire to use more up-to-date material to spread the Christian message. They set up an agency to sell Jesus stickers, posters, tracts and tape recordings, which proved to be a resounding success. Millions of Jesus stickers, sold by the J.L.F. were to be seen everywhere round the country, and it was this which made the breakthrough for the group.

The J.L.F. models itself on the first-century Church, aiming to return to a form of New Testament Christianity based, particularly, on the advice and guidance contained in the Epistles of St Paul.

The communal style of life was tried by the J.L.F. for about a year, but it has since been decided that this is not necessarily the most appropriate life-style.

'We felt that it was not the way God intended,' said Geoff Bone. 'Christians must be the salt in the community, and we believe the Church should be based on the family. This should, however, be an open unit, where those in need feel that they may come.'

The rejection of the commune as the basis of the Christian way of life tends to set the J.L.F. further away from the mainstream Jesus Revolution, and in fact it owes much of its support to members of traditional churches.

Although the J.L.F. does have a few 'House churches', i.e. communities of young believers including families living together, the basis of its support comes from young people belonging to a wide range of churches, such as Baptists, Methodists and Pentecostals. They join the J.L.F. because they see an active and up-dated group with which they can identify, while at the same retaining their links with their own particular churches.

J.L.F. meetings take place in a free and notably participatory atmosphere. There is a great deal of music, mainly consisting of new spiritual songs, and embracing and holding of hands is much in evidence. There is also prayer, normally of the spontaneous nature, and ministry from those 'gifted' in evangelism. Emphasis throughout meetings is on communal participation, an atmosphere in which the participants are made to feel very much part of what is going on. Although there is no set service, the leaders of the meeting have some idea of how things will go, and are able to influence things in a different direction, should they start going 'off the tracks'.

The J.L.F. believes in plural leadership, and distinguishes certain members of the community according to scriptural classes.

These are: (1) Apostles: the 'spiritual statesmen' who go in to 'open up' fresh areas. They encourage members of the congregation to express certain God-given gifts. (2) Elders: the people agreed upon by the community to be set aside to represent the body. (3) Prophets: these work for the 'edification and comfort' of the community through prophecy. They keep the community aware of God's will, and often what they say will be controversial, and serve to shake up the community. (4) Pastors: people who can teach, and also act as shepherds in the community. (5) Teachers: those who are regarded as the strongest teachers, able to 'Make the scriptures relevant and transform lives' . . . 'men of the world'. (6) Evangelists: individuals who have a gift for explaining Christ to outsiders, and drawing them into the community.

The system is regarded as evolving within the whole Christian community, and the J.L.F. feels it is part of a movement which is pulling all the churches together. Members are encouraged to stay in their own churches, and Geoff Bone was at pains to point out that the J.L.F. is not standing off from the rest of the Christian body.

Witnessing for Christ is regarded as a very important part of the J.L.F.'s work, and they teach that all members should be prepared to do this at any time. They sometimes organise 'outreach' activities, which might include public meetings, street leafleting, and door-to-door evangelism. The J.L.F. has its own bulk tape copier, and sends cassettes of music and services throughout the country. The group stresses that it is not only young people who belong to the J.L.F., and say that people are surprised at the number of older people to be seen at their meetings. The basic doctrine of the J.L.F. is something which its members feel is acceptable to most Christians, and includes the belief that the Second Coming is at hand. Talking in 'tongues' is looked upon as a spiritual gift, and sometimes occurs at meetings. If you are interested in the activities of the J.L.F., write to its headquarters at Hemel Hempstead, from where you can be put in touch with a member in your area.

Musical Gospel Outreach

An organisation which, like the J.L.F., grew out of the Jesus Revolution, but has since drawn back to the establishment Church, is *Musical Gospel Outreach*, publishers of the Christian youth magazine *Buzz*.

M.G.O. was founded in 1966 by Peter Meadows and David Payne. Peter Meadows describes its growth:

> Lots of kids in the churches were waking up to the fact that 96 per cent of the people did not go to church. This coincided with the Beatles era, and sparked off something in the kids in the churches, who started using music to spread the message.

> Five to six hundred Christian music groups sprang up all over the country, and we felt at the time there was a need for some form of co-ordination.

The co-ordination took the form of M.G.O., which issued a news-sheet, provided training, and acted as a clearing house for new Christian songs.

Buzz started as a small news-sheet aimed at people playing in the groups, and through it, training sessions and weekends were held. It has long since outgrown its original function, and now acts as an all-purpose Christian magazine aimed at the young, with a circulation around fourteen thousand. Trendy in its layout to the extreme, the magazine contains news of Christian activity, interviews and features on current problems, and also exposés and critiques on Christian and non-Christian spiritual groups. There is still quite a lot of the magazine devoted to Christian music. It regularly gives a page over to publish 'Liberation Communication', the quarterly news-sheet of the Jesus Liberation Front, and this is indicative of the amount of overlap in theology and outlook there is between the two groups.

M.G.O. also organises concert tours all over the country for Christian artists, aimed at converting non-believers, and at encouraging Christians to be positive about their faith. They also run a record company, Key Records, and act for the management side of their performers, through 'Faze Management'. Two regular annual events held at the Royal Albert Hall consist of a concert-style presentation of evangelical material. Two annual training weekends are also held, one for Christian musicians and another for Christian youth workers. There is also a *Buzz* shopping service, which offers Christian books and records.

Peter Meadows, who also acts as executive editor of *Buzz*, outlined the policy and growth of the magazine:

> The message of *Buzz* is the same as the evangelical church, but just in a different language. We are not preaching a new breed of Christianity,

but are bringing the Bible alive through modern communication methods.

The young are seeing the failure of materialism, and there is a growing desire for spiritual values. The Bible has never been more relevant, and many Christians believe that we are now coming to the climax of history, the Second Coming.

At first I think M.G.O. was a challenge to the establishment, but now we have become the establishment.

Younger Christians are not as revolutionary as they were a few years ago, and have stopped fighting the establishment. The Jesus movement has grown up. The baby must stop yelling sometime and start making some sense.

We now have more involvement with the media, and supply them with information. We also work in conjunction with other groups, such as the organisers of the Spree '73 Billy Graham rallies.

Record catalogues are available from M.G.O.'s New Malden offices, as are training brochures, concert details and lists of artists. Individual copies of *Buzz* are available from the same address, price 15p each, or an annual subscription is available for £2.46p.

The Unified Church

It is now some five years since a Christian orientated group, then popularly known as the Unified Family, came to this country from its homeland of Korea. More recently, the movement has officially registered itself as a charity, 'The Holy Spirit Association for the Unification of World Christianity', more simply called the *Unified Church*. The movement has grown up round the somewhat charismatic figure of its founder, a Korean engineer, Sun Myung Moon, who gives a written teaching called 'The Principle'. This Principle, it is claimed, clarifies and reveals the many mysteries contained in the Bible.

According to the Rev. Moon, Jesus appeared to him on countless occasions over a period of ten years. In 1946 Rev. Moon approached the Christian churches in Korea with his revelations, but the reception he received from them was so negative that he decided to take his message north – members of the Unified Church draw a parallel with Jesus, who turned north to Galilee in the hope of finding more of a response to his mission. In fact the whole life story of the Rev. Moon has many parallels with the life of Jesus, and this is undoubtedly something which the members of the Unified Church find significant. His journey north was one which went, quite literally, against the flow, as millions moved south to escape the Communist government and Red Army installed in the north. On his arrival, Rev. Moon formed an underground church, but was betrayed by one of his disciples. The church's literature tells the story:

> The betrayal was soon to come. Judas lurks within every man. The police came, and an innocent man received a terrible beating. His broken body was thrown outside the Daedong police station onto the frozen ground. Other disciples carried it away for a Christian burial. Remarkably it still breathed. In three days he began to preach again.

The underground church began once more but the Rev. Moon was once more captured and thrown into a concentration camp, where he remained for five years. In 1950, he was released when a United Nations force liberated the camp, and he returned to the south, where he founded a church which quickly spread to other towns throughout the country.

But the years of imprisonment had left a deep scar on the movement, which exists as powerfully today as then, tainting its philosophy and outlook with violently anti-communist feelings: 'Sun Myung Moon, engineer, pioneer for God, living saint and saviour is the only Christian leader who voluntarily walked with God into the capital of a Communist Tyranny to found God's Church', reads Unified Church literature. The Tongil (Unification) Church began to grow, despite opposition from the established Church in Korea. Next it moved to Japan, where, once again, in the face of opposition, an underground church was founded. Then came the move to the United States, which proved to be the foothold in the West which the Church sought, and from which it has spread across to Europe. There are now Unified Church communities in more than forty countries, and the movement claims an international following of three-quarters of a million, with four to five hundred members in this country.

The Divine Principle, which forms the basis of the movement's philosophy, aims at uniting all religions by bringing out and clarifying spiritual issues raised in the Bible, particularly those concerning the nature of Christ, God and salvation. It consists of twelve sections dealing with the ideal of creation and the fall of man, and examining the spiritual meaning of history. The Principle itself is not made freely available to the public, and the only way one learns more about it is by attending lectures run by the Church. These are given in the form of 'workshop weekends', held at the movement's headquarters at a farm near Reading – the public are invited to attend the farm for a weekend, where they can not only hear the Principle, but also experience life in a Unified Church community. A small fee of £4 per person, £6 per married couple and £2 for students is made, but this includes food and accommodation. Alternatively, the Principle can be heard over the course of two or three evenings at any of the Church's fifteen centres around the country. After hearing these lectures, in which the Principle is taught, one is allowed to study the Principle alone. It is claimed that without the lectures, the Principle is very difficult to understand.

Mike Marshall, one of the movement's leaders in this country, explained something about the Principle:

> The Principle gives pattern and coherence to the scriptures, and shows that God is working today. It is concerned with how God is changing the physical world, not just the spiritual, and shows how these two must be united.
>
> Central to the book is the idea of the family under God, where two can become one in their relationship. This is God's ideal for man – the family ideal.
>
> Men and women are the two aspects of God, the physical visible expression of Him, and He is now re-establishing the God-centred family.
>
> The theme of the family, and its distortion, is central to the analysis contained in the Principle. We are concerned with the ideal family. Not the traditional institution of the family, but a love relationship in the family situation.

In addition to study weekends at the farm, there are further study courses held during the week. And for those who wish to commit themselves more fully, there is the opportunity to move into one of the Church's centres. These are described as being similar to the communities formed by disciples of Jesus during the early days of the Church.

Worship in the communities does not adhere to any set service, but consists of meetings at which there is singing, prayers and a sermon. Each community makes its own schedule of prayer times, and a certain standard of self-discipline is required of community members. Precise details of life in a community, and what is required of an individual before he can enter one, are not forthcoming from officials of the movement – the argument given is that such facts are meaningless until the Principle is heard.

Another point which members of the Church are reticent to discuss concerns the status of the Rev. Moon himself – is he saint or saviour? Once again, the argument is that the Principle must be heard before this can be known. Rev. Moon himself asks his followers to tell people about the Principle and not about himself, and promises that when the Principle is read, one will understand who he is. It is not difficult to conclude, however, from talking to members of the movement and reading its literature, that at the very least a great deal of divinity is attributed to the Unified Church's leader.

22

Great stress is laid by the movement on creating a practical example by means of farms, businesses, schools etc., run by the movement. The Church has formed the Unified Family Singers, who have produced shows in various parts of the country, and Unified Family Enterprises, who have a printing workshop, make candles, and run a farm and an importing business. The aim here is 'to raise money for the work of the charity, and also to promote standards in business and industry that will be working at a new age.'

An additional organisation formed by members of the Church is the Federation for World Peace and Unification, which produces a weekly paper called *Rising Tide*. It is the Federation which forms the focal point for the movement's 'political' views, which basically boil down to a spiritually justified form of anti-Communism. Europe and, more especially, America, are seen as potentially the divine forces for good on earth. Their great wealth is a blessing from God, which they must use for the sake of the rest of the world. However, because their spiritual priorities are wrong, they are failing in their task, and the Church regards itself as the movement which will correct this imbalance.

Communism is regarded as an increasing problem in the West, and this is 'God's judgement on man'. It is thought to be a philosophy which completely destroys the spirit, making man materialistic, self-centred and without hope. The Western world is 'privileged in God's eyes', and therefore has the responsibility of preserving spiritual values.

Those who wish to know more about the Unified Church should contact the movement's headquarters at Reading. You may then arrange to attend a workshop weekend, or alternatively be put in contact with your nearest centre.

The Pentecostal Church

A movement separated from the orthodox Church by virtue of its emphasis on the experience of spiritual baptism, is the *Pentecostal Church*. Pentecostal is, in fact, a generalised term applied to a group of religious bodies who stress the importance of experiencing the Holy Spirit, or 'baptism by fire' as it is sometimes known. The very name Pentecostal is taken from the phenomenon experienced by Christ's disciples on the day of Pentecost:

> And when the day of Pentecost was fully come, they were all with one accord in one place. And suddenly there came a sound from the heaven as of a rushing mighty wind, and it filled all the house where they were sitting. And there appeared upon them cloven tongues like as of fire, and it sat upon each of them. And they were all filled with the Holy Ghost, and began to speak with other tongues, as the Spirit gave them utterance. *Acts* 2, 1–4.

This description forms the foundation of the Pentecostal belief that there is an experience of God, subsequent to conversion, which is of the utmost significance. The experience takes the form of the baptism of the Holy Spirit, as described in *Acts*, and its climax is a phenomenon known as 'speaking in tongues'. It is the stress which the Pentecostal movement places on spiritual baptism and 'tongues' which distinguishes it.

The phenomenon of 'tongues' occurs when a deeply religious individual is possessed, supposedly by the spirit of God, and like those described in *Acts* begins to produce utterances, which may be coherent or incoherent. Tongues is presumed to contain a message, even if the words appear to be unintelligible, and someone gifted with what is known as the 'interpretation of tongues' is often required to translate what is uttered.

The history of the phenomenon of tongues in the Church is an interesting one. At Pentecost it was regarded as a sign of the indwelling of the Spirit, and *Acts* indicates that speaking in tongues shows conversion and commitment to Christ. In time the Church came to expect 'tongues' to be manifested, virtually demanding it as a sign of possession of the Holy Spirit. It became regarded as a sort of sacrament, and entered the early Christian services at times other than baptism and conversion. The phenomenon of tongues has virtually disappeared from the modern orthodox Church, but many of the more recent Christian movements, attempting as they do to return to the days of the Early Church, have turned again to tongues. The Pentecostal movement, although much older than some of the other groups we have discussed, similarly models iself on the first-century church.

Towards the end of the last century there was a growing feeling among the Church that a revival was in order, and at the same time manifestations of a similar nature to those described in *Acts* began to take place. Pentecostalists pointed out the supernatural and divine occurrences that are described in the Early Church, and argued that there is no reason to suppose that such phenomena are limited to biblical times. Many Pentecostal centres sprang up throughout the country, basically fundamentalist in belief, coupled with an intense pre-millenarianism and expectation of a Second Coming. Healing was frequently practised, as were the 'spiritual endowments' we have already mentioned. But the claims of Pentecostalists, particularly those relating to baptism in the Holy Spirit, caused widespread opposition from the more orthodox body of Christian belief and practice, with the result that Pentecostalists united in separate bodies. In 1924 these various bodies or 'assemblies' came together to form the organisation known as 'Assemblies of God in Great Britain and Ireland', and it is this organisation which still represents the Pentecostal movement today.

The Bible is the infallible word of God for a Pentecostalist, and study of it is given prominence: it is the embodiment of truth, and the exper-

24

ience of the Holy Spirit is in no way meant to supercede its usefulness and validity. Pentecostalists tend to take a straightforward, literal attitude towards the Bible. They believe it is divinely inspired throughout, providing a guide to all aspects of life. It is maintained that the biblical story of the Fall is fact, in which man was marked out as morally responsible for his own actions. Only by the salvation of faith can man be saved, and Pentecostalists believe this takes place in stages. Firstly, by 'conviction', the individual gains a sense of sinfulness; then follows 'contrition', which is sorrow for sin and longing for salvation. Finally the name of the Lord is called upon through prayer and faith. Redemption takes place through the atoning death of Christ, 'regeneration' is the name given to the re-birth which results from the operation of the Holy Spirit towards God and 'illumination', in which lives are changed by Him. 'Sanctification' takes place when a sinless life begins, and finally 'glorification' occurs when we become like God.

Baptism by immersion in water is another practice which distinguishes the Pentecostal Church. Originally, of course, total water baptism was undergone by Christ himself, and according to Pentecostalists the practice has undergone considerable distortion, until it has reached the status it has in the orthodox Church today. They are particularly opposed to infant baptism.

Following the acceptance of Christ in the Pentecostal Church, baptism by total immersion in water is regarded as a public symbol of commitment, as the forerunner of the more important spiritual baptism. The Pentecost is a repeatable experience, it is claimed, through which all true Christians pass.

The symbol of this spiritual baptism is almost always speaking in tongues, a phenomenon which has been explained by non-believers as resulting from religious excitement. There are also a number of other spiritual gifts apart from speaking and the power to interpret tongues, and these include prophecy, supernatural insight into the spirit realm, the performance of miracles, and healing. Healing is widely practised in the Church. During Pentecostal services, letters are read asking for healing help, and all present pray for recovery. Towards the end of the service all those in need of healing are asked to approach the front of the church, where, to the background of hymn singing, the minister passes along the line of sick. He lays his hands on each, as is traditional among many types of healing groups, and prays for their recovery in the name of Christ. The sacrament of the Lord's Supper is also a highly esteemed Pentecostal practice, and the breaking of bread and partaking of wine are considered to be important for the true Christian.

Services take place in the sort of atmosphere which is distinctly communal, in which everybody is encouraged to take part. Shouts of 'Praise the Lord' and 'Amen' are often heard in response to the prayers and preaching of the ministers, and some churches hold special meetings at which ordinary members of the congregation are asked to preach on particular topics of faith. Hymns, bible readings, silent prayers, and fiery sermons all have their part to play in what is largely an unstructured service. Music is normally provided by members of the congregation, and hymn music tends to be of the lively revivalist sort. Ministers will end their sermons by pleading with those present to accept Christ. This is normally the emotional peak of the service, and gives the revivalist and evangelical movements their flavour.

The Pentecostal Church is intensely evangelistic in outlook. The Assemblies of God have a special 'Home Missions Council', whose job it is to establish Pentecostal churches in areas where they do not already exist, while every Pentecostal church organises its own form of local evangelism, including rallies, street evangelism, and door-to-door witnessing. There is also much stress placed on missionary work abroad, and the Assemblies of God have an overseas mission council which selects missionaries, handles the not-insignificant funds set aside for missionary work, and generally supervises work abroad.

Each church within the Assemblies of God is autonomous, and will send its own delegates to a district council, which in turn is part of the general council. Literature about the Pentecostal Church can be obtained from your local assembly or from the head office of the Assemblies of God, who will also be pleased to put you in touch with your local assembly. Visitors are always welcome to go along to their local Pentecostal church, to take part in the services, and to become more fully committed as the spirit dictates.

The Quakers

In many senses diametrically opposed to the views and practices of the Pentecostal movement, on what we might call the 'liberal' or 'left wing' of Christian belief, we find the *Society of Friends*, otherwise known as the Quakers. Deeply opposed to proselytism, Quakers are lacking in the evangelical zeal which is the hallmark of the Pentecostalists. Their whole philosophy is based on the understanding that it is first-hand experience which governs an individual's religion, that it is a matter very much for the individual to discover for himself.

A brief look at the history of the movement throws much light on its present-day structure. Quakerism (a nickname which has stuck for over three hundred years) arose in Britain during a time of considerable religious unrest. Its founder, George Fox, at the age of nineteen, became disillusioned with the gap which existed between Christians' professed beliefs and the way in which they lived, and over the course of four years he travelled from religious group to group, seeking help. Finally, in 1647, after reaching a point of despair, he had a realisation which was to spur him on to found the Quaker movement. In his own words:

26

'... when all my hopes in them and in all were gone, so that I had nothing outwardly to help me, nor could tell what to do, then, oh then I heard a voice which said 'there is one, even Christ Jesus, that can speak to thy condition'.

The teaching which Fox gave was a simple one, and stressed that the divine spirit dwells in every man. Because of the immediacy of Christ's teaching and guidance, there was, Fox claimed, no need for ordained priests, consecrated buildings or outward sacraments. Stress was laid on the need for personal experience, and worship took the form of quiet, expectant, communal gatherings, where God's guidance was awaited, either through silence or through the spoken word. The religion taught by Jesus was thought of as a loving way of life, which should enter day-to-day living.

The Quakers' extreme opposition to a 'hireling ministry', along with their refusal to take oaths or pay tithes, led to persecution at all levels. Parliament passed the Quaker Act (1662), under which many Friends suffered various legal sentences and more than 450 are thought to have died in prison as a result of the Act. In the 18th century the Toleration Act brought an end to the worst persecution, although many disabilities remained. Because of their refusal to take oaths, Quakers were effectively barred from holding public office, or entering Oxford and Cambridge universities. As a result, Quaker intelligence became concentrated in industry and commerce, and when combined with the frugal Quaker way of life and the Society's stern discipline in cases of bankruptcy, small family businesses were quick to grow. Huntley and Palmer, Cadbury, Rowntrees and Horniman are some of the firms originally founded by Quakers. Their reputation for integrity also led neighbours to entrust them money for safekeeping, and out of this grew Quaker banks such as Lloyds and Barclays.

In the nineteenth century tension grew in the Quaker movement between the Quietists' tradition, representative of the conservative wing, and the evangelical tradition. By the beginning of this century there were three discernible movements within the Quaker tradition: (1) the orthodox meetings, which were both pastoral and formal; (2) the 'conservative' meetings, which not only followed the traditional form of Quaker worship, but also the older customs of speech and dress; and (3) a group of Hicksits meetings, rigorously separated from the rest of the Quaker movement for seventy years, interested in 'modern thoughts', and regarded suspiciously as being what we might now term 'revisionist'.

Since the First World War, however, the barriers have gradually been broken down, until today there is a union of all Quaker meetings.

Throughout their history the Friends have rejected the idea of 'creed'. They believe that creeds tend to 'crystalise thought on matters that cannot be embodied in human language' and also restrict the search for a more adequate expression of truth. Creeds are also thought to act as a

27

barrier to many who might otherwise enter the fold of Christianity, and their absence in the Society of Friends means that Quakers represent a far wider range of individual thought and belief than might normally be found within one denomination. For Friends, being a Christian does not entail conformity to doctrines or observance of forms, but 'an overwhelming sense of the nearness of God through the indwelling spirit of Christ'. It is this emphasis on personal experience of God which is the point of departure for Quaker belief, and it was on this that Charles Fox built the Society. He felt that he had rediscovered primitive Christianity, and proclaimed: 'Christ has come to teach his people himself'. This contrasts with a Christianity which had for centuries been dependent on the infallibility of Church and Bible. While rejecting the priestly tradition, Quakerism also rejects total dependence on the Bible as the source of Truth in favour of personal experience of divinity.

In accordance with its lack of doctrine, the Society has never required its members to conform to any particular view about the historical Christ. A wide range of views of Him is therefore to be found among Quakers, some merely accepting Him as a great religious teacher, others regarding Him as something more than this. There are also many Friends who are sceptical about accounts of the physical resurrection of Christ, while for others this is a crucial element of faith. Another factor which distinguishes Quakers from the rest of the Christian Church is their lack of external sacraments. They believe in spiritual baptism and communion, and claim that the whole of life should be a sacrament. They interpret Christ's command 'Do this in remembrance of me' as applicable to every meal, rather than the institution of a symbolic act which is unnecessary for those who claim to experience Christ vividly in their daily lives. In the same way, Quakers do not baptise, and stress that true baptism is not one of water but an inner one of fire and spirit. They point out that Christ himself did not perform baptism. In the same vein of thought, Friends do not generally observe major Christian festivals, preferring to maintain that every day is the Lord's Day, every week Holy Week.

We now turn to the mainstay of the Quaker way of life, the 'Meeting for Worship'. Meetings require no specially 'consecrated' premises, and can just as well be held in a hired hall or private house as in the Meeting Houses which are owned by the Society. They may be held at any time and on any day, but for convenience Meetings normally take place on Sunday mornings. They are held in simple, sparsely furnished rooms, with seats or benches arranged in a circle, hollow, square or oblong. All the trappings of ordinary churches and chapels, including crosses, organs and pulpits, are notably absent. No prayer books are used, no hymns sung, and there is no order of service. Neither are there any priests or ministers, but people sit silently in what is described as 'silent expectancy'. It is out of this silence that communion with God and with each other grows, and it is claimed that the silence of the Meeting provides an ideal setting for the exploration of 'the most profound levels of our existence, and also for the realisation of our loving partnership with others present'. Occasionally somebody will be moved to give a brief spoken contribution, known as a 'ministry'. This will be of an entirely spontaneous nature, and will normally involve a person in talking about something significant, which he has realised within his own spiritual life, using his own words, ideas and feelings. What he says is thought of as being spoken on behalf of the Meetings and accepted by them, because the speaker has been sensitive to the spirit of the Meeting. Occasionally, somebody may choose to read a passage from the Bible, but there are no set Bible readings as such. Overall, the meeting is as spontaneous as possible, and pre-planning is positively discouraged.

It is at a Quaker Meeting that one can gain first-hand experience of what Quakerism is all about, and no amount of written description can replace this. The Society of Friends welcomes new people who are broadly in sympathy with its attitudes and aims, although it is not keen to gain 'converts' merely for the sake of increasing its membership. Those who wish to know more about the work of the Society can write to its London headquarters, who will send literature together with the place and time of the nearest Meeting.

Names will never be sent to local Friends unless an enquirer specifically asks to be put in touch with them. In recent years informal day and weekend conferences have been arranged to give enquirers the opportunity to learn more about Quakerism, and meet and talk with Friends. Enquirers are also always welcome to attend their local Meetings, and talk with Quakers there. Once somebody has been attending a Meeting regularly for some time, they may then wish to become a member, in which case elders or any other members of the Meeting will be pleased to discuss the matter with them. There is then a simple membership process, whereby the aspiring member or 'attender' writes a letter of application to the Clerk of the Monthly Meeting, equivalent to the local governing body. The Monthly Meeting will then arrange for two Friends, one of whom knows the attender, to visit him in order to establish a personal relationship. In this atmosphere they will attempt to discover something of the applicant's feelings and experiences, and answer any questions or problems he may have. They then report back to the meeting, which will usually accept the membership of the applicant. Occasionally the attender may be asked to postpone his application, and only rarely will membership be refused.

The Christian Community

In 1921, a group of young Lutheran ministers in Germany believed that a profound renewal of Christianity could come through the ideas of Anthroposophy (see p. 113) so they approached Dr Rudolf Steiner, who said that religious life could only be renewed through the sacraments. The Christian Community that was thus founded, could not have been formed without Dr Steiner, yet he did not found it. It exists alongside the Anthroposophical Society in Great Britain but separate from it.

The sacraments, as Rudolf Steiner showed, particularly the Eucharist, are deeds to be enacted to establish a communion between the spiritual world, mankind and the earth. When a ritual is celebrated, something happens. The emphasis of the Christian Community is to encourage a new sense of individual dedication and commitment through the experiencing and sharing of the sacraments, and of meditative prayer.

There is a priesthood which conducts the regular services or 'Acts of Consecration'. The Christian Community has at present fifteen congregations in Britain. They are essentially non-exclusive and are quite open to members participating also in other religious groups. In its way the Christian Community, though not as well known as the Quakers, has quite as distinctive and modern a flavour.

The Mormons

The Church of the Latter-day Saints, or 'Mormon Church' as it is nicknamed, is perhaps the largest and most influential religious sect to grow out of America. Although basically Christian, accepting both Christ and the Bible, Mormons are distinct in following the teachings of their prophet and founder, Joseph Smith Jr. This includes acceptance of *The Book of Mormon*, which their founder is said to have discovered and translated. The book is regarded as being on a level of scripture with the Bible. For any real understanding of the Mormon Church one must know something of its background and history, the story of which is fascinating, and doubtless responsible for attracting many to Mormonism.

It was in 1820 that Joseph Smith, at the tender age of fourteen, experienced his first religious revelation. The boy had been influenced by a religious revival taking place locally, and after reading the Bible is said to have realised the need to approach God directly. He was confused, however, as to the best way in which this might be achieved, and was unsure about the varying claims of the many denominations which existed. He went to a grove of trees in Upper State, New York, to pray for guidance, and saw the figures of two glorified men, God the Father and Jesus Christ. He was told that he need not join any existing denomination, but was instructed to prepare himself to become the prophet of a Church which would 'aid the restoration of the pure gospel of Jesus Christ'. When he returned home and told the story of his experience, he was persecuted and criticised by his neighbours who regarded the boy's claims as bordering on heresy. In fact, this earliest reaction was an indication of things to come, for the Mormon Church is distinguished in American history by the vast amount of persecution it was forced to undergo.

Three and a half years later, Joseph received a second vision while at prayer in his bedroom. The figure of an angel, who identified himself as Moroni, a prophet, appeared to him. The angel told the boy of the existence of certain records engraved on gold plates, hidden in a hill near his home. These records were, he claimed, the history of a people originally from Jerusalem, who were the ancestors of some of the American Indians during the period 600 B.C. to A.D. 421. It was not until 1827 that Joseph finally unearthed the golden plates, which were contained in a stone box along with a strange pair of spectacles and a sword. It took Joseph two months to translate the plates, which were written, or so it is claimed, in a mixture of ancient languages, including Hebrew and Egyptian, which the Mormons call 'reformed Egyptian'. At first the translation was done with the aid of the mysterious spectacles, which were in fact two stones mounted in a spectacle frame. It is said that when Joseph wore the glasses he was able to decipher the text of the plates, but that after some practice, translation could be carried on without them. The plates were translated aloud by Joseph, while an assistant, sometimes his wife, transcribed his words.

It is these texts which go to make up the *Book of Mormon* which gives the Church its nickname. They are so called because it is said that it was a man called Mormon who inscribed the plates, which are an abridgement of the writings of a number of men, including Mormon himself. Among the writings of the book is the story of how Christ visited North America after His ascension. *The Book of Mormon* was first published in 1830 after which the plates were taken away by Mormon, although not before they had been seen by eight witnesses. The first Church was established in Fayette, New York, with a few who accepted his testimony gathering there, and missionaries were sent to convert the Red Indians, with some success. From the very beginning, however, Smith's movement was bound to meet opposition and 'Joe Smith's Golden Bible' began to spread, resulting in constant persecution.

The 'saints' gradually grew in number, and settled in Kirtland, Ohio, where the first Latter-day temple was built. But the growth of the Mormon community aroused political and religious tension among its non-Mormon neighbours, and the Mormons were forced to move on. Around the same time another Mormon community was growing on the banks of the Mississippi where a new town, designed by the prophet himself, was laid out and called Nauvoo. Founded in 1840, the town soon became one of the largest cities on the American frontier, with a population in excess of 15,000.

Throughout the growth of the Church, Smith himself had been no less a target of persecution than the movement as a whole, and was arrested more than thirty times on various charges. Once again, after settling into Nauvoo, persecution was just around the corner, and the growth of the

Mormon community, linked to Smith's growing political power, finally took its toll. The fatal step came when Smith, as mayor of the city, closed down a newspaper which he claimed was a public nuisance, but which was actually an anti-Mormon paper which had been campaigning against Smith's power and calling for a revocation of the city's very liberal charter. The destruction of the newspaper presses, on Smith's orders, brought a state of mob violence uncomfortably near, and in response to this Smith called out the city's militia to keep things in order. This was the final move in what many saw as a political challenge to the state government, and even to the presidency itself, by the Mormon community. Smith's political power was too real to be allowed to continue unchecked, and he was arrested for treason in 1884. He was removed to a state prison, along with some of his leading followers, under a pledge from the state governor that they would be protected. The pledge was broken, and a mob attacked and broke into the prison in which Smith was being held, and he and his brother, Hyrum, were shot dead.

Following the death of Smith, the leadership of the Church was taken over by Brigham Young, who was responsible for laying the foundation of a permanent home for the Mormon community. Forced out of Nauvoo, some 30,000 Mormons made a mass exodus west, travelling 1,400 miles across a vast unsettled wilderness. Seventeen months later they arrived in remote wasteland in the valley of the Great Salt Lake. 'This is the place – move in,' Young told his followers.

Mormons believe there are two sources from which doctrines spring. Firstly through the written word of God, and secondly through direct revelation from God to man. We have already mentioned that Mormons accept the Bible, both the Old and New Testaments, and also the *Book of Mormon* as being the word of God. There are also two other volumes, both written by Smith, which are similarly regarded. One of these, *Doctrine and Covenants*, is a record of 130 revelations received by Smith, most of which deal with the way of life which Church members should follow. They lay out details for the organisation and government of both Church and community. The *Doctrine* also includes an important instruction known as the 'Law of Health', which instructs members to refrain from the use of tobacco, alcohol, tea and coffee, while encouraging them to eat grains, fruit and wholesome herbs. The revelations talk about the world after death, as well as dictating the life-style to be adopted in this one. The fourth written source of doctrine, known as *The Pearl of Great Price*, consists of records of revelations given to Moses and purportedly revealed to Smith. There are also some writings of Abraham, which, it is claimed, Smith translated.

Regarding direct revelation, Mormons believe that there is continuous revelation between God and man, in which impressions are made on his mind through God's spirit. Every member of the Church has the right to receive divine guidance through revelations relating to their own personal life, but the President of the Church is the only individual who may receive revelations for the guidance of the Church as a whole. For this reason he is regarded as a seer, and his pronouncements are accepted as God's word.

Mormons maintain the apostasy of the Christian Church after the death of the apostles, and claim that the Church as a whole has lost its authority. The restoration of the priesthood and the 'Keys to the Kingdom' came, they believe, to Smith and some of his associates, and has been handed down through the leadership of the Mormon Church. Even today, Mormons challenge all other denominations who officiate in the name of God. They say non-Mormons do not have the authority to carry out ordinations, and challenge the right of other denominations to baptise and bless the sick.

The Church of the Latter-day Saints has more than fifteen temples throughout the world, one of which is near London, and it is in these that some of the most important work of the Mormon faith is carried out. They are regarded as very sacred places, so much so that even a Mormon may not attend one until he has proved his worth during a probationary period following baptism. Baptism for the dead, a sort of 'baptism by proxy', is one aspect of the work performed there, and is aimed at those who have died without having a full opportunity to hear and accept the gospel during their lives. After death, according to Mormon teaching, the individual enters the spirit world to await the resurrection. While there, all are taught the gospel and given the opportunity to accept or reject it. Rejection of the gospel after death does not lead to hell, as one might expect, but results in the cessation of progress on the spiritual path, which is hell in itself. Marriages, known as 'sealings', also take place in temples, and it is believed that these are literally eternal ties, which bind the couple together after death, as well as in this life.

The ultimate aim for a Mormon is the union of spirit and body, and it is thought that resurrection in an immortal body and an everlasting life with one's loved ones follows death for those who lead a righteous life according to gospel teachings. Universal salvation will take place when all men are resurrected through the atonement of Christ, and this is connected to the Mormon belief in an imminent Second Coming, when the dead will be resurrected to live again in a golden age. Mormon meetings are simple affairs, which take place in centres built more as community centres than churches. This underlines the central role which the Church plays in the life of the Mormon community. Although most Mormons no longer live in exclusively Mormon communities, the Church is nonetheless regarded as the mainstay of social life, and is organised in such a way as to respond to this. There are Mormon Sunday schools, educational institutions and primary associations for the young, relief societies for women and mutual improvement associations for teenagers, with the Mormon 'way of life' stressed throughout. This Church influence on all aspects of life is negligibile in the Mormon community in this country, compared to the United States and Salt Lake City, where the Church acts as a government, a social services organisation, a cultural and sporting board, as well as many other roles.

The government of the Church is carried out by the President, who is regarded as the only revelationist on Church matters, and is traceable in direct line back to the first prophet. He is advised by two councillors, and all three figures hold all Church authority. Below these leaders come twelve apostles, who have the same authority as the President and his advisers, but hold it only as a group. When the President dies, it is the eldest of the apostles who takes over the leadership. The Church has no professional clergy, but regards all its male members as worthy of priesthood. The normal age of entry into the lesser or 'Aaronic' priesthood is twelve, and it is the responsibility of this priesthood to deal with temporal matters. Spiritual affairs are dealt with by the higher or 'Melchizedek' priesthood, which is entered, only by the worthy, at eighteen or nineteen. Within the lesser priesthood there are the roles of deacon, teacher and priest, while within the higher there are elders (who deal with welfare matters, home teaching and the visiting of families) and high priests (who deal with work to the dead), and 'seventies', who are the missionaries.

Mormon churches have the character of community centres, and house sporting, cultural and social activities. Simple services are also held there on Sunday evenings, and are similar to Methodist or Baptist ceremonies, but carried out by a lay clergy. There is no set service of prayers, and no hymn and prayer books, but hymns and songs are sung, addresses given, invocation made and the sacrament given. The Church does baptise its followers, but rejects infant baptism with the argument that children are already saved by the atonement of Christ. Baptism, therefore, only takes place above the age of eight, and is carried out through total immersion and the laying on of hands. This latter act is regarded as a 'baptism of fire', in which the gift of the Holy Ghost is given, and it is only after a water and fire baptism that a person is regarded as belonging to the Church.

Most Mormons are very missionary conscious, and believe that their Church will eventually envelop the earth. Many young Mormons volunteer for full-time missionary work, men for two years and women for eighteen months. This work is normally undertaken around the age of nineteen for men, possibly a year or two older for women, and is regarded as an important part of spiritual training and preparation for later married life. The heads of the missions are normally older and more experienced men, but all major posts in the mission outside America, and certainly in this country, are held by teenagers and those in their early twenties. The missionaries live together in small centres, adhering to strict schedules and life-styles involving full-time missionary work, study and prayer. There are seven missions in the British Isles, one in Ireland, one in

Scotland and five in England, and within the missions, centres are spread widely throughout the country, covering most major population areas.

An introduction to the Mormon faith is given to those who are interested in the form of a set of seven lessons, which cover aspects of the Mormon religion such as the role of Joseph Smith, life after death, final resurrection, etc. These are normally given at home and the Mormons prefer to talk to whole families wherever possible. In this country, however, people sometimes prefer to go to the Mormon chapels and centres for instruction, and this is arranged where more convenient. Those interested in knowing more about the Church of the Latter-day Saints can write to the Secretary at the London headquarters, from where their address will be forwarded to the nearest centre. A member of the Church will then call to arrange lessons.

Christian Science

A group which looks to the Early Church for its initial inspiration, although not in the same sense as some other Christian groups, is the Church of *Christian Science*. Although it does not attempt to return to the early Christian way of life as such, it does regard itself as representing the recovery of certain emphases which were current at the time of the primitive Church, in particular the emphasis on healing. Healing is the cornerstone of Christian Science, but it is important to understand that healing is by no means solely what Christian Science is about. Furthermore, the term 'healing' is employed in its broadest sense. Although healing of the physically sick is a central part of the Church's ministry, healing also extends to the mending of 'family and business problems, of social injustices, intellectual limitations, psychological tensions and moral confusions'.

The Church of Christ, Scientist, was founded in the latter half of the nineteenth century by a New England woman, Mary Baker Eddy. Following an unhappy life in which widowhood and illness were both features, she began to seek for a more complete understanding of God, and in 1866 had a revelation which was to form the basis of the Christian Science philosophy. While suffering from the effects of a serious accident, she was healed while reading in *St Matthew* 9 of Jesus's raising of a man suffering from palsy. Flooded with the presence and power of God, she found that she, too, was able to rise from her bed healed. The story might well have ended at this point, had she not determined to understand the power which healed her.

In 1875 her study came to fruition with the publication of her book, *Science and Health with Key to the Scriptures*, which has since become the basic textbook of Christian Science. Four years later she met fifteen of her students and decided to organise a Church which would reinstate

35

the relatively forgotten practice of healing which Jesus practised. In a few years the Church took its permanent and present form as The Mother Church, The First Church of Christ, Scientist, in Boston, which together with its branches throughout the world forms the Christian Science denomination.

The basic tenets of Christian Science are:

1 'As adherents of Truth, we take the inspired Word of the Bible as our sufficient guide to eternal life.

2 'We acknowledge and adore one supreme and infinite God. We acknowledge His Son, one Christ; the Holy Ghost or divine Comforter; and man in God's image and likeness.

3 'We acknowledge God's forgiveness of sin in the destruction of sin and the spiritual understanding that casts out evil as unreal. But the belief in sin is punished so long as the belief lasts.

4 'We acknowledge Jesus's atonement as the evidence of divine, efficacious love, unfolding man's unity with God through Christ Jesus the Wayshower; and we acknowledge that man is saved through Christ, through Truth, Life, and Love, as demonstrated by the Galilean Prophet in healing the sick and overcoming sin and death.

5 'We acknowledge that the crucifixion of Jesus and his resurrection served to uplift faith to understand eternal Life, even the allness of Soul, Spirit and the nothingness of matter.

6 'And we solemnly promise to watch, and pray for that Mind to be in us which was also in Christ Jesus; to do unto others as we would have them do unto us; and to be merciful, just, and pure.'

Although Jesus's ethical teachings are accepted by Christian Scientists in much the same way as in the orthodox Church, there is, nonetheless, a very distinct theology attached to Christian Science. The fact that familiar Christian terms, such as 'Christ', 'God', 'salvation', etc., are employed by Scientists may prove to be misleading, and it should be borne in mind that very distinct and unorthodox definitions are applied to these words. The term 'Christ', for example, is not synonomous with Jesus, although He did, it is believed, manifest 'Christ' fully. Christ is the 'Wayshower', and it is through Him that salvation is obtained. But 'salvation' is in no way a 'magical deliverance from sin'. According to Mrs Baker Eddy: 'The way to escape the misery of sin is to cease sinning. There is no other way'. Thus the Bible is basic to the study and belief of Scientists, but always in the light which *Science and Health* throws on it.

Perhaps the most basic assertion made by Mrs Eddy was her denial of the reality of the phenomenal and material world, and of the existence of evil. In *Genesis* it is stated that man was created in the image of God, and that He pronounced all that He had made 'very good'. Man in the image of God must be wholly spiritual and perfect; therefore, it is argued, it must follow that the sick and sinning mortal who appears to us is a false representation of the real man. It is when we grasp the falseness of the apparent man, put aside this material sense of him and 'put on the new man', that 'healing' takes place. The core of Christian Science is, therefore, the rejection of the material, imperfect and evil world for the 'reality' of God's perfect creation. It was because of Christ's ability to perceive the 'real' man that healing was possible: 'Jesus beheld in Science the perfect man, who appeared to him where sinning mortal man appears to mortals. In this perfect man the Saviour saw God's likeness and this correct view of man healed the 'sick'. In this way the 'Science' of which Christian Scientists talk draws an absolute distinction beween the divine mind, God, and the false mentality which most people possess. For Christian Scientists, spiritual healing is not a question of 'faith healing'. What is required is that the individual should turn understandingly to God, whose nature he understands through Christ. To know God as Truth is to look beyond material appearance to spiritual reality, and glimpse the true nature of the man He has created. Healing is simply the result of the change from material-mindedness to spiritual-mindedness, from self-centred to God-centred thinking.

But healing is only regarded as incidental to the larger purpose of coming to know God, a by-product rather than the ultimate aim of a Christian search for God. Yet Scientists regard it as the most obvious proof of the validity of their belief, and consequently give it an important place in the Church. Every Christian Science church holds regular mid-week meetings in which spontaneous testimonies of healings are given. Verified healing stories are printed in nearly all the Church's periodicals, and the last hundred pages of *Science and Health* consist of testimonies by those who have been healed by simply reading and studying the book. The Church carries out healing through its own accredited practitioners, and there are even Christian Science nurses, qualified to look after the sick, but who give no medication. Christian Science sanitoriums are also sponsored by the Church. Stress is always laid on total reliance on Christian Science healing, and medical assistance is frowned upon.

Government of the Church is determined by the *Church Manual*, as divinely revealed to Mrs Eddy. It states that a board of five directors should administer the affairs of the Church, and when a vacancy occurs it should be filled by a person elected by the remaining members of the Board. Each branch of the Church has its own democratic government, and is only subject to the Mother Church in matters pertaining to the *Manual*. A Christian Science 'society' is a branch of the Church which has not yet attained church status. The Church has no clergy, and anyone, without distinction of sex, may rise to any position. Services are conducted by a First and Second Reader, elected by the church membership, for a limited period of time only. Sunday services consist of the reading of Bible passages, followed by correlative passages from *Science and Health*. There are twenty-six subjects which Mrs Eddy chose for these lesson sermons, each of which are repeated twice a year, although the citations chosen to illustrate them are varied.

It is important to say that Christian Science is a way of life, which determines the day-to-day attitudes and behaviour of its followers. Through discipline it attempts to develop serenity, encouraging an optimistic outlook as most favourable to the functioning of the organism. It is, according to Mrs Eddy, mental and spiritual factors which determine our health.

There are Christian Science reading rooms throughout the country, where you can drop in to read more about Christian Science – the addresses of these, along with the address of your local Christian Science church, will be found in the telephone directory. Visitors are always welcome to attend services, although it may be best to phone first in order to check dates and times. Alternatively, write to the head office in London, who will send you Christian Science literature, and help you to locate your nearest church.

The Unity School

The term 'Christian Science' was originally used to describe a much larger movement of 'Christian metaphysics' which grew up in America in the latter half of the nineteenth century. Sometimes known as 'New Thought', many varieties of healing groups grew up around the general sort of philosophy described under Christian Science, although each differed in emphasis and possessed its individual features. One Christian metaphysical group still active today is the *Unity School of Christianity*.

Unity, like Christian Science, was founded as the result of a miraculous healing, when in 1886 Myrtle Fillmore attended a lecture in Kansas City on 'New Thought'. She was seriously ill, but as she left the hall the thought 'I am a child of God and therefore I do not inherit sickness' stuck in her mind. The idea, common to most Christian Science groups, transformed her self-concept, and she gradually became cured of a disease which had dogged her all her life. It was as a result of this cure that Myrtle, with her husband Charles, founded the Unity School.

Describing the cure, which took two years to complete, Mrs Fillmore outlined the way in which thought is employed to bring about healing:

> How do we communicate intelligence? By thinking and talking of course. Then it flashed upon me that I might talk to the life in every part of my body and have it do just what I wanted. I began to teach my body and got marvellous results. I went to all the life centres in my body and spoke words of truth to them – words of strength and power. I did not let any worried or anxious thoughts into my mind. I let a little prayer go up every hour that Jesus Christ would be with me and help me to think and speak only kind, loving, truth words.

In this way Mrs Fillmore believed she had discovered a law of healing, which she employed with those who came asking for help. Gradually her husband, Charles, also came to believe in the ideas which his wife held. A man who had long been interested in philosophy and religion, Charles became the philosopher of the Unity School, articulating a philosophical framework for its beliefs, and also providing the major part of its biblical interpretation. Unity was so called because it claimed to 'borrow the best from all religions'. It did not require its students to sever their connections with their own churches, and it maintained a 'liberal' outlook. Those taking part in Unity were invited to accept what they found to be true and reject the rest, and no particular idea or practice was forced upon them. They were welcome to practise Unity's healing in conjunction with other forms of medical treatment if they so wished, and although its founders were both strict vegetarians, they did not insist that their students should follow this example.

Prayer is an important element in the Unity scheme of healing, and this is generally undertaken in groups, who gather for absent healing sessions. They are taught to relax in mind and body, to turn all thoughts to God, and to think of Him rather than of their individual problems. In order to help students maintain concentration on the power of God, they are taught to use affirmations and denials, which are repeated over and over. The words themselves have no particular power, but continued concentration on them enables the student to realise the Truth contained in them.

Unity claims there is power in unified prayer, and for this reason meets together in groups, which pray for individuals all over the world. It is estimated that Unity receives six hundred thousand requests for prayer every year, and although many of these deal with physical healing problems, the majority deal with emotional problems.

Throughout their lives the Fillmores claimed that they were establishing a school rather than a Church. They taught that man has in him divine potentials far beyond any that he usually expresses, the potentialities of the Christ. They believed that throughout the body there are spiritual centres, and that by concentrating on these in prayer one can realise the spiritual force contained in them. Charles wrote a book on this idea, *The Twelve Powers of Man*, in which the centres are named and described. Both Fillmores regarded Jesus as the Son of God, the Master, who demonstrated His Sonship in His life, acting as a perfect channel of God's power and love. They claimed the teachings of Christ had been misunderstood for centuries, and thought of Unity as a return to the original teachings. A twenty-four-hour prayer vigil is maintained at Unity headquarters, and all requests by telephone or letter are answered. Regular weekend courses are run at Unity House, as well as at various points round the country, and guests are welcome to visit the centre for a period of rest and renewal. There are local study classes and prayer groups, and a postal library for books and tape-recorded talks. Unity produces a large amount of printed literature of various types which will be sent on request. All enquiries should be addressed to Unity House.

Science of Mind

A third group belonging to what we have loosely defined as the 'New Thought' movement is the *Science of Mind* centre in Bournemouth. Although it does not operate in this country as a Church as such, the Centre is associated with a number of Religious Science Churches in America which teach the same philosophy. Adhering to the basic tenets of Christian metaphysics, the New Thought Centre stresses what is commonly called the power of positive thinking, reiterating the claim that creation is dominated by eternal law and order. Founded some eleven years ago, the Science of Mind teaching is based on the principle that there exists only one infinite creative intelligence which permeates everything. This is the only mind which exists, although it expresses itself individually through each of us.

Science of Mind teaches that the ideas emanating from this one mind adhere to the laws of cause and effect, stressing the truth contained in the Bible that 'As a man thinketh in his heart, so he is' – in other words, thought makes us what we are. Thus negative thoughts produce negative results, while positive thinking, backed up by absolute conviction, produces positive experience. For the adherents of Science of Mind this is an exact law, which can be harnessed to produce the desired results.

By teaching an individual to handle his own thoughts, Science of Mind claims a man can begin to control his own fate. As long as he believes, and denies all doubt, he is able to control his own experience, and in this way lose his helplessness.

A number of practical techniques are taught to enable such 'positive thinking' to be applied to everyday life. This includes a special form of affirmative prayer, in which the power of mind is directed, rather than a power outside beseeched. By making positive, definite statements it is claimed that the subconscious mind has no choice but to respond in a positive way, because it adheres to an exact law in a mechanical way.

The Science of Mind centre holds regular meetings for lectures and discussion at 3 p.m. on the first, second and fourth Sundays of every month, except August and September. Like most Christian metaphysical groups, it also practises healing, and the services of its healing ministry are available for anybody. There is also a library of metaphysical works available to members. In addition to the Sunday meetings, the Centre holds classes for students who wish to study Science of Mind in more depth – these form the preliminary stage for those wishing to attain ministerial status.

The President of the Centre, Mrs Kathleen Green, is also willing to lecture to interested parties, but these would have to be not too far from Bournemouth.

Association for Promoting Retreats

The idea of 'retreat' is usually associated with priests, monks and nuns who withdraw from the world in order to pursue a totally spiritual life. In fact there has been a movement in this country for over sixty years to encourage lay people to make retreats, to spend some time living in a spiritual atmosphere, away from the day-to-day pressures and responsibilities in an environment of peace and quiet.

In 1914 the *Association for Promoting Retreats* was founded, in order to encourage people to make retreats, and also to persuade the Church to support more retreats. Although, at the time, the Association was entirely a Church of England affair, the Roman Catholic Church was simultaneously sponsoring the same kind of development. The Quakers are the third main group with a long tradition of retreats, although these differ from the Catholic and Church of England concept of retreat, in that they generally involve groups of people going off to pray together. These three groups are the only Christian organisations which have 'purpose built' buildings available for retreats. About half the Anglican retreats are run by religious communities, while the other half are the responsibility of the diocese in which they fall. All Catholic retreats are owned and run by religious communities, while Quaker houses tend to be reserved for the specific purpose of retreat and conferences.

In 1969 the Association became inter-denominational, and since that time its approach has tended to be heavily ecumenical. Every six months it publishes a journal called *The Vision*, which it now shares with the Catholic National Retreat Council. *The Vision* consists mainly of a list of retreats available over the coming six months, but also includes reports from various conferences, meetings and retreats, and also articles on prayer, meditation and silence. The Christian basis of the Association is reflected in the journal, which is written by and aimed at Christians, although 'liberal' in its approach.

The Association is financed entirely by its members, who pay an annual subscription of £1, for which they receive copies of *The Vision* twice a year. Although membership is open to everyone, the 4,000 or so members are predominantly Anglican, and almost entirely Christian. However, the Association caters for anybody who is interested in retreats, either as individuals or as members of a religion. All the retreat houses are run by Christians but anyone, from Buddhists to atheists, may make use of them. In fact, although *The Vision* contains only Christian houses, the Secretary of the Association does try to maintain records of retreats run by other religions, such as Buddhists and Jews.

Traditionally, the retreat is silent, with little or no discussion except perhaps for talks on various spiritual topics given by the retreat conductor. There are, however, other traditions of retreat, and nowadays there is more experimentation with group participation within the retreat situation. Modern retreats are sometimes led by teams rather than individuals, with stress laid on shared experience through prayers and meditation. Many more people using retreats now are uncommitted to any religious belief or church.

Basically the retreat is a period of withdrawal from everyday life, which may go on for twenty-four hours or a number of days, or even weeks. It may consist of either a shared experience of God, or an individual deepening of personal relationship with Him. Silence is generally an essential ingredient, and discussion, where it does take place, will normally be at a deeper and more spiritual level than usual.

There are two basic types of retreat houses among the hundred or so available in this country. Firstly there are the larger houses, which cater almost entirely for groups, whether they be parish groups, professional groups, or even yoga groups. Groups book the house, and once installed are allowed to do what they like with the facilities, organising their own timetable administered by their own leaders. These large houses may also provide open retreats, where the leaders are provided and individuals can book in to take part. The second type of house is the private retreat, which is usually run by a small religious community. Visitors go as guests of the community, and while normal community life goes on around them they can choose whether or not to take part in these activities. The monks or nuns of the community will generally make themselves available if you wish to talk to them, but if you prefer to remain alone they will certainly not force their attentions on you.

This second type of retreat is becoming more popular, as more and more people prefer silence and contemplation to organisation. There is, in fact, a widening of interest in retreats, particularly among the uncommitted and the young, who may be drawn to prayer and meditation, but not necessarily through Christianity. There is also a growth of interest among committed Christians, who recognise the importance of sharing and community life. The retreat offers a spiritual environment, where Christians can meet together on a deeper level.

Although all retreats are happy to have non-Christians staying, it should be pointed out that some are better at handling them than others. An important function of the Association is to put people in touch with the right sort of retreat, and free advice and guidance are available from sympathetic staff. Be warned, however, that some of the more popular houses are booked eighteen months in advance. Advance bookings are not so important for the smaller retreats, but these do tend to get quite full in the summer, particularly if they are situated in the middle of beautiful countryside. Although *The Vision* contains lists of the houses available, the magazine is more suited to those interested in group bookings. Individuals might be better advised to contact the Association directly for advice.

Generally, retreats are excellent value for money, with the all-in cost of twenty-four-hours' stay varying from £2 to £3. Some do not even have a fixed charge, but ask people to pay what they can afford. A recent article about the Association in *The Daily Telegraph* brought more than 650 telephone enquiries, which gives some idea of the extent of growing interest in retreats. Almost fifty thousand people retreat every year, and interestingly enough about three-quarters of these are women.

Some retreats are able to cater for families, while others have leaders available to undertake counselling. If you are interested in going on, or organising, a retreat, contact the head office of the Association, who also publish a number of booklets on various aspects of retreat.

The New Church

Emmanuel Swedenborg, a Swedish mystic, philosopher, scientist and theologian, was born in Stockholm in the late seventeenth century. In his early years he travelled through Europe studying mathematics and the natural sciences, and his status as a scientist is attested to by his publication of Sweden's first scientific journal. In 1740 he became interested in anatomy, physiology and psychology, and undertook a detailed study of the brain. His avowed purpose in this work was to locate the soul, which he wanted to prove was immortal. In fact his whole interest in physiology was based on his interest in the body as the 'kingdom of the soul'. He was later to describe this early work as 'the years of preparation'. From 1743–5 Swedenborg underwent the early stages of what has been described as a 'protracted spiritual and emotional crisis'.

During this time he received three visions of Christ, and became convinced that he had a divine commission to give the world a new religious dispensation. His *Journal of Dreams* gives a detailed report of his spiritual experiences, including his first vision of Christ in 1744, as well as descriptions of dreams recalled from earlier years. In 1745 Swedenborg received a definite call to abandon worldly learning, and for the remainder of his career he devoted his time to interpreting the Bible and relating his experiences of the world of spirits and angels. On several occasions he is reported to have manifested clairvoyant powers, and claimed to be in continual communication with spirits for thirty years. Besides his Biblical commentaries, he also published a number of formal theological treatises, producing thirty bulky volumes, all written in Latin, between 1749 and 1771. He died in London in March 1772.

Swedenborg taught that because man had strayed so far from the truth, the Lord himself had allowed himself to be born through mortal woman. Thus, central to his teachings, was the rejection of the doctrine of Christ as the Son of God, and also of the Trinity. Also rejected were the Church's teachings on vicarious atonement, the devil and eternal punishment. Swedenborg proclaimed that God forever manifested in Christ spiritual freedom and responsibility, and that eternal life is an inner condition which begins at the start of earthly life. Man, individually and collectively, undergoes an evolution of stages in spiritual development, in which gradual redemption comes about through personal regulation of spiritual states. Also stressed is the need of practical love in all relationships.

Swedenborg himself never aimed to found a new cult or sect, but gave his books to influential figures in the hope that they would gradually disseminate his new revelations. Nonetheless following his death a body of those who read and accepted Swedenborg's writings did spring up, and were known as the Church of the New Jerusalem. Although the Church itself is not vast in size, it is generally accepted that Swedenborg's work has had a wide and considerable influence.

Swedenborg's followers regard the Second Coming as having already occurred in 1757, when the interior meaning of the Scriptures was revealed to him. Thus they claim that his teachings overturn and recast the former religious beliefs, and view the new dispensation as having the same relationship to the New Testament as the New Testament has to the Old. Within the Church of the New Jerusalem (or New Church) Jesus is directly worshipped as God, and is regarded as Creator, Redeemer, the Word and the Revelation. The usual view of the Trinity is reversed, with its concept of approaching God through Christ. Rituals within the Church are similar to the Anglican, but with obvious variations in interpretation – for example, baptism is regarded as forming angelic associations.

The New Church teaches that salvation is the deliverance not from the consequences of sin, but from sinning itself. Atonement is not, as in the traditional Church, regarded as the reconciliation of God to man, but of man to God. The idea of chance is rejected out of hand, with the teaching that Divine Providence rules all things, in this world and elsewhere. Stressing the reality of the spiritual world, the reality of life after death is also taught, with the understanding that all men are immortal. All are also created for heaven, and those who love goodness and serve God will go to heaven where they will be eternally happy. Only those who choose to lead an evil life will go to hell, of their own accord. Judgement is the disclosing of character, and our final fate following death is dictated by our simple desire to 'be with our own kind'. As we have said, the New Church believes the Second Coming was effected when Swedenborg revealed the spiritual sense of the Bible, and claims it is the fulfilment of John's vision, when he saw the New Jerusalem coming down from God out of heaven, and heard the divine declaration, 'Behold, I make all things new'.

The largest New Church body in Britain is the General Conference, which has more than forty churches throughout the country. The Church also runs study circles in a number of centres, and provides literature to interested parties. Addresses of local churches and further information can be obtained by contacting the *New Church Enquiry Centre* in London or *New Church House* in Manchester.

An organisation independent of the New Church, although obviously linked with it, is the *Swedenborg Society*. Founded in 1810, the main purpose of the Society is to translate, print and publish works of Swedenborg, and to make them known to the general public. It also maintains a reference and lending library at its headquarters in London, where there is a reading room open to members and friends.

The Society organises occasional meetings, lectures and conferences to promote the work of Swedenborg. But its work is largely concerned with the printed word. As some of its literature explains: 'The New Church, if it is to be anything, must be a reading Church, and it is vital that the works of Swedenborg be kept in published form, so that they are there for men to read.' The Society is not a missionary organisation, and annual membership costs £1. For further details of the Society, and a catalogue of publications, contact the London headquarters.

2 Eastern Oriented Groups

Hinduism

Of all the world's religions, Hinduism is probably the most difficult to define simply because it lacks dogma, allowing the individual a wide degree of personal religious belief and practice. Lacking a founder and a creed, to state what a Hindu is presents a virtually impossible task, and the situation is further confounded by the fact that throughout its history the philosophy of Hinduism has varied, sometimes admitting certain concepts and approaches which were later replaced. The roots of the religion seem to stretch back as far as three thousand years before the birth of Christ, and the word *hindu* itself is Persian, meaning simply 'Indian'. Thus Hinduism is the religion of the Indian people, and it is estimated that approximately one in nine of the world's population is a Hindu. Of those spiritual groups which have found popularity in the West, it is probably fair to say that the vast majority have a Hindu foundation, and even if they do not label themselves Hindu, many of them introduce Hindu concepts and ideas into their philosophy.

Hinduism is at once a way of life and a highly organised social and religious system, but to the Westerner the social aspect is of little more than passing interest. The brand of Hinduism taught in the West tends to concentrate on the spiritual and metaphysical aspects of the religion, largely disregarding the social structures traditionally allied to it. The reasons for this are self-explanatory, as there would be little interest for the Westerner in a teaching which concerned itself with a caste system with no meaning outside a Hindu society. Indeed, even within India itself, there has been widespread rejection during this century of the caste system, as witnessed by the reform movements which reached their zenith with Mahatma Gandhi.

It was these movements which denied formal and institutionalised Hinduism, reasserting in its place the spiritual essence of the religion. Thus where at one time it would have been possible to define a Hindu as one who observes his caste duties, this no longer holds true. Within the vast and apparently incoherent religious complex of Hinduism, dogma has never held much sway. There are, however, certain essential beliefs which underlie the various manifestations of Hinduism, one of which is the belief in an Absolute which permeates creation. This is the equivalent to 'God', is called Brahman, and is essentially neuter and abstract. Brahman is formless, although many Hindus believe he may take form and descend to earth in order to fulfil his purpose. He may manifest himself in any form, at any time and at any place, and in this way the Hindu accepts the idea of God incarnating in human form. There is also the belief that this is not the first time that God has created the world, but that he is continually creating and dissolving the world as well as individual bodies.

A central distinguishing concept in Hinduism is that of reincarnation: the belief that the spirit is a continuous entity. Just as a person changes his clothes, so the Hindu believes that the spirit changes bodies. It cannot die, but when the body it is occupying dies, the spirit is born again elsewhere. Closely related to this is the idea of karma, which teaches that every action has its reaction (i.e. 'whatsoever a man soweth, that shall he also reap'). Thus the soul is reincarnated into a new body according to the actions of the individual in his previous incarnation. It is karma which leads the soul from body to body, until the individual reaches a point of spiritual development where he becomes purified, and realises God.

This liberation from the cycle of rebirth is called *moksha*. The complete union of the spirit with God, of the individual self with the Universal Self, known as *mukti*, is the aim of the Hindu. Hindus also believe in the oneness of life, i.e. that life is essentially one, although it takes many forms. For this reason, the majority of Hindus are vegetarians, refusing to hurt any creature in order to obtain their food. Almost all Hindu-based groups encourage their followers to take up a vegetarian diet.

Hindus believe in the absolute authority of their scriptures, the most ancient of which are the four Vedas. These four books, containing 20,000 hymns, are said to have been given to the first four human beings. As well as prayers, they also contain descriptions of rituals, and traditionally their commands cannot be questioned. They are a sort of natural law within themselves. More popular are the later scriptures, such as the two great Hindu epics, the *Ramayana* and the *Mahabharata*. Perhaps best known in the West is the *Bhagavad Gita* (Song of God), which is the teaching given by Lord Krishna to his disciple, Arjuna. These later works are widely available in various translations and are worth looking at for the insight they give into Hindu beliefs and lifestyle. Also available are the Upanishads which are more on a par with the Vedas, but are very beautiful and appealing.

No discussion of Hinduism is complete without mentioning the 'guru' or teacher, literally, the one who takes us from darkness into light. The importance of the guru, who is notably missing from most of the world's religions, is clearly described by a fifteenth-century Indian saint, Kabir, who says: 'In the midst of the highest heaven there is a shining light; he who has no guru cannot reach the palace; he only will reach it who is under the guidance of a true guru.'

For most religions revelation occurred at one particular point in time, with the coming of the religion's founder. But for the Hindu the situation is very different. He believes that there are continually on the earth self-realised persons, with whose aid it is possible to achieve liberation. They are always there to provide inspiration, and in the face of complex ideas and philosophies act as intermediaries in resolving problems of doctrine. Outside these questions of belief and knowledge, there has always been a strong strain in Hinduism which stressed the importance of achieving liberation through 'bhakti', or devotion. It is believed that through pure love of God the mind can be cleared of doubt, bringing about union with God. It is this aspect of Hinduism which has placed the guru in a position of importance, as he often becomes the focus for the disciple's devotion.

There are many varieties of guru, but basically he is a person who has achieved a high spiritual state, and is able to help his disciple to attain similar heights. Although some gurus are little more than teachers in the normal sense of the word, others are known as 'Satguru', or true teachers. These are considered to be the embodiment of truth, the teacher of reality, who answers the disciples' need for surrender. They are the living truth, able to unite the disciple with God, and claim total devotion and surrender.

Often the guru succeeds his own guru in an initiate chain stretching back, sometimes over centuries. He usually initiates his disciple in some way, traditionally by giving him a mantra (*anavi*). This is usually given in secret, and becomes the centre of the disciple's spiritual strivings (*see* Transcendental Meditation). The guru may also give some other technique in his initiation (*see* Divine Light Mission). *Sambhavi* and *shakti* are other forms of initiation which may be given. The first comes about through some contact between the guru and the disciple – a chance word or glance – which invokes a divine revelation. The guru's own divine power (*shakti*) may also enter the disciple unexpectedly, and the physical presence of the guru is not necessary for this to take place.

Many of the Eastern groups operating in this country also adopt the guru-disciple relationship, although sometimes this is adapted to meet Western conditions. For many the concept of the guru, involving as it does the 'worship' of another human being, is a difficult one. However, as with many of the ideas discussed in this book, it is only through personal experience that a true judgement can be formed. For many Western disciples it is a case of 'to know him is to love him'.

As Christianity has its official and institutionalised face, so too does Hinduism, and this is probably best represented in Britain by the *Hindu Centre* in London. Before 1962, despite the immigration of large numbers of Hindus to Britain, there was no organisation which represented

48

and served the interests of the community. In particular, many Hindus were concerned at the lack of facilities where they could pursue their religious practices. For this reason, a number of elder members of the community formed the Hindu Centre, which organised regular Sunday religious meetings in hired church halls. In 1968, the Centre took over its own permanent building, which includes a meeting hall, shrine room and library.

Representatives from the Centre present the Hindu point of view to a number of official bodies (e.g. U.N. Religious Advisory Committee, I.L.E.A. Religious Advisory Council). On the spiritual side, the Centre has a full-time Hindu minister, who is able to perform all the Hindu religious ceremonies, including marriage. As well as celebrating the Hindu Holy Days and Festivals at the Centre, there are regular Saturday meetings, between 7.30 p.m. and 11.00 p.m., which include lectures on the scriptures and the singing of devotional songs.

The Centre's priest, Dr Sharma, also carries out quite a lot of work outside, performing ceremonies and delivering lectures on Hinduism throughout the country. This is an important part of the Centre's work, and those wishing to arrange for a speaker should contact Dr Sharma at the Centre. It is also possible to arrange for parties to visit the Centre itself, where the Sunday proceedings may be witnessed. In addition, the Centre distributes large quantities of booklets and literature on Hinduism to interested parties, and once again, all queries should be addressed to Dr Sharma at the Centre.

Periodically, special classes are organised to teach yoga, Hindi and Sanskrit, and occasionally special groups examine a particular Hindu scripture in some depth. All activities at the Centre are open to anyone, and there is generally a friendly and welcoming atmosphere. There are Hindu temples up and down the country in most major cities where sizable Hindu populations are gathered, and generally visitors are welcome to attend. For details of your nearest temple, write to the Hindu Centre in London.

The *Sai-Hindu Centre* is a similar organisation, but is dedicated to the Hindu saint, Sri Sai Baba of Shirdi, who died in 1918. A simple, uneducated man, Sai Baba gave an essentially non-sectarian teaching which stressed the importance of faith in human relationships and in man's attitude to God. He also taught his followers that while they followed their own religion they should above all serve humanity, without restriction of caste, creed or religion, and this is reflected at the Centre. It aims to provide a service which will be acceptable to all Hindu sects, and towards this end of 'universal Hinduism', many different Hindu gods are represented in the statues and pictures which decorate the Centre.

The Centre was founded in 1965 by an elderly Indian woman devotee of Sai Baba who received a vision in which she was asked to open the

Centre in a small semi-detached house in Golders Green. It was felt by devotees that Sai Baba's following in this country was sufficient to warrant the Centre, and it now draws its membership largely from the Indian community. The Centre claims a membership of over one thousand, about half of whom live in the locality. Spiritual discourses are held every Sunday evening at 7.00 p.m., and meetings also involve the singing of devotional songs.

The Centre is at its best during the special festivals which are celebrated, and these often attract large numbers of people. Largely social gatherings, these are colourful events involving singing, music recitals, and the performing of religious rituals such as Arti, with lots of nice food thrown in for good measure. If you would like to visit the Centre, it is advisable to write first or telephone for details of any special events that may be coming up. Otherwise you are welcome to attend any of the Sunday evening *satsangs*.

An expansive Hindu sect with a following of more than twenty-five thousand in Britain is the *Swaminarayan Hindu Mission*. The Mission, which has been operating in this country since the early 1950s, draws its membership from Indians and East African Asians, and operates internationally in India, North America and throughout East Africa. It claims to be the largest Hindu religious organisation in the U.K. with a large temple in north London, branches in major cities throughout the country, and plans to purchase properties in towns such as Wellingborough.

The basic tenet of the Mission's faith is the belief in a continuous succession of divine incarnations in the movement's leaders, ever since Swami Sahajananda (now known as Lord Swaminarayan) in the nineteenth century. Swaminarayan is regarded as an avatar who incarnated for the sake of his disciples' salvation. Since then, successive heads of the movement have been regarded as Divine, including the current head, Shri Pramukh Swami, who is fifth in line. He became the movement's head in 1971, after the death of its former leader, and according to followers has, since then, 'begun to manifest divine attributes'.

Another distinctive feature of the movement is that its leader and his monks uphold a rigid code of absolute celibacy, which goes as far as avoiding contact, or even looking at women. The theory is that the monks are set apart from all normal relationships between the sexes in order to ensure their sexual energies are sublimated to their spiritual progress. It must be stressed, however, that the rule of celibacy is strictly limited to the monks, and that householders are encouraged to lead a normal family life. At the same time, the movement claims it was among the first Hindu sects to accord a respectable status to women, ordaining women preachers as early as the mid-nineteenth century.

The Mission is trying to set up a Joint Hindu Council which will bring together all the Hindu groups operating in the U.K. It is also pushing ahead with plans to extend its own organisation by starting up new branches and strengthening existing ones. Services at the temple in London are open to the public, and visitors are also welcome to go along to meetings of the movement elsewhere in the country. In the first instance, those who wish to know more are recommended to write to Mr Praful Patel, chairman of the movement, at the London temple.

Krishna Consciousness

Any visitor to London's West End in the last few years has probably come across the Krishna Temple – it is hard to avoid. The devotees of Krishna are young, shave their heads (girls excluded), wear saffron robes, and constantly sing and dance. They are to be seen every day, weaving their way through the traffic, the tourists and the shoppers, chanting the praises of their Lord, Krishna. They also go in for 'personal encounter' conversation, with evangelical fervour. The devotees will tell you the praises of Krishna and invite you to buy the literature they carry.

Krishna is the most common form of God worshipped in India, and is the basis of the Hindu religion. He is said to have lived about five thousand years ago, and the story of his life is told in the pages of the *Gita*. *Krishna Consciousness*, as its followers usually call it, was brought to the West by His Divine Grace, A. C. Bhaktivedanta Swami Prabhupada, the spiritual Master of the movement. He had been converted to Krishna while a student in India, and rose to the head of the branch of Hinduism that we now know as Krishna Consciousness. For years he felt an inner call to spread the message of Krishna beyond the East, but always resisted it, feeling the task to be beyond his capabilities. However, in 1965, at the age of seventy, he set out on the spiritual pilgrimage of his life. The path of the guru from India to America was a well-worn one by the time he trod it, but never before had a seventy-year-old man left the comforts of a high position and set out almost penniless. He landed in New York with hardly a cent to his name, and his only luggage was a caseful of literature about his Lord. He knew nothing of the American culture, and began to spread Krishna Consciousness by the traditional Indian method of approaching people in the street and singing the praises of God.

Perhaps it was this strength of devotion that attracted followers to him. But whatever the reason, he worked hard for the success Krishna Consciousness enjoys today. After a year he was able to afford a room in a waterfront tenement where he would sit and chant. But the noise of the tiny silver cymbals and bells he used to accompany his devotions were too much for the upstairs neighbours: they poured boiling water through the floorboards on top of him.

His earliest followers quite literally lived in the gutter. But in contrast, in America today the movement is rich. The Los Angeles-based Spiritual Sky incense factory finances it, and it can afford to run a free school for

51

members' children from all over the world.

In Britain, this success has not been paralleled. Krishna Consciousness first came into prominence when one of the Beatles, George Harrison, became interested. The basis of the movement's devotional activities is a simple chant, known as the Maha, or great, Mantra. It goes: 'Hare Krishna, Hare Krishna, Krishna, Krishna, Hare Hare', and is repeated, substituting Rama, the name of the second most popular Hindu deity, for Krishna every second verse.

Harrison got them a record contract, and their Mantra made the Top Ten. It was followed by an equally well selling L.P. Apart from the enormous publicity – the movement performed their hit on several TV shows – the records made a lot of money. With the proceeds, Krishna Consciousness was able to offer free meals, and sometimes accommodation, to those who would follow them from the *maya* of the West End back to the movement's temple in Bury Place.

At a time when mantras, drugs, music and general 'freedom' were at a peak, the life-style of Krishna Consciousness was enormously popular. Great feasts, particularly on a Sunday, were held, with much singing, dancing, and festivity. But the money ran out and so did the fair-weather friends. Until last year times were tough and only the genuinely devoted stayed. Then Harrison again lent a helping hand. He bought the movement Bhaktivedanta Manor, a large country house set in seventeen-acre grounds, and devotees were able to live there in peace.

Following the example of their spiritual master, many of them set out on the road each year, armed with records, leaflets, books and the standard saffron anorak in case rain strikes. Apart from London, the movement is well established only in Edinburgh.

If you do make it to a centre, the routine will probably be similar to the Bury Place Temple, which is open from 4.30 a.m. to 9.30 p.m., and longer if your interest is strong enough. You can talk to the residents and ask questions. Off the streets and on home territory, a lot of the frantic evangelical style goes out of the devotees and they show up as friendly and very human.

To move into a temple, only the desire is necessary (followers can also live 'normal' lives). Once inside a temple, there are four basic rules: (1) No animal foodstuffs (excluding milk products, which are highly recommended); (2) No intoxicants (which includes tea, coffee and cigarettes); (3) No illicit sex life (i.e. outside marriage); (4) No gambling.

Those that live in the temples support themselves by donations and selling literature (printed by the movement on its own presses in America), or else by packing incense. Those that live outside the temples work at normal jobs, but try to make their homes as much like temples as possible.

The devotees wear Jappa beads similar to rosaries around their necks. But instead of chanting Hail Marys, they work their way round the 108 beads (with number 109 as the starting point), chanting the Maha Mantra at each bead. This is done a minimum of sixteen times a day. They also study the *Bhagavad Gita*, but only use the 'As It Is' translation written by their Master. They claim it is the only accurate one.

The day starts at four in the morning and vegetarian food that has been purified by being offered to Krishna is eaten. This ceremony of eating sacred food is known as *prasadam*. The morning devotions are open to the public, but visitors are encouraged to come in the evenings between 7.00 p.m. and 9.00 p.m. There they experience chanting, dancing, and what is called 'deity worship', where the temple idols are glorified.

The life-style of the Krishna Consciousness movement can be summed up by calling them practisers of Bhakti Yoga. *Yoga* means to link with, and *bhakti* devotion. So they aim at reaching the Supreme, Krishna, through devotion. They also expect that the time for the deliverance of the world is at hand, when Krishna will come swooping out of the sky in a great fiery chariot to rescue them. This is the reason for their shaved heads and topknots: they believe Krishna will pluck them up by the hair, and that if they have a good, long topknot he will not drop them.

Further information can be obtained by writing to Bury Place or Bhaktivedanta Manor. The movement employs a small full-time staff to answer queries and to send out literature.

Divine Light Mission

There can be few people in this country who have never heard of the *Divine Light Mission* or its teenage spiritual leader, Guru Maharaj Ji. This is due partly to the considerable amount of attention paid to the movement by the media, and partly to the evangelical zeal of its followers. There can be few towns in Britain which have not been plastered with pictures of the Mission's head, whom the press have dubbed 'the chubby faced boy God'. Every day Guru Maharaj Ji's followers, known as 'premies' ('lovers of God'), took to the street selling the Mission's newspapers and distributing leaflets telling of the peace of mind which, they claim, Maharaj Ji is able to give. They organised scores of public meetings, which in London were held seven nights a week, at which colour films of the Guru were shown, and glossy magazines containing his discourses were on sale. In the summer of 1973, a spiritual festival organised by the Mission and attended by Maharaj Ji attracted capacity crowds of more than fifteen thousand for three days running. In fact, it is probably true to say that in this country the Divine Light Mission is the nearest thing to a non-Christian spiritual mass movement, with the possible exception of the Transcendental Meditation Movement. Estimates vary, but during its few years of operation here, probably more than ten thousand people have been initiated into the movement, while many more have come into varying degrees of contact with it.

Guru Maharaj Ji was born in Hardwar, India, in December 1957, the youngest of four sons. His father, Sri Hans Ji Maharaj, was a spiritual Master in his own right, with thousands of disciples. After taking up the spiritual path, Hans Ji spent several years walking on foot from village to village initiating aspirants into the 'Knowledge', until his disciples persuaded him to set up the Divine Light Mission.

The Knowledge is a phrase often used in the Divine Light Mission, and refers to the method of initiation whereby four techniques of meditation are taught. It is claimed that the Knowledge is an ancient technique, taught through the ages by the Perfect Master. At all times in history such a Master has been on earth teaching the same Knowledge, although often following the death of the Master the essence of his teaching has been lost, and a religion formed in its place. Among those who have taught the same Knowledge, say members of the Mission, are the founders of the world's great religions, such as Christ, Buddha, Krishna and Mohammed, as well as a number of lesser known saints.

The Knowledge is passed from generation to generation through a succession of Masters, each of whom is its source while he is on earth. Only one Perfect Master (or *Satguru*, meaning 'true teacher') is alive at any one time, and thus to find the Master and receive his Knowledge is regarded as the aim of the spiritual aspirant. Followers of Sri Hans Ji Maharaj believed that he was the Perfect Master of his time, in the same way that devotees of the present Guru Maharaj Ji believe him to be the Satguru of today. When Sri Hans Ji died in 1966, it was to his youngest son, Guru Maharaj Ji, then only eight years old, that the mantle of the Satguru was passed.

The Mission first came to the West in 1969, when a *mahatma* (or apostle) arrived in London to begin initiating people there into the Knowledge. Although it was generally thought that Maharaj Ji himself would not come to the West for some time, in June 1971 the then thirteen-year-old jet-age boy guru arrived in London.

Maharaj Ji and his Divine Light Mission seemed to arrive at just the right time in the history of the hippy movement, as hundreds flocked to join it in the early months. Over the years the movement has undergone a number of changes and developments, which have had the effect of altering its character. Premies who had previously 'dropped out' were encouraged by the movement's leaders to cut their hair, give up drugs, get jobs and generally give the organisation a respectable front. A number of older people have also joined, although it is still true to say that the followers are mostly under thirty.

In 1974 Guru Maharaj Ji, who was then sixteen, appeared in the world's press once again, this time in the role of bridegroom to a twenty-four-year-old American disciple. Since that time there are signs that the Mission is changing once again, as it moves away from its former militantly purist and evangelical approach towards a more 'Westernised' attitude. This is reflected in its efforts to move into the fields of social service and community work, and in its generally far softer sell.

The Knowledge itself, as we have said, consists of four simple meditation techniques, taught to the aspirant at a secret initiation, by a mahatma. The techniques are said to enable the mediator to turn his senses within, and perceive four things: (1) Divine Light – said to be an eternal and self-effulgent light shining within everybody; (2) Divine Nectar – this is known elsewhere as 'ambrosia' or 'the water of life', which flows within, and can be drunk; (3) Divine Harmony – aspirants are taught to meditate on the inner sound, sometimes known as the music of the spheres; (4) Holy Name or Word – this is described as the 'primordial vibration', which is constantly vibrating within everybody, thus providing the perfect object for meditation.

It is said that by the practice of these meditations the mind is stilled, great peace is achieved, and finally God-realisation is reached. It is not simply claimed that the Knowledge brings the individual calm – something which could be said of many human pursuits. But premies claim that the Knowledge is *the* perfect God-given form of spiritual practice, supreme in that it reveals perfection within every individual.

Many people have been disturbed by the attitude of reverence and devotion which premies adopt towards Maharaj Ji, and particularly by their claims that he is the Messiah, or God incarnate. Maharaj Ji himself has often refuted these claims, saying that he is no more than a humble servant of God with the ability to reveal the Knowledge. There is, nonetheless, a strong element of devotion shown by followers of Maharaj Ji, which stems from their belief that he has shown them the 'perfect path'.

Another important aspect of the premie's life is known as *satsang*, which means literally 'company of truth'. This usually consists of spiritual discourses, held at the Mission's centres and ashrams throughout the country, in which devotees and mahatmas talk about their spiritual realisations and the Knowledge. Premies are also encouraged to 'give *satsang*' to others, so that they can hear about the Knowledge and develop a desire for it.

For the person who decides that he wishes to be initiated into the Knowledge, *satsang* is generally a prerequisite. In this country there is usually a resident mahatma (the only person authorised by Guru Maharaj Ji to initiate others) who will give Knowledge in London, although occasionally this also happens in the provinces. The procedure is normally that those asking to be initiated are asked to listen to *satsang*, until the mahatma judges they have understood enough of its meaning and implication. Those waiting to receive Knowledge are also normally required to give up eating meat, drinking alcohol and taking drugs for a period before initiation. If the mahatma is satisfied that an individual is prepared enough to receive Knowledge, he will select him to attend a Knowledge session with a small number of others. The session can last up to eight hours or longer, and no financial charge is made for initiation.

Those premies who wish to dedicate themselves totally to Guru Maharaj Ji's work, and wish to live a 'monastic' life, move into the organisation's ashrams, of which there are approximately forty up and down the country. These are houses where devotees live a communal life dedicated to Guru Maharaj Ji. *Satsang*, including the singing of devotional songs, is normally held every evening. The public are always welcome to attend these and to talk to devotees. Ashrams are situated in most population centres, but if you do not happen to live near one the Mission will be pleased to give you the address of a premie living nearby, who will be able to tell you more. The majority of premies do not live in ashrams but lead family lives (as 'householders') or live together in communities of devotees. In London, the Mission's activities centre on the Palace of Peace, where *satsang*, concerts and film shows are held. Enquiries should be addressed to the Divine Light Mission's national headquarters in London.

Sai Baba

'When someone asks you in great earnestness where God is to be found, tell them that He is here in Prasanthi Nilayam. Direct them to come to this place and share your joy'. These are the words of *Sathya Sai Baba*, 'Man of Miracles', probably one of India's most widely known and highly respected living saints. Although the fact that he has not yet visited the West, coupled with his dislike of organised publicity, means that Sai Baba is not among those gurus well-known in the West, his following in India is massive, including prominent statesmen, academics and professional people.

Sai Baba's ashram, situated just outside the village of Puttaparthi in southern India, is known as Prasanthi Nilayam ('home of highest peace'), and has become the centre of pilgrimage for thousands of devotees. Founded in 1950, the ashram and its compound was declared by the Indian government to be a legal township in 1966, and as Sai Baba's popularity has spread, so the 'Sai Baba' industry has developed. Even in the north of India, one can see portraits of Sai Baba on sale alongside the more ancient deities such as Krishna. Yet Baba himself discourages his devotees from undertaking organised publicity, and strictly forbids any money to be raised in his name.

Undoubtedly it is Sai Baba's miracles which are responsible for spreading his fame. Born in Puttaparthi in 1926, it is said that a cobra was found beneath the infant, thus signifying the royal status of the baby, named Sathyanarayana. The early life of Sai Baba (a title which loosely translated means 'saintly father') is not easily established, largely due to the degree of romantic legend which inevitably clouds the truth. Sai Baba himself forbids his devotees to discuss his early life, in order to discourage distortion and embellishment. However, it seems fairly well established that at the age of seven he began to compose religious songs, and soon afterwards started to perform miracles, by materialising objects out of thin air for his friends. It is this ability of materialisation which has now virtually become Sai Baba's trademark.

At the age of fourteen the boy fell into a state of what appeared to be unconsciousness, followed by days during which his behaviour became odd and inexplicable. He would scream, sing religious songs nobody had ever heard, talk gibberish, or begin a high level discourse on the scriptures. Doctors, astrologers, priests, and even exorcists were called in to treat the boy, although none were successful. Then on 23 May, 1940, the boy got up from his bed, appearing normal and happy for the first time in months. Calling his family around him he began materialising sweets and fruit.

He then announced that he was a reincarnation of Sai Baba of Shirdi, a spiritual Master living in Bombay, who had died in 1918, with the declaration that he would reincarnate after eight years. His announcement was made even more peculiar by the fact that nobody in his village had ever heard of Sai Baba of Shirdi. 'What are we supposed to do?' asked the boy's bemused father. 'Worship me every Thursday and keep your minds and houses pure', the boy replied. From that time Thursdays were to become of special significance to Sai Baba devotees.

Sai Baba then continued his schooling, although his fame was already beginning to spread, bringing many to him in order to ask for his blessing. Throughout this period Sai Baba continued to perform his miracles, manifesting *vibhuti* (sacred ash) and even pictures of Shirdi Sai Baba.

Finally, on 20 October, 1940, Sai Baba broke with his family and home ties, throwing away his books and declaring, 'I am no longer your Sathya. I am Sai.' He announced that he would leave to undertake his work, for the sake of his devotees. It is reported that many friends and relatives saw a bright halo around the boy's head, as he declared: 'Maya (illusion) has left. I am going. My work is waiting.'

From the day that Sathya broke with his past to become Sai, an ever-increasing number of devotees have been drawn to him, and the stories of the miracles which he has performed are numerous enough to fill volumes. Every Sai Baba devotee has his particular miraculous occurrence to relate, and Baba has often performed his miracles before crowds of thousands.

Baba himself claims that his miracles are his 'visiting cards' which draw people to him and instil them with faith. They are the foundations on which he builds his work, and not, he claims, a form of publicity: 'Those who decry the super-human are the ignorant or the wicked, that is, those who have no authority to judge the spiritual. The establishment of dharma (spiritual teaching) is my aim; the teaching of dharma, the spread of dharma is my object. These miracles are just a few means towards that end.'

Sai Baba teaches his devotees the importance of controlling the mind and turning it towards God through repetition of His name, the study of scriptures, the adoption of regular prayer and the singing of *bhajan* (spiritual songs). Good deeds, such as the observance of vows, are all thought of as aids along the spiritual path, and the importance of surrender is also stressed by Sai Baba.

As one can imagine, the disciple-guru relationship is of vital importance among followers of Sai Baba, who regard their teacher as God. Disciples will travel thousands of miles just to get a glimpse of their Lord, and *darshan* (physical presence of the Master) is considered a vital part of the devotee's life.

Sai Baba encourages his devotees to lead a clean and upright life, avoiding alcohol, drugs and meat, and eating only pure food. He teaches them to reduce their speech to a minimum, and thus avoid needless hatred, jealousy and anger, while always seeking the company of good men. Stressing the importance of faith, he tells his disciples to cultivate a patient and loving attitude towards others, while maintaining the purity of their own lives.

Despite the fact that there are numbers of Indian Sai Baba devotees throughout Britain, there is no central organisation which co-ordinates activities. Devotees seem to hold their own local meetings spontaneously, although in certain areas these take place on quite a regular basis. However there are signs that this situation may be changing. Sai Baba has appointed Sitaram, an Indian devotee living near London, to supervise the activities of devotees in Britain, and has instructed him to start the process of drawing things together, to begin some kind of Sai Baba organisation – speculation is that this may be in preparation for Sai Baba's first visit to the West.

Originally meetings were held each Sunday at Sitaram's home, but due to the great interest shown, particularly among young Westerners, these have now had to be moved to a public hall. These meetings, like others around the country, include a large element of singing and chanting, as well as readings from Sai Baba's discourses.

Those who would like to know more about Sai Baba, or would like details of the meetings of his devotees, should contact Sitaram. There is also a very good book on Sai Baba, called *Sai Baba: Man of Miracles*, by Howard Murphet.

Sri Chinmoy

Of those Hindu gurus who have come to the West, none have received more recognition and acceptance than Sri Chinmoy Kumar Ghose. Born in Bengal in 1931, Sri Chinmoy is said to have had a childhood filled with deep mystical experiences, at the age of twelve achieving the highest level of consciousness, known in the Indian scriptures as 'Nirvikalpa Samadhi'.

Soon afterwards he entered the Aurobindo ashram at Pondicherry where he remained for the next twenty years. During this period Chinmoy claims he expanded and perfected his inner realisations through prayer and meditation, and in 1964 he travelled to America.

Since coming to the West, Sri Chinmoy has attracted many followers, nearly all of whom are the young, ex-hippie type. However his influence in America seems to be more widespread than in Britain, where his devotees number around a hundred.

In 1970 he was invited to conduct regular weekly meditations for delegates and staff at the United Nations Church Centre in New York, and this led to his selection as the first Director of the U.N. Meditation Group. During his time in the West, Sri Chinmoy has lectured at more than a hundred and fifty universities around the world, including Oxford and Cambridge. He has also had private meetings with the erstwhile U.N. Secretary-General U Thant, as well as a private audience at the Vatican with Pope Paul, who presented him with a papal medallion.

Chinmoy claims that the ultimate aim of his teaching is union with God. Although there are many roads which reach this same goal, the path taught by Chinmoy is the 'path of the heart' – 'love, devotion and surrender are the three elements which lead us most swiftly to this goal'. It is admitted that this path is not for everyone, and Sri Chinmoy is very selective in whom he accepts as his disciples. He does not seek to gain a large following, but is at pains to ensure that those who are accepted really are 'his' disciples.

Drug addicts, alcoholics and hippies will not be accepted by Sri Chinmoy, who teaches a way of life in which drugs, alcohol, tobacco and meat are banned. These may, however, be given up by degrees, and devotees try to lead a balanced rather than a fanatical life. Great stress is laid on cleanliness, and devotees are expected to bath and change their clothes before attending meditation sessions. Sri Chinmoy likes his female devotees to wear saris and the males to wear white when attending meditation – this is not a rule, but Chinmoy teaches that anything which lifts the consciousness for one second is desirable.

Sri Chinmoy teaches that there are three stages of meditation: (1) concentration; (2) meditation; and (3) contemplation.

He does not teach a specific outward form of meditation or give a mantra. He claims that a real spiritual Master is someone who is inseparable from God, and thus can easily enter into a person, see his growth, development and aspiration, and know everything about his inner and outer life. Such a Master can, he claims, teach you to meditate merely by his gaze.

When Sri Chinmoy holds a public meeting, he generally will say very little. He prefers to work through meditation sessions rather than lectures, and apart from chanting *Om* two or three times there may be silence in the hall for half an hour or more. During this period Chinmoy will sit and meditate with his audience, and it is said that he enters *samadhi*, where he becomes one with the Ultimate Reality which is absorbing his attention. Many meditating with him have intense experiences, feel tremendous forces or energies, and may be profoundly moved. Some find their lives strikingly changed by the experience, and go through something akin to 'conversion'. Those who wish to become followers of Sri Chinmoy must ask his personal permission. If accepted, the disciple must meditate every day, for fifteen minutes, early in the morning and also in the evening. He is also expected to do some work for the Sri Chinmoy centre which is nearest to him, but otherwise he continues his normal life. Stress is laid on inner values, and the teaching is based on the fact that devotees meditate to receive guidance, and then use it. There is no question of withdrawal from the world, and disciples try to be gentle, restrained and unassuming, which describes well the atmosphere of the centres.

Centres house a handful of disciples, act as the 'temple' for followers, and accommodate group meditation. There are only four centres in England, one in Ireland, and three in Scotland – for addresses write to Mrs Mary Plumbly at the London centre, which is the headquarters of the movement in Britain. Visitors are always welcome at the centres, but it is best to check first on times and dates. In London, visitors are welcome to attend regular Sunday meditations, and are asked to arrive between 6.30 and 6.45 p.m. Sri Chinmoy himself pays regular visits to Britain, generally during June and July. Meditation lasts about half an hour, and also involves the reading of poems and other writings by Sri Chinmoy, a little chanting, and the singing of an invocation.

Rajneesh Meditation

One normally associates meditation with the stilling of the mind, but quite the contrary is true at the *Rajneesh Meditation Centre* in London. The Centre teaches what it calls the 'chaotic breathing technique', as devised by its leader, Bhagwan Shree Rajneesh, who is said to have reached total enlightenment at the age of twenty-one while sitting under a tree in Jabalpur, India.

Followers of Shree Rajneesh believe that in the past various spiritual Masters have developed certain techniques for spiritual advancement, but because man has changed, these are no longer effective. Their Master's technique, however, has been specially designed to help modern man overcome his problem.

The method takes place in four distinct stages, each lasting about ten minutes. The first consists of fast 'chaotic' breathing, in which the whole body is used. This aims to produce a total breathing which will break tension spots and emotional blocks which result from a lifetime of repression. In the second stage, what, in psychoanalytical terms, is called 'catharsis' occurs, i.e. a sudden and often violent release of emotional energy. Again, this 'explosion into total emotional and physical expression' is aimed at releasing pent-up tensions, frustrations and repressions. Not unlike the Subud *latihan*, the individual is encouraged to express anything he feels freely, and the energy released by the technique may give rise to fits of laughing, crying, screaming or dancing. In the third stage the Sufi mantra, Hoo, is shouted intensely, in order to raise the energy level still further. The sound is said to hammer just above the sex centre of the body. According to the Centre's literature, 'Most of our hang-ups are sexual ones, and while we have these hang-ups we are crippled physically, emotionally and spiritually.' In the final stage comes total silence and stillness. It is in this silence, which is deeply experienced, that meditation occurs, and one feels the emptiness of becoming part of the whole of existence.

As one might imagine from the above description, the technique taught by Shree Rajneesh is a physically demanding one, but apparently individuals eventually adapt to it. The breathing in particular may present problems at first, because it involves muscles which are usually dormant. The chaotic meditation technique is usually taught during a specially structured course lasting fourteen consecutive days, including weekends, during which time you may expect a day-to-day progression. There are two meditation sessions, one in the morning and another in the early evening, and each session lasts between $1\frac{1}{2}$ and 2 hours. Following the sessions, taped lectures by Shree Rajneesh are played, and these are said to help the student understand his experiences and progress. A charge of £12 is made for the course, but included in the price is use of the Centre (and of a sound-proof room!) for a further fortnight. If you wish to continue using the Centre for meditation after this, you are asked to contribute £2 per month. The course is taken by groups of six people at a time.

The aim of the course is to unify the body, soul and mind of the seeker. Shree Rajneesh teaches that the body is the base of our existence, that it has its own wisdom, and that it is necessary for us to return to it. Our minds have evolved from our bodies, but still have their roots in the body – in the West, however, we tend to operate almost exclusively with our minds. Chaotic meditation gets you 'out of your mind and into your body'.

Once the course is completed, students are encouraged to do meditation three times a week, normally at the Centre. Group meditation is supposed to create a lot of energy, which in turn aids meditation, and for this reason regular weekly meetings are held in church halls, enabling larger groups to meditate together. These meetings provide the newcomer with an opportunity to see the technique in action (a 20p donation is asked for admission).

For those who wish to become more deeply involved with Shree

Rajneesh's teachings, a visit to India seems essential. Meditation camps are regularly held in India for large numbers of students, providing a means of going deeper into meditation. Programmes at the camps (which are conducted either in Hindi or completely in English) are intense, and include three dynamic meditation practices a day. Shree Rajneesh also lectures regularly every morning and evening, and it is said that just being in his presence boosts personal meditation. Those who wish to commit themselves still further may be initiated by Shree Rajneesh into *sannyas*. These are the 'full-time followers', who renounce everything to follow their Master. They must show a willingness to practise regular meditation, feel a desire to surrender to Shree Rajneesh and become his disciple; be prepared to wear orange clothes and to carry a locket with his picture.

Throughout the teaching of Shree Rajneesh runs the theme that one should never negate anything, but say yes to the whole of existence. His way is described as 'tantric', in that there are no rigorous rules, no dogmas, no negation of life, and above all, no suppressions of natural instinct. Instead he encourages 'understanding and awareness, and a joyful acceptance and oneness with the whole of existence – the only god that there is, is life'.

At the Centre every Thursday at 6.30 p.m. there are taped lectures by Shree Rajneesh, in which he discusses methods of meditation and other spiritual topics. The Centre also sells books of his talks, as well as a wide range of taped lectures.

Transcendental Meditation

Transcendental Meditation, or T.M. as its followers call it, has come a long way since the days of Flower Power, when the Beatles, the Rolling Stones and film stars proclaimed its wonders to the world. Maharishi Mahesh Yogi, the Indian swami who brought it to the West from India, was virtually unknown when he first arrived in Britain in 1958. He had been encouraged by the response he received teaching T.M. in India, and built up a steady following by several world tours. However it was not until the late 1960s that he came to the attention of the world at large through the 'conversion' of the Beatles, following a meeting he had with them in Cardiff. At the time they were deeply involved with drugs and Eastern mysticism, and meditation was a natural progression. They sang the Maharishi's praises and T.M. became a household word.

T.M. has grown dynamically since those early days, and today Maharishi, as his disciples call him, has established centres in more than sixty countries and boosted his following in England and Wales to about thirty thousand. This was done mainly through the vehicle of S.C.I., the Science of Creative Intelligence, which he began to evolve in 1970 with the help of scientists and psychologists who practised T.M. S.C.I. is defined as a system for studying the origin of creation and intelligence. Its appeal lies in the use of rational, scientific terminology to explain the benefits of T.M.

T.M. is said to be a completely natural technique for controlling the mind and the nervous system. Maharishi makes no claims to have invented or discovered it, but says it is part of the ancient Vedic knowledge of India. He has merely revived its use.

Popular opinion holds that the meditation revolves chiefly around a mantra, but other followers say mantras play a small part in the process of meditation. The techniques are secret – to preserve their power – and are a subtle means to experience a refinement of the thinking process and take the meditator's attention to the source of energy and intelligence within. But whatever T.M. comprises, it works. Science has proved that through T.M. thought becomes clearer and more powerful, mental and physical tensions decrease, blood pressure is lowered, and tranquillity obtained.

A list of benefits includes reduced nervousness, reduced aggression, reduced depression, reduced irritability, increased sociability, increased self-assuredness, decreased tendency to dominate, decreased inhibition, decreased self-doubt, increased outgoingness, decreased emotional instability, increased staying power and efficiency, etc. The list is, in fact, virtually endless. New research statistics are published daily, and widely circulated by the movement's administration.

T.M. itself is defined as 'a simple mental technique that anyone can learn quickly and easily. It is not a philosophy or religion, requires no control or effort, no concentration or contemplation. It is an effortless process of the mind that produces cumulative benefits from the first day of practice'. The idea is to meditate first thing in the morning and last thing at night for twenty minutes. The effects last through the day and night and accumulate. The longer T.M. is practised, the better the result.

Maharishi has a world plan with seven goals:
1 To develop the full potential of the individual.
2 To improve governmental achievements.
3 To realise the highest ideal of education.
4 To solve the age-old problems of crime and all behaviour that brings unhappiness to the family of man.
5 To maximise the intelligent use of the environment.
6 To bring fulfilment to the economic aspirations of individuals and society.
7 To achieve the spiritual goals of mankind in this generation.

He aims to train one teacher for every thousand people in the world. To do this his lessons are recorded in colour video tape and flown to each country and any questions arising from the lessons are answered by qualified teachers. None of this is cheap, however. T.M. is expensive to spread, and so it is expensive to learn. The basic techniques cost at least £20, cash in advance. But there are no further costs, and the pupil is allowed as much of the teacher's time as he needs. Also, there are reductions in cases of need. The initiation takes place on four consecutive days, and lasts about two hours a day.

S.C.I. comes next. For thirty-three colour video lessons and the personal instruction of a teacher, the aspirant pays over £30. Again there are reductions, for those that qualify. The next stage is a six-month residential, teacher-training course. Courses are held in various European cities with Maharishi himself present, and the price varies with the city.

T.M. and S.C.I. will provide free speakers, films and exhibitions at public lectures, colleges and schools for any interested groups. At the numerous centres round the country, the introductory lectures are being standardised, as are the teachings. This means that any centre will offer the same facilities. These centres form the Spiritual Regeneration Movement (S.R.M.), a registered charity set up to promote T.M. and S.C.I. in Britain.

There are three recommended books: Maharishi's introduction to the Penguin edition of the *Bhagavad Gita*; *Seven States of Consciousness* by Anthony Campbell, published by Victor Gollancz, and *Transcendental Meditation* by Jack Forum, an American publication available from the main centre. A full list of recommended reading is also available.

Another organisation which teaches the Maharishi's form of meditation, and has done since it was first set up in 1961, is the *School of Meditation* in London. The organisation is non-profit making, and is staffed by volunteer workers, but nonetheless, you will be asked to donate one week's wages to the school before beginning the meditation. According to literature: 'The School, for its part, undertakes to guide the development of the practice of meditation in relation to the needs and wishes of the individual for as long as the individual may require.' The School holds regular public meetings where more information may be obtained; alternatively write or telephone. The School is open to callers from Monday to Friday, between 10.30 a.m. and 4.30 p.m.

Meher Baba

Among various spiritual groups one finds a great many differing claims made about the status of the Master himself. Some modestly claim to be merely ordinary men who are divinely inspired, while others claim to be something greater. None is more candidly outspoken about their own status than *Meher Baba*, who told his followers: 'From the beginningless beginning I have asked one question, "Who am I?" and I gave one answer, "I am God".'

Merwan Sheriar Irani, known as *Meher Baba*, was born in India in 1894 of Persian parents. In 1913, while attending college, he met with Hazrat Babajan, an ancient Mohammedan woman who was said to be one of the five Perfect Masters of the age. It is claimed that she gave the young man God-realisation, and made him aware of his high spiritual destiny. Eventually, Merwan sought out another Perfect Master, Upasni Maharaj, a Hindu who gave, over the course of seven years, 'gnosis', or divine knowledge. In this way Merwan attained spiritual perfection, and in 1921 he began his mission by gathering together his first disciples. It was these men who gave Merwan the name 'Meher Baba', meaning compassionate father.

Life with Meher Baba, from all reports, was by no means easy. The history of the Master and his disciples seems to consist of a number of phases, each with its own particular tenor and mode of life. During these periods, Meher Baba would treat his disciples in different ways, and it is said that each of the phases corresponds to different stages in the development of the disciple.

During the early period, an extremely rigid and demanding discipline was maintained among followers, who were banned from so much as reading a newspaper. During this time, Baba was often very fierce, until he announced one day that he was going to establish a school. He built a colony near Ahmednagar, called Meherabad, and there founded a free boys' school (where spiritual training was stressed), a free hospital, and shelters for the poor. After two years the colony was dissolved, and then began what is known among disciples as the 'new life period'. The disciples broke all family and other ties and roamed the country for three years. Throughout this time they were under the impression that they had left their homes for good, and it was not until the end of the period that Meher Baba announced they should return to their villages. During the period, conditions were often hard, and the disciples frequently went hungry. They wandered from place to place, begging for their existence, and underwent demanding tests of devotion. Often the Master would deliberately stir up and activate situations, just to test his followers. However, in the midst of the hardship, Meher Baba would suddenly announce a holiday, during which the disciples would rest from their wanderings and regain their physical strength.

The period is regarded by disciples as a highly significant one, during which work for the whole of mankind was carried out. For followers of Baba, the end of the period marked the end of all ceremony and religious rites – from that time all need of ritual has been abolished. Baba told his followers that he would string together all the religions of the world like beads on a string.

In 1925, Meher Baba announced he would observe a silence, and this he maintained until his death in 1969. He dictated many spiritual messages and discourses by means of an alphabet board, but later discontinued the use of this and reduced all communication to hand gestures. He first visited the West in 1931, when he contacted his first Western disciples. Before he died, he paid a number of further visits, and in

Myrtle Beach in America established a centre for his work.

In India an important part of the Master's work through the years was concerned with the 'masts'. These are pilgrims on the spiritual path who have become 'crazy' with their love for God. For this work Baba travelled throughout India and Ceylon, seeking out and caring for those 'God-intoxicated' pilgrims. Other work in which he involved himself personally was the washing of lepers, the washing the feet of the poor, and the distribution of grain and cloth to the destitute. Baba taught that the Master awakens love in those who are ready, and it is love which is the cornerstone of his teachings.

Baba said quite plainly that he was God, the Avatar, and that through compassion the Avatar returns to earth to rescue it. There is a cycle of God incarnating himself in human form – the Avatar, Christ or Buddha – and he comes at the time when the world is at a spiritual low ebb. It is his task to revitalise and regenerate, and for this reason Baba said he had come to awaken, rather than to teach.

Baba said that we are all God but are unconscious of it. Awakening is the process of becoming conscious of it. Followers of Baba claim that one gradually becomes more open to this awakening. They believe Baba gave what is termed an 'Avataric push' in everyday life, and that the very material matter of the universe receives a push in its evolution from the appearance of the Avatar. In this sense, he works simultaneously on every level of creation, and is aware of every single individual. Thus he gives each person a push in his own personal terms.

Modern followers claim the stages which the early disciples went through in the presence of Baba are still experienced by them today. For them, his power and his love is as strong and tangible as ever, and they feel the minute details of their lives all have some significance in their relationship with Baba. They are constantly looking for guidance in what Baba said, and also spend much time trying to catch a sense of his love from the devotees who knew him. Western devotees sometimes travel to India to be with the original disciples, and are always hungry to hear *darshan* stories about the Master himself. Every detail and story of the Master's life is cherished by the disciples.

In accordance with the teachings of their Master, Baba-lovers try to be honest, and avoid thinking of themselves as special or holy. Baba taught no creed or practice, and for this reason most Baba-lovers eat meat, and generally lead normal Western lives. The only absolute rule is the ban on drug taking.

Baba-lovers aim to achieve balance in their lives, and recognise the dangers of becoming attached to unattachment. They do not try to be 'good', but attempt to go beyond this by completely trusting in Baba, who taught that a man becomes more and not less human on the spiritual path. They claim that Baba uses their individual situations to draw them closer to him by presenting them with challenges. But there is no set

66

pattern to what the devotee will experience, and no part of an individual's experience need be negated. Baba taught his disciples to judge people by their heart, and not by external appearance.

There are probably around two hundred Baba-lovers in Britain, although there is a varying degree of commitment among them. The *Meher Baba Association* is a relatively small and loosely run body, which does not undertake any sort of 'evangelisation', which on the whole was discouraged by Baba himself.

The Association is not exclusive, although it is usually publicised only by word of mouth. There are various forms of commitment among the lovers, and some prefer to relate to Baba alone, buying his books and studying them individually. However, the Association is run by a hard core of committed members, who maintain a centre in London. On Mondays at 6.30 p.m. sessions on Baba's discourses are held, and at the same time on each Thursday there is an open night, which sometimes involves tapes of informal discussions. At 3 p.m. on Saturdays the largest meeting of the week is held, at which there are films of Baba, music, readings, talks and visits. There are no religious ceremonies held at the centre, and visitors, who are always welcome, will not be 'got at'. The atmosphere is warm and friendly. Literature will be sent to those who request it, and if required you can be put in touch with any lovers who might live nearby. There is a wide range of reading material available from the Association, including books on various topics by Baba himself.

Aurobindo Society

Another Indian spiritual teacher who, like Meher Baba, spent much of his life observing a rule of silence was Sri Aurobindo, whose teachings are presented in this country by the *Sri Aurobindo Society of Great Britain*. Aurobindo was born in Calcutta in 1872, and at the age of seven was sent to England to be educated. After a successful academic career, during which he studied languages at Cambridge University, he returned to his native land at the age of twenty-one and joined the Baroda State Service. It was during his thirteen years working in political administration that he had his first spiritual experience, and he used the time to develop his cultural, political and literary interests.

In 1906 his political interests took him to Calcutta, where, as principle of a college, he became the leader of the Indian independence movement in Bengal. This led to his imprisonment two years later, accused of sedition and conspiracy, and this period proved to be the turning point in his life. During his year in prison he spent much time in contemplation, resulting in a number of spiritual experiences. Soon after his release he withdrew from political life, 'in answer to an inner call', and in 1910 arrived in Pondicherry, the present centre of the Aurobindo Society.

After four years of what he described as 'silent yoga', Aurobindo began a philosophical magazine entitled *Arya*, which became the major medium for his writings, ranging across topics such as yoga, the scriptures and human unity. It was in 1926 that he withdrew into a silence which was to last until his death in 1950.

No discussion of Aurobindo is complete without mentioning the Mother, the individual on whom the task of implementing Aurobindo's vision has devolved. The Mother was born in Paris in 1878, and had a childhood which was full of unusual 'inner' experiences. She first met Aurobindo in 1914, and immediately recognised in him a person of whom she had repeated visions. She returned to India in 1920, where she has remained since. Following Aurobindo's withdrawal into silence, she took over the running of the ashram, and her leadership of the movement remains to this day. There is a strong element of 'mystical unity' between Aurobindo and the Mother.

Aurobindo's teachings centre round the concept of the evolution of man. Adopting the traditional Hindu teachings, he claimed that behind the veil of appearance there exists a 'Reality of a Being and Consciousness', a true eternal self. Although we are all united in this one spirit, we are ignorant of this fact, divided by our separate consciousness. By psychological discipline it is possible to remove this veil, and thus become aware of the true self and divinity within us all. Aurobindo teaches that this One Being and Consciousness is involved in matter, but through the process of evolution becomes liberated from it. Life is the first step in this liberation, mind is the second – now we await the next step. This is its movement into something greater, a consciousness which is spiritual and described by Aurobindo as 'supramental'. Only when this next step has been taken towards the development of the Supermind and spirit as the dominant force in man, will the divinity within everything become manifest. It will then become possible for life to manifest perfection.

It was towards this end that Aurobindo taught his form of yoga, so followers could develop themselves to the point where they evolved a consciousness which would transform and 'divinise' human nature. Man has not reached the final goal, but is a transitional being.

In the same way, Aurobindo taught that the world too is in a transitional state, but it is possible for man, through conscious effort, to accelerate this process. Rather than allowing the transformation to evolve through a long and painful process, the development can be enhanced by man becoming the conscious creator of the 'New Being' or spiritual superman. This self-transformation would in turn manifest itself on earth, and in this way Aurobindo foresaw the establishment of the perfect spiritual society, the kingdom of heaven on earth, occupied by a new species of superman.

Aurobindo in no sense demanded withdrawal from the world as the price of spiritual development. He repeatedly stressed that the object of his yoga was self-perfection and not self-annulment; perfection in the universe rather than withdrawal from it. The term 'yoga', as used by Aurobindo, is defined as a methodised effort towards self-perfection, although it does not involve any set teaching or prescribed form of meditation. Instead it calls upon the seeker to open himself to the divine power and presence within him, through a combination of faith, aspiration and surrender. One way of opening the consciousness to the divine is through meditation or contemplation. Another is through service and dedicated work, and a third is through *bhakti* or devotion. Contemplation alone is not sufficient to reach the desired point – work too is necessary, indeed indispensable in order to follow the dynamic yoga of action.

The task of implementing Aurobindo's vision of the new society has fallen on the Mother, who, even while Aurobindo lived, was responsible for founding and developing the original ashram at Pondicherry. It was only after her arrival in 1920 that numbers began to increase and a community life began to develop. From that time the Mother has guided the development of the community, until it has now grown to a population of about eighteen hundred residents, with an additional floating population of two hundred. In accordance with Aurobindo's teachings, the ashram has never conformed to the traditional image of a spiritual shelter. Its members are not renunciates, do not wear special coloured robes or practise asceticism. Instead they lead a life based on their Master's spiritual teachings, with the ideal of attaining the divine life here on earth.

In 1964 the ashram took a step towards realising its aim of creating a new world when the idea of 'Auroville', a town based on the teachings of Aurobindo, was first developed. Auroville, although still in its early stages, will be a 'universal town', set up near Pondicherry, where men and women will live in peace and harmony – thus demonstrating Aurobindo's vision of Human Unity. The project is designed to create something akin to a spiritual twentieth-century Utopia, and Aurobindo followers throughout the world are setting up groups to support the scheme which will demonstrate the practicality of their Master's dream.

Followers of Aurobindo are few in Britain, although the Aurobindo Society does have a centre in London. This has a collection of books and literature on and by Aurobindo and the Mother, and also information on Auroville. Visitors are welcome to use the centre for reading on any Friday between 7.30 p.m. and 9.30 p.m. The centre also has a collection of films and photographs, and will supply lecturers to interested parties.

Twice a week followers meet at the centre, and anybody is welcome to join them. If attending for the first time, it is probably best to go to the Tuesday meeting, which begins at 8 p.m. It includes readings from writings of the Mother and Aurobindo, meditation, music, and open discussion, where you will be welcome to ask questions. The Saturday meetings, which begin at 5.30 p.m., usually involve less discussion and more study, but visitors are nonetheless welcome, and are invited to stay after the meeting for tea and discussion. The meetings usually only attract about a dozen people, except for special occasions when forty or fifty people attend. Occasionally public meetings are held when special visitors are in the country, or when new films of Auroville are available. The Society also has small groups which meet monthly in Cambridge and Colchester – for details of these or any further information contact the secretary at the centre.

Self-Realisation Fellowship

One of the first Indian holy men to come to the West and remain for any length of time was Paramhansa Yogananda, founder of the *Self-Realisation Fellowship*. Yogananda's teaching was wide ranging, with much emphasis on the unity of all religions, but his main aim was to spread the practice of meditation and yoga, and of 'kriya yoga' in particular. Followers of Yogananda believe he was the fourth in line of great Hindu Masters, whose mission it was to spread the Self-Realisation Fellowship's message throughout the world. The first of these Masters was Mahavatar Babaji, who was responsible for reviving kriya yoga, and in 1861 permitted his disciple, Lahiri Mahasaya, to teach the technique openly. It is claimed that before this the technique had remained a closely guarded secret, but Mahavatar Babaji recognised that in the coming age large numbers of people throughout the world would seek a technique which could bring them liberation and the realisation of God's imminence.

It was one of Lahiri Mayasaya's most advanced disciples, Sri Yukteswar, who became the spiritual teacher of Yogananda himself. Yogananda was born in 1893 in Gorakhpur, India, and came to his guru in 1910. For ten years he was given a severe spiritual training in a hermitage in Bengal, where in 1914 he joined the monastic Swami Order. In 1920 Yogananda was sent by his guru to the West, as a delegate at the International Congress of Religious Liberals in Boston. Soon after his arrival he founded the international headquarters of his Self-Realisation Fellowship in California, where it still exists today. Paramhansa began a mission which was to last for more than thirty years, taking him throughout the United States lecturing on the 'universal science of yoga'.

As well as wanting to disseminate his specific yoga techniques, which he claimed enabled one to achieve direct personal experience of God, he also preached the harmony and basic oneness of Christianity and Hinduism. He believed that the Christianity taught by Christ and the yoga taught by Krishna were one, and that the principles of truth were common to the foundation of all true religions.

Followers of Yogananda point to the *Book of Revelations* in support of their claim that Christ taught yoga methods to his close disciples. They argue that when John talks of seven stars and seven churches he is in fact referring to the seven *chakras* or energy centres of the body, described in yoga. All religious paths, Yogananda taught, lead to the same 'divine highway', that of daily devotional meditation on God.

When Yogananda died in 1953, it is said that during the ten days prior to burial his body showed no signs of decay, and this is taken by his followers as a further demonstration of the truth of the yoga which he taught. However, the death of the Master did not diminish the devotion of his followers, or their enthusiasm to spread his teachings and mission. They believe that although it is a great blessing to come personally into contact with a guru, the real happiness and advancement is in the inner attunement which comes through daily meditation and following the guru's instructions.

Followers point out that many great Christian saints were born centuries after their guru, but through devotion and obedience to their ideals became holy. Thus one can, by following the S.R.F. path of meditation, expand one's consciousness until it becomes eternally united with that of the guru – who is 'ever-living omnipresent'. Those who follow this path are said to achieve the two blessings of peacefulness of mind and blissful awareness of the soul.

One now becomes a student of S.R.F. by studying a course of tuition organised by the Fellowship. It consists of printed lessons covering the various phases of spiritual development, and combines philosophical teachings about the spiritual laws which govern life with practical techniques of yoga to 'awaken soul awareness'. The lessons are based upon the writings and transcribed oral teachings of Yogananda, and include poems by him, stories from Hindu scriptures, prayers and affirmations. Lessons are grouped in six steps, and after the first, second and sixth of these one can return report forms to the Mother Centre in California, who will give any special guidance which one might need.

It is only after the completion of the second step that students are initiated into the highest form of the meditation techniques, kriya yoga. This takes place only after the student has been studying for a minimum of six months, but it is more likely that students will have to wait at least a year for this initiation. It is regarded as the spiritual baptism of the Fellowship, and in accepting it students formally enter the disciple-guru relationship with Yogananda and S.R.F.'s other Masters. If one fulfils the necessary qualifications for initiation, then this is performed by a minister of S.R.F. – in this country there are no resident ministers, and so students have to wait for the visit of a minister from America, which only happens about every other year.

All activities of S.R.F. are controlled by the renunciates of the Self-Realisation Order in California, who include both monks and nuns who have taken monastic vows. In Britain followers of Yogananda are few in number, but there is an S.R.F. group which meets once a week for meditation. However, the printed lessons are only available from the international headquarters in California. If you are interested in knowing more about S.R.F., literature can be obtained by writing to the Secretary of the British group. But perhaps the best introduction to Yogananda and his work is his autobiography, *Autobiography of a Yogi*, considered a spiritual classic, and widely available in Britain. The book gives an extremely good grounding for those considering pursuing the S.R.F. course of study, and is also rewarding for those with a more general interest in yoga and the spiritual life. Application forms for enrolment are available from the international headquarters of S.R.F., and the lessons are available to all who sincerely seek spiritual understanding, and are prepared to make a real effort. S.R.F. is always happy to welcome new students. Among the subjects dealt with in the S.R.F. teachings are meditation, heredity and reincarnation, life after death, karma, correct breathing and divine healing.

Vedanta

An Indian saint whose philosophy is still being taught in the West almost ninety years after his death is Sri Ramakrishna. Ramakrishna spent most of his life teaching in the grounds of a temple near Calcutta – a realised soul who succeeded in attracting a considerable following in his native land. After his death, eighteen of his closest disciples, according to his instructions, met together to form a small monastic order which later became known as the Ramakrishna Order. The most prominent of these founders was Swami Vivekananda, who was one of the first men to bring Hinduism to the West when he addressed the World Parliament of Religions in Chicago in 1893.

Perhaps because of its intellectual appeal, the teachings of Ramakrishna, known as *Vedanta*, succeeded in attracting the attention of a number of prominent Westerners. In fact, Vedanta was one of the first Eastern spiritual movements to have an influence in the early years of this century. Among its supporters were Aldous Huxley and Christopher Isherwood, who wrote one of the best biographies of Ramakrishna.

The philosophy of Vedanta is evolved from the Upanishads, which form part of the ancient Hindu scriptures known as the Vedas. It forms the common basis for many Hindu sects, and accepts all the great prophets and teachers of history as manifestations of the one Godhead.

For this reason it does not attempt to make converts, but provides a rational basis for principles acceptable to followers of any religion. Vedantic philosophy teaches that the basic reality underlying man's consciousness is the same as the ultimate reality which underlies the whole universe. Man's real nature is divine, and the aim of human life is said to be the unfolding and the manifestation of this nature.

The practical techniques by which Vedantic theory is realised are called yoga, but this term is used in its broadest sense, the original meaning of the word being 'union' with God. Followers of Vedanta teach that there are four main types of yoga, each suited to individuals of particular temperaments.

Jnana yoga is the yoga of the intellect, which is refined to discriminate between the real and unreal. Bhakti yoga is the yoga of devotion, where, with the aid of rituals, music and prayer, the emotions are directed to a personal God. Karma yoga, the yoga of action, asks the aspirant to purify his active nature by performing service in the spirit of detachment. Finally, raja yoga is the 'science of psychic and psychological control', where the development of concentration of mind is employed in order to bring about a transformation of consciousness.

The ethics of Vedanta also play an important part in the life of the aspirant, teaching him that if he injures another he injures himself, while if he helps another, he helps himself. Thus Vedanta is defined as a 'philosophy, religion, psychology and ethics in one, integrated in a metaphysic which fulfils reason'.

The Ramakrishna Order is represented in the West by a number of centres throughout America, France, Switzerland and Argentina. In Britain the only centre affiliated to the Order is the *Ramakrishna Vedanta Centre*, which has an ashram in London. The London Centre was started in 1948 by Swami Ghanananda at the invitation of a number of interested people, but like all swamis of the Order living abroad, his task was not to convert. The ministry of the Order is to help individuals to develop spiritually, while at the same time promoting mutual understanding between the followers of different religions. Thus the swamis are in no sense missionaries.

The Centre is now run by Swami Bhavyananda, a member of the Order for more than thirty years. Each Sunday at 5 p.m. he gives public lectures at the Centre, which cover such areas as Vedanta, India philosophy and comparative religion. The lectures begin with the chanting of Sanskrit verses, and are usually followed by a brief period of meditation. A programme giving more precise details of talks can be obtained on request from the Centre, where special occasions, such as the birthday of Ramakrishna, are also celebrated.

The Swami occasionally addresses meetings in the provinces, and will give personal interviews, by appointment, for spiritual guidance. He will be happy to answer letters from interested enquirers, and sometimes runs special study classes for those who wish to study Vedanta in more depth. The Centre has a meditation room with a shrine, which is open to the public every day from 10 a.m. to 7.30 p.m.

The Ramakrishna Order publishes a large amount of literature on various aspects of its spiritual teachings, and the Centre has a book department which provides the Order's publications to callers or through the post. A comprehensive catalogue can be obtained on request. A bi-monthly magazine, *Vedanta for East and West*, is also published by the Centre.

Sikhism

A relatively recent religion – at least in comparison to the other world faiths – is Sikhism, which was originally founded a little under five hundred years ago by Guru Nanak. Nanak emphasised the fundamental truth of all religions, and his mission was to put an end to religious conflict by preaching the gospel of universal toleration and stressing the oneness of God. In an age when class distinction and the caste system flourished Nanak taught brotherhood and equality, opposing the formalised aspects of the two main 'competing' religions of India, Hinduism and Islam. He also spoke out against the custom of *purdah*, and gave women equal status with men.

Sikhism is essentially a practical religion, which teaches its followers tolerance to others and calls upon them to give service to the community. Nanak stressed that retirement from the world was not necessary in order to realise God, but that ordinary people could reach him while leading normal family lives, following normal occupations and taking part in worldly affairs.

Nanak himself was born in Lahore in 1469 of a hight-caste Hindu family. He married, had two children, and worked in commerce, but at the age of thirty is said to have received God's command to go out into the world to give His message. He consequently set out on a missionary journey which took him through the whole of the Punjab and as far away as Tibet. He taught that the human body was a special blessing only given to man after an evolution through 8,400,000 lives, and that therefore man should make use of the special opportunity given to him to work his way to salvation and union with God. During the latter half of his journey, Nanak settled at Kartarpur, where he was joined by his family, and founded a community of followers.

The Sikhs have ten gurus, each following in succession to the previous guru, and each said to possess the spirit of Nanak – this is stressed, for example, in the way that each of the gurus signed their writings 'Nanak'. One of the most notable of the gurus, the fifth, Guru Arjan, was responsible for compiling the Sikh holy book, the *Adi Granth*. He collected the hymns of the four previous gurus, added many of his own poems, included works by fifteen other saints whose sentiments were in accord with Sikhism, together with odes by Sikh bards, and produced one volume. This remains unaltered today, except for the addition of hymns by the ninth guru, Teg Bahadur.

The tenth and final Sikh guru, Gobind Singh, brought about many changes in the religion, giving it much of the character which it has to-day. Guru Nanak had always taught simplicity in all things and had rejected rituals as unnecessary. But Gobind Singh was a soldier, and believed that through the teachings of the gurus sufficient stress had already been given to the moral and spiritual aspects of the faith. Thus he ended the line of gurus, claiming it was no longer necessary to perpetuate the cult of human leadership through a single living guru. In 1699 Gobind Singh gave the Sikhs a form of democratic organisation, introduced baptism, and called upon Sikhs to follow certain disciplines and to wear a uniform.

All Sikhs were to adopt the family name of 'Singh', meaning lion, and to regard themselves as belonging to the same family. All baptised Sikhs were forbidden to cut their hair, told to wear a pair of shorts as underwear, and to carry a comb, steel bangle, and a short sword. They were also instructed to rise early, and to say certain prayers at sunrise, sunset and before going to bed. They were forbidden to smoke tobacco, take drugs, eat meat killed according to Moslem rites or commit adultery. Their moral behaviour was always to be of the highest order, and they were to fight fearlessly in all righteous causes and for the defence of their religion against tyranny. In this way the more formalised Sikh religion which exists today was instituted.

The Sikh temple is called a *gurdwara*, and normally contains one large room containing the *Granth Sahib* (sacred book) which is used for worship. Services begin with the singing of hymns, and may consist of lectures, poems or stories from Sikh history. The service always ends with the Ardas, a prayer invoking God's grace in granting the Sikhs His blessing. A final verse is then read from the scripture, and the distribution of *prasad* (sacred food) follows.

The two most important ceremonies in a Sikh's life are baptism and marriage. The former is similar to Christian confirmation, in that it brings the Sikh into full membership of his faith. Marriage was highly regarded by the Sikh gurus, and was given a spiritual significance. Husband and wife are called upon to seek the union of their two souls. Apart from regular services, baptism and marriage, other festivals are celebrated at the Sikh *gurdwara*, such as the guru's birthdays. On these occasions members of the congregation will normally eat a meal together after the service. Sikhs are generally well known for their hospitality and openness, and visitors are always welcome to the *gurdwara*.

There is a fairly large Sikh community in Britain, and organisations exist to foster outsiders' interest in the religion. The *Sikh Cultural Society of Great Britain* was formed in 1960, and soon afterwards began to publish *The Sikh Courier*, a quarterly magazine designed particularly for non-Sikhs and containing articles about the Sikh faith and history. The Society also has a temple in London, where it holds a special service in English on the first Sunday of every month, to which all interested in learning about Sikhism are invited. The Society can also accommodate organised groups of visitors, and produces free literature on the faith in English. The

Society also provides lecturers, operates a lending library, and has new books on Sikhism for sale. All enquiries should be addressed to the Secretary of the Society.

The object of the *Sikh Missionary Society* is to advance the Sikh religion in this country, and consequently much of their work is carried out within the Sikh community itself. This group does not seem so active in the field of public relations with non-Sikhs, but it does produce literature in English about the religion. It is also keen to encourage branches to start up throughout the country to serve the local Sikh community. There are some fifty or sixty Sikh temples in Britain, but there appears to be no central organisation which has a comprehensive list. However, the Missionary does have some addresses, and will help you to contact your nearest Sikh temple if they can. The Society also tries to arrange lectures on Sikhism, as well as celebrations of various religious functions.

3HO Foundation

A group which combines the enthusiastic practice of yoga with the Sikh religion is the *3HO Foundation*, which runs the Guru Ram Das ashram in London. 3HO (which stands for 'healthy, happy and holy') was founded in America in 1969 by Yogi Bhajan, who, it is claimed, is the only teacher of tantric yoga in the world. Full-time members of the group, who are almost always young Westerners, and nearly always ex-hippies, are easily distinguished by their traditional Sikh dress. Both men and women wear white, while the women also wear white veils. Men do not cut their beards, and wear their hair tied up in turbans. The fact that they follow these strict rulings concerning dress, reflects their attitude towards tradition.

Thus all the basic ideals of the Sikh religion are pursued: only natural, pure foods are eaten, drugs and alcohol are banned, and males do not cut their hair. This latter rule is followed for both health and psychic reasons. It is said that the turban helps to channel psychic energy around the head, while symbolising at the same time the brotherhood to which Sikhs belong.

Kundalini yoga is the main form of yoga taught and practised by followers, and it is, they claim, the root of all yogas. It was kept a secret for thousands of years, although the few schools which did teach it gradually allowed the teaching to become polluted. Basically, it is concerned with purification of the system in order to 'receive the liquid light of pure consciousness'. It is a massive system of yoga, and consists of more than 108 basic exercises, with an almost infinite number of variations. Breath is the key, but asanas, exercises and postures are also involved, as well as mantra chanting and meditation.

Kundalini is sometimes described as the serpent power – it is visualised

76

as a coiled serpent which lies sleeping at the base of the spine. Certain spiritual practices are said to arouse the kundalini – representing psychic energy – which then passes up through the body *chakras* or energy centres until it reaches the top of the head. At this point, it is said, God-realisation occurs.

The effect of practising kundalini is said to be an extremely powerful one. It cleanses the blood and the organs of the body, as well as strengthening the mind. The chanting of mantras is particularly important in order to obtain the mental effects of kundalini, and for this reason mantra meditation is widely practised by 3HO followers. They believe certain ancient mantric chants are particularly potent in carrying the individual beyond the physical sound and back to the source of the sound, which is the primordial vibration. Thus sound plays an important part, whether the individual is chanting aloud, singing, or even chanting silently. The chant of *sat nam* (meaning 'true name') is particularly important, and followers of 3HO always greet you with these words in an attempt to keep the vibration of the mantra going all the time. This is, in fact, the final aim of the 3HO followers – to extend the chant to their whole lives, so that the vibration of it is always around them. This, they believe, is most important in order to keep the mind constant and controlled.

Most members of the 3HO ashram are trainee yoga teachers, and every evening except Sundays, kundalini yoga lessons are given. The classes are not progressive, and so beginners just start in with others who have been coming for longer periods. A 40p donation is asked from students, but this will be waived for anybody who really cannot afford it. Kundalini yoga requires a great deal of application, and is very demanding – members of the ashram openly admit that the exercises are difficult, and for this reason only those who are determined are likely to stick things out.

The other method of yoga taught by Yogi Bhajan is known as 'Tantric yoga'. This differs from kundalini in that it requires the presence of a Maha Tantra, a master of Tantra, before it can be taught, and so it can only be taught when Yogi Bhajan himself is present. The aim of Tantric yoga is to clear the subconscious mind, and it is practised between partners. Couples sit and look at each other in particular *mudras* while in the presence of Yogi Bhajan, who is said to 'channel the energy'. Yogi Bhajan generally visits Britain twice a year, and courses in Tantric yoga normally take place on a number of consecutive evenings. A charge of £15 was made for the last Tantric yoga course held in London. Those who practise kundalini and Tantric yoga, or who are Sikhs, do not have to move into ashrams, but those who wish to dedicate themselves totally may do so. As well as the kundalini yoga lessons offered at the ashram, special classes in childbirth and cooking are occasionally held. For those who wish to commit themselves further, the ashram offers two-week programmes of residential study. The student takes part in all the activities of the ashram, attends meditations and yoga classes, and learns about natural food preparation. Special times are also set aside for reading and study. If after this the student wishes to stay on and live permanently in the ashram, he may do so – there is no membership or initiation into 3HO.

Subud

Compared to many of the Eastern-orientated groups which exist today, *Subud* is a relative 'old timer', making its first appearance in England in 1957. It was then that Subud's leader, an Indonesian monk known as Pak Subuh, arrived to take up residence at a large house in Surrey.

The early history of the group in England is surrounded by an atmosphere of sensation. Many of those who originally came to Pak Subuh believed him to be the Messiah, despite his constant denials. There were also large numbers of followers of the late Gurdjieff, who believed that Pak Subuh was the great successor to whom their teacher had referred during his lifetime. When stories of miraculous healings and sensational spiritual experiences began to leak to the press, Subud was soon to be the subject of many newspaper headlines. Interest was further inflamed when a well-known film star was miraculously cured after being initiated into Subud. The extent of the publicity which Subud received can be gauged from the fact that during 1957 some five hundred newcomers were initiated into the brotherhood. In 1959, a lengthy world tour was followed by a giant international congress in England, with representatives from about forty countries.

This really marked the high point of the movement as far as external growth is concerned. In 1960 Pak Subuh left Britain, and since that time the movement has been keeping a 'low profile'. Throughout the 1960s, propaganda for Subud was regarded unfavourably and actively discouraged, but now the movement appears to be coming increasingly into the open with its activities.

Subud originally began in 1933, when the movement's founder Muhammad-Subuh (known to his followers as Bapak, meaning father) received a revelation of the power of God. It is said that this experience initiated a three-year period of intensive development within Bapak, during which he is said not to have slept. He was told in answer to prayer that he would be able to transmit the same experience he had received to anyone else who wished to share it. He was instructed not to attempt to seek these people out, but to wait until they found him. Because Subud, unlike some spiritual groups, has not tried to go out and look for new members, it has spread mainly by person to person contact, another factor which has added to its rather exclusive image.

The word Subud is a contraction of three Sanskrit words: *susila*, which means right living in accordance with the will of God; *budhi*, meaning the inner force residing in the nature of man; *dharma*, which means surrender and submission to the power of God. Taken together they mean 'right

78

living according to the highest that is possible for man in submission to God's will'.

The basis for Subud is the *latihan*, an Indonesian word meaning an exercise or training. It is the *latihan* which forms the initiation for those who wish to become members of Subud, and is regularly practised by those who have already joined. Initiation itself is carried out in a special *latihan*, and is known as 'opening'.

The transmission of the Subud initiation generally takes place through 'helpers', who are specially authorised by Pak Subuh to represent him in this way. These helpers are not necessarily of any great spiritual development, but are chosen from among those who are available with sufficient experience of Subud.

The *latihan* is not something that can be taught, but is said to arise spontaneously within a person who receives the power of God by transmission through a person in whom it is already established, i.e., a helper. The exact experience may differ according to the needs of each individual, but it does not come about through human action or volition. It is something totally dependent on the will of God.

It is said that the experience of the *latihan* only continues so long as the person inwardly submits to it, and the will is free at any moment to intervene and stop its action. When 'opening' a new aspirant, helpers do nothing for them other than doing their own *latihan*. Of its own accord, the same process at work in the helper begins to take place in the initiate.

The experience of the *latihan* varies greatly between individuals: some experience something powerful and overwhelmingly profound almost instantly, while others have to wait for long periods before consciously perceiving the effects of 'opening'. While 'opening' is taking place, the hands may rise, or the body begin to sway, and during this time the state of mind is described as 'free wheeling'. There is no conscious effort or prayer necessary, but those taking part spontaneously become channels for the power of God. Healing also sometimes takes place at 'openings'.

Once an individual has been 'opened', he is asked to attend *latihans* twice a week in company with other members. Men and women practise separately, and are accompanied by one or more helpers, whose job it is to time the *latihan* and generally ensure that things do not get out of hand.

During the *latihan* members do not go into a trance, but are fully conscious. Although the experience varies between individuals, and also from *latihan* to *latihan*, to begin with it usually takes the form of physical movements and sounds. These are, it is claimed, outward manifestations of an inward action too deep to be directly experienced. As time goes on, the experience should become more inward. The experience is said to bring a great feeling of peace to the individual, which stays after the *latihan* itself is over. The purpose of the *latihan* is one of purification, and worship of God through surrender to His will.

Subud has no creed or dogma, rules or regulations attached to it. Neither does it interfere with the practice of any religion, although yoga and meditation are discouraged. Pak Subuh is regarded as a spiritual guide, rather than a teacher, and he explains that all the teachings necessary for mankind have been given in the religions of the world. It is said that the experience of the *latihan* is the true essence of all religions, and is available for the first time to all mankind through Subud. Experience rather than theory is stressed. Pak Subuh himself is held in great esteem by his followers, who believe that he is divinely inspired and a channel for the power of God. He himself says that he is a man, and fallible, but claims he is a messenger of God.

Newcomers are always made welcome by Subud followers, who will be pleased to talk about Subud and their experiences through it. However warning is given that Subud is in no sense an easy option or a way out of the problems of life. Often it may present individuals with difficulties, and many members report having undergone physical illness 'as part of the purification process'.

Subud can also bring out any inherent mental or nervous disorders, and those with a background of mental illness are not encouraged. Members give the impression of being friendly and open, and will not argue or try to embarrass newcomers. If you take drugs you will have to satisfy the helpers that you want to give them up. Heavy drinkers and outspoken agnostics will also find it a very difficult task to be 'opened'. Stress is laid on practical living, and those initiated will be asked to get a job and work hard, if they are not already doing so.

Subud is open to everyone over the age of eighteen who is prepared to make the affirmation: 'I believe in God and His power and will worship none other than the one Almighty God.' Unless you are over sixty-three, you will be asked to wait for three months after applying for initiation. If after this period you are still of the same mind, then you will probably be 'opened'.

Approximately two thousand people in this country have been initiated into Subud. Many of these have just passed through, but equally there are those who have devoted their lives to its practice. Groups have now sprung up throughout the country, wherever there are people who want to do a *latihan* together. There are six regions in the British Isles, each with its own organisation, and the various groups meet in rented halls and members' homes. Applicants will be put in touch with their nearest group, which may vary in size from a handful of people to a hundred. However, for Subud to be really effective in your life, you must be prepared to sacrifice much. According to a Subud spokesman:

It is important that one has the right attitude to *latihans*. One must want to do the will of God more than anything else, even if this means sacrificing things. The process requires great patience, and it takes a

80

lifetime. You cannot fit Subud into your life – you've got to fit your life into Subud.

Baha'i

A religious movement which began more than 130 years ago in the turmoil of nineteenth-century Persia, and now claims to be the fastest growing religion in the world, is the *Baha'i* faith. Taking as its central message 'the oneness of mankind and the fundamental oneness of all religions', followers of the faith forcefully maintain their independence as a world religion. Today they have representatives in more than three hundred countries, and their literature has been translated into almost four hundred different languages.

The Baha'i story begins with a young Persian merchant, known as the Bab (the gate), who in 1844 proclaimed himself to be a messenger of God. Not unlike John the Baptist, the Bab was the forerunner of the faith, proclaiming that he was the herald of a greater one than himself – 'one who would inaugurate a new era in religion and civilisation'. Opposed and denounced, the Bab and his followers were persecuted for six years. More than twenty thousand of his followers were put to death, and in 1850 the Bab himself was publicly martyred at the age of thirty.

The founder of the faith, Mizra Hussayn Ali, was a Persian nobleman born to a wealthy family in Iran, who in 1863 proclaimed in Baghdad that he was the one of whom the Bab had foretold. Many accepted him and he left Baghdad in triumph, but there followed forty years of exile and imprisonment, during which he frequently underwent torture. Like his predecessor, he was violently opposed and persecuted, and attempts were made on his life. Finally he was banished to Palestine, and it was there, in 1892, at the age of seventy-four, that he died in the prison city of Acre.

During the long years of his banishment he was treated as an object of violent disdain, but after his death the majority of the followers of the Bab accepted him as the 'promised one'. Thus he was formally installed as the head of the Baha'i faith, and given the title Baha'u'llah, meaning 'the Glory of God'.

Following the founder's death, Baha'u'llah's eldest son, Abbas Effendi, was appointed successor, according to the wishes expressed in the old man's will. The son became 'the Centre of His Covenant and the one to whom all must turn for guidance and instruction', and was known as Abdul-Baha ('the Servant of Glory'). He is now regarded by members of the faith as 'the Interpreter'. Remaining a prisoner until the overthrow of the Turkish regime in 1908, Abdul-Baha was released under an amnesty for all political and religious prisoners in the Turkish Empire. It was he who first took the Baha'i faith to the world, travelling in Egypt, Europe and America spreading its message.

Following his death in 1921, his grandson, Shoghi Effendi, who was then a student at Oxford University, was appointed guardian of the faith and interpreter of the scripture. Until his death in 1957 the faith spread rapidly, expanding its following, then his task was taken up by a group of appointees known as 'Hands of the Cause'. In 1963 members of the fifty-six national administrative institutions of the movement, in accordance with the plan laid down by Baha'u'llah himself, elected the Universal House of Justice, and it is this body which today still acts as the supreme legislative and administrative body.

The Baha'i faith takes its teachings from the principles, laws and ordinances laid down by its founder in over one hundred volumes of writings. These include letters sent to kings, rulers and religious leaders of the world by Baha'u'llah, proclaiming his station and calling. The basic tenet of the teaching is that religious truth is relative and not absolute. Divine revelation is regarded as a continuing and developing process, whereby man is educated through a series of prophets. These prophets include the great religious leaders of history such as Buddha, Christ, Mohammed and Moses who, according to the Baha'i teaching, gave the world the same fundamental teachings, but also revealed the specific laws and principles suited to the age.

Differences between religions have arisen because of their followers' failure to understand the teaching, and because the message is revealed according to the stage of development reached by mankind in each age. Man has evolved through progressively fuller revelations of the mysteries of God, and each messenger has given a fresh impulse to his endeavour, teaching love of God and social virtues. In time religion becomes corrupt, and then God sends another messenger to revive things and begin a new era. Baha'is claim that the messenger promised in all the holy books has appeared, bringing the same message, but suited to modern needs.

Baha'is believe that Baha'u'llah is the prophet for our time, whose job it is to fulfil the revelations of the past. It is he who reconciles the divergent beliefs of the age, with the aim of reinstating fundamental truths in conformity with the particular situation of the present age.

The principle around which the Baha'i belief pivots, applicable specifically to present times, is that of the oneness of man. The present stage in man's evolution is 'the coming of the age of the entire human race', and this involves the abolition of racial, religious, class, national and colour prejudice, realisation of equality of the sexes, prohibition of slavery and the elimination of the extremes of wealth and poverty. Accepting that all problems are spiritual in nature and have a spiritual solution, Baha'is believe in the inevitable unity of mankind, and claim that only the 'transmuting spirit of God' can bring this about.

Thus the Baha'i mission is to unite mankind, and in addition to spiritual teachings, the writings of Bah'u'llah lay down the institutions and attitudes which will prevail in the new world commonwealth. He calls for a world superstate, an international executive, a world parliament, and a supreme tribunal, the functions of which are clearly described. A universal auxiliary language is also advocated for the unification of mankind.

Within the Baha'i faith itself, consultation is said to be the keynote of its administration. The faith has no clergy and no ritual, and is supported entirely by voluntary contributions, which may only be made by its own members. While all bodies are elected, no 'politics' are allowed within the movement, and those in authority are considered to be answerable to God. Support and obedience to the elected administration is regarded as the foundation of community life, and Baha'is attempt to achieve a balance between authority and freedom. Teachings on the individual life encourage strict obedience to the laws of one's country, chastity and decency, discouragement of divorce and encouragement of family life. A high moral standard and right dealing in all affairs are called for. Baha'is claim their faith is only in its infancy, but already there are some five hundred assemblies of Baha'is in Britain, where followers meet regularly. These meetings follow no fixed pattern, but generally include prayers given by the Founder as well as readings from his works. The address of local centres can be obtained from the National Spiritual Assembly of the Baha'is in London, who also hold regular meetings at their headquarters at 8 p.m. every Thursday. Followers always welcome enquiries, and you will be encouraged to examine the faith for yourself, rather than blindly accept any dogma. The Baha'i Publishing Trust publishes a wide range of literature, and a complete catalogue of publications available can be obtained on request from the Trust.

Sufism

A school of Eastern mysticism which has found favour in the eyes of many Westerners in recent years is Sufism. The word *sufi* is derived from an Arabic word meaning wearer of wool, which was once taken as a sign of spirituality and austerity. Sufism began to develop in the eighth and ninth centuries A.D., and was the mystical offshoot of Islam. Not unlike the first Christian communities, the first Islamic generation formed a fairly homogeneous body of belief, with a strong mystical bias. But after the second generation, the 'rot' began to set in, and the spreading of worldliness caused a falling away from the purist Islamic belief and practice. This left a distinct class of Islamic mystics, who became distinguished by the name 'Sufi'. Within the Sufi community itself, different groups quickly formed, and this in turn led to the formation of a large number of Sufi orders, many of which survive today.

Deeply rooted in Islam, Sufis sought much of their support in the Koran, and differed from Muslims in their understanding of religious practice, rather than in the practice itself. Today there are Sufi orders in most Islamic countries, and in recent years small Westernised versions of these orders have begun to appear in Britain and other Western countries.

One group which, although Sufi in inspiration, chooses not to use the phrase about itself, is *Beshara*. They believe that the word has become devalued in the West, because of fake Sufi orders, but nonetheless differentiate between two types of Sufism. The first is the traditional Sufism, which is a religion connected to Islam. The second they refer to as the 'real' esoteric Sufi tradition, which is free from religions, and it is with this that they associate themselves. They think that the various Sufi orders, formed after the death of particular saints, have deteriorated through time, until today they have become shallow and have lost contact with the source of their original inspiration. In contrast, they see themselves as the possessors of the true Sufi esoteric tradition.

Beshara began in Britain five years ago, when a mysterious Turk was sent here with the sole purpose of initiating the group. The origins of this man are a mystery, but he is still around in the wings, and helps things along behind the scenes. However, he is in no sense a guru, a concept which absolutely contradicts the Beshara philosophy. Members of the group believe that no single figure should dominate, and this idea is a central concept which is regarded as an idea of the coming age.

Beshara's teaching is based upon the writings of two great Sufi saints, who lived during the twelfth and thirteenth centuries – Jalall-udin Rumi and Muhyiddin Ibnul 'Arabi. These two men represent a synthesis of a certain stream of prophets, beginning with the Jewish, passing through the Christian and reaching completion with the Islamic, a progression considered as summarising the essence of the teaching, which is the perfect and complete man.

Beshara's work falls into four main areas: *zikr* or remembrance, study, meditation and service. *Zikr* is practised regularly by Beshara members, who kneel in a circle or straight lines and chant Arabic names of God. The names are actually ancient dervish forms of God's various attributes, and pertain to His beauty. They are supposed to help the individual reach a constant awareness of reality and of God, and in fact all work in Beshara is towards this end. Any 'experiences' which a person may have as a result of *zikr* are regarded as incidental. The aim is to return to the source and merge with it, thus fulfilling man's destiny.

Study is regarded as a vital part of the Beshara path, in that it enables one to relate experience to the greater whole, and understand the details of the Unity. Arabi is studied in the first instance, and it is only later that the student progresses to examine Rumi, who is regarded as the more sophisticated of the two.

Students are first introduced to study in Beshara via an introductory paper called the 'twenty-nine pages'. This explains the symbolism and

84

outlines the concepts with which Arabi works. Initially it is very difficult to come to grips with this sort of philosophy, which is intensely intellectually demanding and requires great clarity of mind. But members of Beshara claim that the writings do justify the effort, and that once the unfamiliar concepts are understood, the noble nature of the writings may be perceived.

Meditation is not thought of by Beshara members as being a particular technique, and the less emphasis laid on technique the better. At first students are introduced to meditation through very simple methods, learning to slow down the breathing rate. Gradually individuals develop their own techniques, which suit them best, but again, these will be very simple. Meditation is regarded very much as a preparation for *zikr*, helping to make the individual calm, so that *zikr* can be practised in the correct manner. The aim of the *zikr* is to give praise and worship, rather than to attain experience.

Service is probably the most difficult aspect of Beshara's work to define.

> It (service) is the only step we can take to change our situation and go beyond the laws that govern our 'ordinary life'. Service is the principle of aligning ourselves to the will of God . . . until we understand the true meaning of it, which necessarily entails sacrifice and commitment, we cannot begin to change.

Beshara does not claim to be a spiritual path, but a means of bringing oneself to see what is already there. This ability comes from study, which gives discretion and enables one to avoid various pitfalls. It develops the correct mental attitude necessary to comprehend one's experiences, and provides a framework into which these experiences fit.

The word 'Beshara' means messenger of God, and the long-term aim of the group is to prepare for the Second Coming of Christ. This event will herald the end of a great cycle in man's evolution – whereas the First Coming brought the possibility of going straight to the Creator, the Second Coming will see the fulfilment of this.

Although Beshara is intellectually very demanding, members stress that the prerequisite for understanding is to question one's own existence. The very intellectual may not be able to comprehend the teachings, whereas the less intellectual may be able to understand because of their desire to do so. Generally followers are under thirty, although they come from a broad spectrum of educational and class backgrounds. There is no set doctrine maintained by the group, but as a person gradually comes to know himself, he will find his place in the group. Although thousands are believed to have come into contact with Beshara, only about a hundred people are totally committed.

The organisation runs Swyre Farm in Gloucestershire, where people can go for any length of time from a weekend up to six months. There is a daily routine at the farm, which includes meditation, study, exercise and farming work. The atmosphere is very relaxed, and members try to maintain an open, undogmatic environment. An early visit to the farm probably offers the best introduction to the group. Otherwise, there are Beshara centres in other parts of the country. These differ immensely, and are run autonomously. Some offer a wide variety of activities, including study, discussion, *zikr*, meditation, and even yoga and pottery classes, acupuncture and theatre workshops. Visitors are always welcome to call, and may join in study and *zikr*. Further details about Beshara can be obtained from the London address, although visits to the farm are probably best arranged directly.

Beshara are now organising special training courses in Wales for those who wish to commit themselves to a more concentrated period of study. Information on these courses, which last two weeks, is available from any Beshara centre, or Swyre Farm.

The group have also recently acquired a large country house, near Selkirk, which they are preparing for use as their 'School of Intensive Esoteric Studies'. This will offer people who have undertaken short-term studies through the various Beshara centres the opportunity to develop their work. It is hoped the community will become self-sufficient, and thus provide the opportunity for individuals to achieve a different perspective on life. The courses at the new school began in October 1975. Each course will accommodate fifty students and will last for six months. There will be both a resident staff and visiting lecturers on specialised subjects, and emphasis will be placed on the personal development of each individual. Further details are available from the Secretary of the school.

Perhaps the longest established Sufi organisation in the West, tracing its beginnings back to 1910, is the *Sufi Order*, whose head is Pir Vilayat Inayat Khan. Its teachings are said to originate from the philosophy of the Zoroastrian Magi, which was later communicated to the esotericists of Islam. Thus members of the Order claim that Sufis existed before the advent of Islam, but that they came to it, and were accepted into the inner circle of Mohammed. Over the centuries the Order's philosophy became a blend of a wide range of religious teachings, and finally, through the efforts of Khwaji Muinuddin Chisti, a Sufi Order was founded in India. The aim of the Order's work was said to be to bring together different forms of religious thought, an aim which survives today.

In 1910, Hazrat Pir-o-Murshid Inayat Khan, a mystic and descendant of the Order's founder, was sent to carry its teachings to the West. A spiritual pioneer as far as Sufism was concerned, Hazrat travelled through Europe and America, lecturing. He also wrote a series of books now regarded by many as Sufi classics, and his teaching very much reflected the traditional Sufi emphasis of teaching through music and sound.

After living in Paris, where he held an annual pilgrimage and retreat, Hazrat returned to India in 1927, where he told his eleven-year-old son, Pir Vilayat, that he was to be his successor. Trained by his father, Pir Vilayat now heads the Chisti Order, and is said to have inherited his father's mystical and spiritual qualities.

The organisation which Pir set up grew largely from his sponsorship of a number of inter-denominational congresses. One of his central messages is that of the universal religion – 'God is One'. The Sufi Order, therefore, stresses the Sufic element which says there are no barriers between religions. To this end, inter-denominational congresses, on a wide number of themes, have been organised by the Order in London, Paris, Milan, Geneva, New York and Los Angeles. There are also youth camps in America, and in Chamonix, where Pir has an ashram, retreats and seminars for people of all ages are held.

About five years ago the Sufi Order had a considerable following in Britain, particularly among the young, but this has largely declined, due in no small part to the creation of the Beshara movement. But now there are moves afoot to revitalise the Order, and its first centre, Sufi House in London, has just been opened.

In contrast to Beshara, the Sufi Order is a far easier set-up for the average outsider to accept. It is less demanding and dogmatic, and lacks the element of commitment and group identification which Beshara sometimes exhibits. It is intellectually less rigorous, and is more concerned with trying to be universal and open in outlook, than with plummeting metaphysical depths. The emphasis is on living and enjoying life, and fanaticism and asceticism are not encouraged. Meditation is a very important aid to the enjoyment of life, and as such is an important part of Pir Vilayat's teachings. He teaches a wide range of techniques, beginning with simple breathing practices. Later, more sophisticated techniques are taught, but the point of meditation is always that it enables us to lead our lives more happily. Thus, it is always practical.

Life is seen by Sufis in terms of the relationship between man and God, referred to as the relationship between king and vassal. Life on earth is thought of as an act of chivalry, whereby man undertakes to struggle for a great cause – to manifest the harmony of God on earth. It is this which gives purpose to our lives, and allows us to make sense of it.

Although Pir Vilayat has a following of thousands in America and Europe, there are probably only two hundred people who closely follow him in Britain, but it is hoped that the new centre in London will encourage a resurgence of interest. The centre includes a library and meditation room, and there is even a small retreat shed at the bottom of the garden for those who want to get away from it all.

On the first and third Sundays of each month there is all-day meditation, and every Thursday a Sufi Evening is held. This includes meditation and study, where the writings of Hazrat, Rumi and Gibran are among works examined. It is also planned to begin a regular introductory group for those who are coming to Sufism for the first time. The atmosphere is generally free and easy, with no fixed schedules. This is in line with the belief that Sufism is not a dogma but a way of thinking. For further details about the Order, contact Joyce Purcell at the London centre.

Another Sufi group which claims to have its origins in the work of Hazrat Inayat Khan is the *Sufi Movement*, whose most active branch is the *Sufi Cultural Centre* in east London. Following the death of Hazrat Khan, there was considerable internal dissension among his followers, resulting in a split in the order which gave birth to the Sufi Movement as a separate entity.

Although the Sufi Movement is the parent body, its offspring provides the focus for its activity in this country. The Movement itself is not very organised and consists mainly of older people. With its international headquarters in Geneva, its stated aim is to 'realise and spread the knowledge of unity, the religion of love and wisdom, so that the bias of faiths and beliefs may of itself fall away, the human heart may overflow with love and all hatred caused by distinctions and differences may be rooted out'. It also aims to discover man's potential power of mysticism, and to bring together East and West into a universal brotherhood. Although the Movement does arrange occasional study groups, most of its work is done through the Cultural Centre, from where details about the movement can be obtained.

The Cultural Centre was first opened in 1971, and functions as a bookshop specialising in religious, mystical and philosophical subjects. But the most important work undertaken at the Centre revolves around music, which is traditionally of importance to Sufis. Much of the Centre's work is devoted to selling and teaching classical Indian instruments. The instruments are specially imported from India; many of them are unique and built to the Centre's own specifications. Others are rare, even in India, but have been specially rebuilt by the Centre because they believe them to be of special value. In addition to the instruments themselves, which are kept on display at the Centre, there are also teaching materials in the form of books and tapes, plus a wide range of accessories.

The Centre arranges tuition in small groups at its premises, making no charge for its services. Fees for classes (which are very low) are paid direct to the instructors, and the Centre also produces a list of teachers of Indian instruments, vocal music and dance. At present, sitar is taught on Tuesday evenings, tabla on Thursday evenings, and on Saturdays there are Indian classical voice classes. Check with the Centre in order to get up-to-date details.

In addition to the bookshop and musical business, the Centre also runs an adjacent health-food store, call 'Healing and Health'. This enterprise reflects the interest of the Centre in various forms of alternative healing, including massage, music therapy, colour therapy, herbalism and alpha-wave therapy. Every Friday evening is a special healing evening, during which 'massage may be demonstrated and taught, colour therapy may be examined and experienced, music therapy explained and felt, or any other form of healing may be introduced in a dynamic way'. As well as stocking the usual range of health foods, the Healing and Health shop also imports special oils and herbal treatments from India.

Lectures on Sufism are given every Monday evening, and on Wednesday evenings a meditation group meets, and visitors are always welcome. The meditation sessions usually involve the chanting of various mantras in small groups, but there is no set form for these sessions, and what goes on really depends upon the individual who is taking the group. The atmosphere is very informal, and there are plenty of opportunities for those who wish to get more involved – people are welcome to drop round for dinner and chat.

All members of the community at the Centre play some part in the running of its business, but there is no regular schedule governing life in the community, which does not advertise its activities or seek to convert others. They merely claim to be trying to lead a spiritual life, and do not have a standard platform.

The Sufi Movement also runs a farm near Farnham, Surrey, known as Khankah Abadan Abad, which acts as a training centre for the Movement. It has a community of between twenty-five and thirty, enrolled for periods of one or two years. The Khankah is a closed community, and does not cater for 'spiritual tourism or curiosity seeking'. Visits can be arranged with the director by letter or telephone, but visitors must undertake to play their role in the daily routine of work and follow the community's rules. As well as the normal rules against smoking, drinking and drugs, 'anger, lack of consideration, looseness, dullness, egoism and lack of creativity' are also outlawed. The positive rule is 'participate in the group' – follow the instructions of the leader and give yourself. Visitors staying more than three days will be required to pay £1.50p per day for their keep, while those who stay less than three days are expected to make a donation towards their expenses.

The Movement also organises a work-camp every year, held either in England or Holland, which is basically informal and open to all, and involves work on music and meditation. These provide a somewhat more intense introduction to Sufic teachings, as do the regular summer and autumn schools held in Europe. It is not unusual for some parts of these schools to be closed to the general public, but other parts of the programme, especially lectures, are open to all. For details of study groups run by the Movement, write to the Cultural Centre – but bear in mind that as yet the Movement is not very organised in Britain.

A small Sufi organisation based round one man is the *Sufi Society*. The Society's founder and president is Dr Sufi Aziz Balouch, who has, to say the least, a colourful and varied history. Born on the Persia-Pakistan border, Dr Balouch numbers among his accomplishments ordination as a Muslim priest, appointment as cultural attaché in the Pakistan embassy in Madrid, and a career as a flamenco singer in Spain. He has studied Islamic literature and philosophy at a number of universities, and has spent three years studying Sufism under Akhund Lutf-Allah, a Sufi saint in India. He first came to England in 1947, when he set up the Sufi Society, and has lived in London since 1955. He has also published a large number of books, not only on Sufism, but also on music. Among his other interests, Dr Balouch lists languages, law, medicine, medical-astrology, psychology, naturopathy, homeopathy and healing.

The Sufi Society aims to promote Sufi philosophy, which it does through the organisation of occasional concerts of Sufi mystic music, and also by lectures given by Dr Balouch. Members, who pay only a pound or two per year, are entitled to one free consultation with Dr Balouch on the topic of Sufi mysticism and meditation.

Idries Shah is one of the leading exponents of Sufi thought in the West. He has written more than a dozen books on the subject, including *The Sufis*, regarded by many as the classical reference book in the field, and his work has made a major contribution to the dissemination of Sufi thought to a wide public.

A nobleman, born to a distinguished Afghani family in Simla, India, in 1924, Shah is regarded as having successfully bridged the gap between Western and Eastern outlooks by relating Sufi teachings in a way acceptable to the Western mind. Although a direct descendant of the Prophet, Mohammed, he has always energetically rejected the guru role, resisting the temptation to form his own organisation or cult. Instead he has chosen to reach people through his writings. Despite this he has inevitably attracted a following, particularly in America, and among those attracted have been distinguished poets, novelists and scholars.

Shah employs traditional Sufi methods in his teaching, in particular making full use of stories as a means of helping the individual overcome his conditioning. Less socially conventional methods are also employed, typical of the techniques used by Sufi masters down the centuries.

Although Shah does not rely on formal organisation to get his message across, he does teach selected pupils and runs occasional courses in various centres. In this country there is a number of small groups following his teaching and working weekends are held at Langton House, a fifty-acre estate in Kent from which he runs his Institute for Cultural Research.

Some newspaper reports talk of a 'lightning training system' developed by Shah, claiming that the Rand Corporation in America has adopted his methods. But Shah himself is reticent to discuss his work in detail, refusing to allow his methods to be pigeon-holed. 'The activity in which we are engaged is represented in the totality of what we do,' he explains. 'What we do will depend upon the environment, including the people involved, and so on. We do not work with formal organisation but organise in response to possibilities.'

The best introduction to Shah's work is undoubtedly his writings.

Yoga

Of all the aspects of yoga which are practised in this country, the most widely known is hatha yoga. Basically, hatha yoga is concerned with the body, and its function is to make it healthy and to prepare it for further or 'higher' yogas which lead to spiritual enlightenment. At the same time hatha yoga is often regarded as a purely physical practice which may be followed simply for the improvements it brings in bodily health and well being. While this is a perfectly permissible view to take, it should be borne in mind that physical improvement in health is really incidental to the original aims of hatha yoga. Although there is no well defined point at which yoga merges into a higher discipline, and although yoga and keep-fit both concern themselves with the health of the body, the two are really poles apart.

When the British first moved into India they brought back not only goods but also part of the culture. In this way yoga reached Britain, some say, as far back as 1785. The British in India practised it and also brought it back to their friends, and many Indian yogis came here to hold lectures and demonstrations. But it was not until after the last war that yoga began to take on the form which is so widely practised today.

There are two main ways in which one can set about learning hatha yoga – either through a teacher or from a combination of books, correspondence courses, and demonstrations on television. The best and easiest place to find a teacher is at your local adult education centre, where classes are cheap and instructors are generally well trained. Most centres provide these classes, and they are now becoming so popular that they are available virtually throughout the country. Addresses can be found in your local telephone directory, generally listed under facilities provided by the Education Department of the local Council. Other classes are run by independent teachers, or by teachers who also instruct at adult education centres. Most of these will be trained by one of the two main independent yoga groups – the *Wheel of Yoga* or the *B.K.S. Iyengar Yoga Group*.

Both these groups have common ground, and use the same basic posture and breathing exercises. But while the Wheel says that the physical practice of yoga and the study of the philosophy from which it

91

emerged are inseparable, Iyengar holds that Western man's spiritual development is as yet too slight for him to be able to grasp the subtleties of spiritual enlightenment. Indeed, some members of Iyengar go as far as to claim that anything beyond postures and basic breathing exercises is dangerous, but nonetheless, Iyengar teachers include some philosophy with their physical exercises. Thus if you feel yoga should have the spiritual aim of enlightenment you will probably be more interested in the Wheel, although the organisation does not push the philosophical aspect, but prefers it to go hand-in-hand with the physical.

A further source of information on teachers and hatha yoga methods is the monthly magazine *Yoga for Health,* which is widely stocked or can be ordered from most newsagents. This also contains lists of yoga groups and teachers.

B. K. S. Iyengar is an Indian yogi who came to England several years ago to hold lectures and classes. Among those attending the class was Miss Beatrice Harthan, who had had great difficulty in walking after her spine was damaged in a bus accident some twenty years before. Iyengar's yoga exercises gave her back freedom of movement and took away her pain. Others who attended those early classes were equally impressed, and Iyengar was invited again and again, until a group was founded.

Today it has three main centres, in London, Brighton and Manchester. Beyond those areas it has made little progress. But Iyengar visits Britain about once a year to instruct new teachers, and it is slowly spreading. Many of Iyengar's original pupils have now become full-time teachers themselves.

One drawback to the group is that it is very poorly organised. There is no central address to write to and there are no full-time workers specifically to handle correspondence. Added to this, they issue no publications, lists or guides. But individually, followers of Iyengar have a full grasp of the basic postures and breathing exercises that make up hatha yoga, and an Iyengar-based class is highly recommended.

The Wheel is a much larger and better organised group. Together with its affiliated bodies it covers most of Britain, providing teachers, magazines, correspondence courses – for teachers as well as students – and information in the form of handouts, lectures and seminars. To join the organisation costs about £2, which includes two quarterly magazines: *Yoga*, which gives news of current events and items of general interest, and *Yoga Educational Supplement*, which gives an in-depth account of various aspects of yoga for teachers and serious students. However, it is in the process of decentralising itself. Acacia House will not deal directly with enquiries, but will put you in touch with your nearest regional representative (you must write with an s.a.e. for this information).

Although the Wheel has been included in the hatha yoga section, that is slightly unfair to it. Its creed encompasses all forms of yoga, and it is connected with several other spiritual groups.

Martial Arts

The 'martial arts' are probably as popular now in Britain as they are ever likely to be. Karate, judo and kung-fu are being taught in classes throughout the country, as Westerners try to master the ancient Chinese and Japanese methods of self-defence in emulation of television and cinema heroes.

However another martial art has developed beyond its probable origin as a fighting technique towards an almost totally non-violent form, and this is the *Tai Chi Ch'uan*. Tai Chi was first taught publicly in Peking in the middle of the last century – before this it had taken the form of a secret and esoteric teaching which was restricted to the males of certain Chinese families. Although it may well have begun as a self-defence technique, it is now rarely taught as such, but takes the form of a graceful, flowing, meditative dance, or 'yoga in motion'. The student of Tai Chi moves slowly and consciously through the various postures and movements which constitute the dance, many of them being highly symbolic. Tai Chi is very closely related to Taoist, Confucian and Zen philosophy, and some teachers use the *I Ching* and other philosophical works in order to interpret and explain the dance itself.

Although rather different from Indian forms of yoga, Tai Chi does represent a synthesis of yoga techniques, particularly through its stress on breathing. Breath is the key to Tai Chi – at first one starts with the physical breath, but eventually the rhythm of one's own nature is perceived. When one becomes an advanced pupil, it is claimed that the *chi* (*prana* or life force) is experienced. The dance itself is very simple, with no frills, decoration or superfluous movement. It is about finding the centre of balance, with the physical centre gradually leading on to the spiritual centre. It teaches the individual "containment', the way to build up energy in the body, and then to direct and control its release through movement.

To describe what is basically a visual art in verbal terms is exceedingly difficult, and the only way to get an authentic impression of Tai Chi is to watch it being performed. Teachers claim that the dance is very powerful, and certainly when watching it one experiences the highly charged atmosphere which is created. Tai Chi exhibits continuity of movement throughout, and this is said to represent the constant movement of existence. One is struck, however, by the fact that it does not require a great deal of physical exertion, as do many other forms of yoga. Because Tai Chi excludes all elements of rush, competition, strain and fatigue, it is suitable for a wide range of people, including the elderly.

The overall effect of Tai Chi is said to be harmonisation of mind, body and spirit, a balance between 'yin' and 'yang'. Tai Chi can be approached on any level one desires, and can be regarded as therapy, artistic dance form, physical exercise or meditation. However, many claim that it is a great aid to spiritual development, enabling one to gain a 'heightened spiritual perception'. At the same time it undoubtedly brings physical benefits.

Learning Tai Chi may prove to be a problem, especially if you live outside London. Experienced teachers are few and far between, and many of them are not anxious to publicise their activities. For one thing, their classes are already overfull, but more especially they are anxious to avoid any institutionalisation. They feel that the search for a teacher is of value in itself, and that once something becomes institutionalised it loses some of its value. For this reason there is no one centralised body from which details may be obtained – it is just a case of hunting a teacher down. There are, apparently, various teachers of Tai Chi in certain parts of the country (Manchester and Cambridge, for example), but it is up to the individual to track them down.

Probably one of the most experienced Western teachers of the dance is Mrs Gerda Geddes, who stresses that she gives classes but does not have a group or membership. Mrs Geddes lived for ten years in the Far East, and studied Tai Chi under an old Master in Shanghai. Another full-time teacher, who was originally a pupil of Mrs Geddes, is Beverly Milne, who probably does more public teaching than anyone else. She conducts classes at the City Literary Institute, New College of Speech and Drama, Theosophical Society and Acacia House. However her classes and seminars are usually packed to overflowing, and you will have to be quick to get a place. She also teaches Tai Chi privately.

A third teacher is Mr Lui Hsui-Ch'i, a Chinese Master who is a little different from the previous teachers. He takes a much more serious and traditional approach to the art, and demands a great deal of commitment from his students. He will only take long-term, serious pupils, whom he also encourages to study Chinese philosophy.

A relatively recent arrival on the Tai Chi Chuan scene is the *International Tai Chi Chuan Association*, which gives private tuition at their Wembley headquarters for a fee of about £2 per hour. Group tuition is also given in the evening in hired halls in London and Oxford, for a charge of about £2 for a two-hour session. Venues and times of meetings are likely to change, so you are advised to write to the Association for its latest programme of instruction. All students are required to pay an annual fee of £10 to register as a student of the Association.

Aikido is a relatively recent Japanese martial art which is also said to be a path to spiritual harmony. The techniques of the art are derived from ancient techniques of Japanese sword fencing, although no sword is used. The circular hip movements employed are based on the principle of non-resistance – turning when pushed and entering when pulled, harmonising with one's opponent so as to draw out his force in the same direction as he attacks. The practice of aikido is said to be concerned with achieving unity with nature, and thus it excludes elements of struggle or opposition.

The stated objects of aikido are to teach the oneness of all beings and to assist individuals to unite with nature through self-control. The techniques employed enable one to change the balance of the opponent's motion, and once again there is no dualistic opposition: '. . . one's opponent is under one's control in complete unity'.

Aikido can be very graceful to watch, and is said to be a great boon to physical health by helping to correct certain bone structures, particularly the spinal column, to stimulate blood circulation and to exercise normally dormant muscles. Ideally training should include the four elements of bodily realisation, spiritual realisation, moral realisation and wisdom realisation. Also employed is the power known as 'ki', the energy of breathing.

Aikido was developed by Professor Morihei Uyeshiba, whose place as Master was taken by his son following his death in 1969. Until the Second World War the art was not open to the public, but was taught only to a small group of carefully selected students. After the war, Professor Uyeshiba decided to spread aikido throughout the world, and in 1952 it was first introduced in Europe. Fourteen years later Professor Kazuo Chiba, an instructor in Tokyo, was sent to Britain, and it was he who formed the *Aikikai of Great Britain*, the principle teaching body in this country.

The organisation holds aikido classes every weekday evening at its London headquarters, and in addition has a number of teaching centres throughout the country, including Scotland. For details write to the Secretary in London.

The Sati Society

The Sati Society is a Buddhist-orientated group concerned with 'Satipatthana', the 'way of skill'. The Society has close links with O.R.D. (*see* Development Groups), and is led by John Garrie. It consists of individuals who base their personal and professional skills on the practice of sati, which is in itself an art of living. To define the art of sati presents great obstacles. According to its literature: 'Its very essence IS the practice of it. It points to a level of awareness and integration of the human being which can only be known by experience of it. It is for this reason that the sole requirement for it is that of practice in everyday life'.

Although at first teaching in the Society begins with discussion and reading, the ultimate aim is to reach a wordless state. To this end various forms of meditation play an important role. The philosophical basis of the Society is one of flexibility and freedom of being, with the goal of achieving freedom in action: 'Good humour, a sense of humour and flexibility of mind and body are continually given priority in all Sati Society activities.'

Those wishing to become members of the Society must first complete a basic course of instruction, which may take the form of either basic workshops or private sessions. You will be expected to translate the methods learned during this time into everyday life. Once a member, individuals join one of a number of groups. The development group, lasting five months, studies meditation, healing techniques and philosophy. Regular discussion groups consist of members who each have a personal programme, and attend twice-monthly meetings and monthly private instruction sessions.

Other groups come together at mutually agreeable times to study subjects of interest such as oriental methods of relaxation, respiratory and massage therapies, healing, etc. Personal meditation instruction is available, and retreats are held occasionally to allow members a sustained period of meditation in a secluded environment. Introductory evenings and basic courses are held at varying intervals, but anyone is welcome to enquire further about them or apply for a place on them. John Garrie prefers to meet people for an informal chat before they begin the course. He can be reached at the address given.

The Society publishes a quarterly magazine, *The Sati Journal*, which provides a good introduction to the group. Copies are available from the editor, Eve Godfrey, at the address given. The journal illustrates the group's oriental, and particularly Buddhist leanings, with much of the material by John Garrie himself.

Buddhism

Buddhism arose in northern India in the sixth century B.C. against a background of Hinduism. Its founder was a wealthy prince, Siddhartha Gautama, who became distressed at the illusion and suffering of the world, and left his palace, family and possessions to wander the world in search of Truth. After six fruitless years as an ascetic and religious hermit, he is reputed to have sat under a Bo-tree, and there realised the causes and cure of suffering. It was as a result of this 'enlightenment' that he became known as the Buddha or 'Enlightened One'. The story of how Buddha reached his own enlightenment tends to be less important in Buddhism than the actual teachings he gave, and in this sense Buddhism stands apart from most other religions – Buddha is regarded as an example, rather than an incarnation.

Buddhism teaches a way of liberation through ethics and discipline, and in the system there appears to be no part for a universal God. In fact many Buddhist nations lack a word for such a concept, which the Buddha himself neither confirmed nor denied during his life. He simply chose to ignore God, claiming that he himself was no more than an ordinary man. However, in some countries inevitably, superstition and deification of the Buddha has taken place, wth the result that one may still see certain

Buddhists saying prayers and performing rites to Buddha. This is a feature which generally seems to be missing from the Buddhism which has found its way west. The fact that Buddhism is largely a personal religion has helped to give it widespread influence in the West, where the cult of the individual is highly regarded. Even in the short time that Buddhism has been practised here, it has gone through a number of changes and developments, with the result that today it is less of the intellectual rationalisation it once was, and more of a practical guide to life, based upon the mind-stilling properties of Buddhist meditation.

The basis of Buddhism is that the world is a prison in which we are bound by the 'wheel of karma', or the circle of life and death. The concept behind this notion of karma is that every action we perform – good or evil – has an equal and opposite reaction. Thus because we are trapped into performing actions, we become bound to rebirth. The way to escape the prison is to live the life of the 'middle-path' or 'middle-way' between good and evil, and this is the way to reach 'liberation' or what Buddhists call 'nirvana'. The middle-path is achieved by realising the wisdom of the 'four noble truths' which Buddha taught. These are:

1 The noble truth of pain (or suffering) – birth is pain, old age is pain, sickness is pain, death is pain. Union with the unpleasant is pain, separation from the pleasant is pain, not obtaining one's wishes is pain. In short, the five groups of clinging to existence is pain.
2 The noble truth of the cause of pain – the craving that leads to rebirth, accompanied by delight and passion. Rejoicing at finding delight here and there, namely the craving for lust, for existence, for non-existence.
3 The noble truth of cessation of pain – the complete cessation of that craving. Its forsaking, relinquishment, release and detachment from it.
4 The noble truth of the path that leads to the cessation of pain – right view, right thought, right speech, right action, right livelihood, right effort, right mindfulness, right concentration.

These may sound simple and straightforward, but to achieve these aims is difficult. The eightfold path is not learned parrot-fashion, but must be lived, and the strength to do this comes from meditation. Buddhist meditation has one basic form – concentration on the flow of breath. Beyond this are many other forms, but different groups all practise this basic form from which beginners start. After breath concentration it becomes clearer which type of meditation best suits each individual.

The above 'four noble truths' are given in their encyclopaedic form, but the definitions change shades from group to group. Like other religions, Buddhism is split into factions, of which two basic types are discernible – Mahayana (the greater vehicle) and Hinayana (the lesser vehicle). Mahayana is the more outgoing, loving and 'gentle' form of Buddhism. Its emphasis is on the development of loving kindness, and the fact that it leaves room for the 'emotions' makes it more acceptable to the Western mind. In contrast, Hinayana can be thought of as the 'purer', stricter, more rigorous form of Buddhism, with its stress on the intellect and self-discipline. Far more analytical and 'cooler' in approach, Hinayana orders are more likely to have rules and to demand sacrifice from their followers. Beyond these two main forms there are a number of other groups which follow particular regional forms of Buddhism, i.e, Sinhalese, Tibetan, Thai and Japanese (usually called Zen).

Strength of commitment is undoubtedly the most important factor in determining how much a person gets out of Buddhism. Commitment is made to three things, called the Threefold Refuge or Three Jewels. The Threefold Refuge is: 'I go to the Buddha for Refuge, I go to the Doctrine for Refuge, I go to the Order for Refuge'. The Three Jewels are the Buddha (as an example rather than an incarnation), the dharma (sacred law and duty, the path of right action, which varies from individual to individual) and the sangha, or spiritual community, which represents the contribution Buddhism makes to the world. This contribution is also thought to help the individual as a karmic effect.

One should try and grasp at an early stage that the apparent simplicity surrounding Buddhism is illusory. Whereas other religions have a fairly complex, yet tangible code of behaviour, Buddhism is what you make it, and for this reason only by participating in a particular Buddhist group can you really come to understand what it is about. The best way to go about finding the group most suited to your needs is to approach them personally, rather than depending on the information given in their literature, or even contained in this book.

Several groups run retreat courses at regular intervals. These are relatively cheap and are recommended as an excellent introduction to Buddhism. Full lists of Buddhist groups in Britain can be obtained from The Buddhist Society, the Mahabodhi Society and The Friends of the Western Buddhist Order. Do not be surprised, however, if they all give you the same address, for shortage of teachers in certain parts of the country may mean a virtual sharing of facilities. You may find you have a choice of groups in your area, but it is just as likely that there will be no local Buddhist group, or at least no group with a teacher. In this case the various societies normally suggest an alternative course of action.

Researching Buddhism through books is a difficult task and really no substitute for first-hand experience. There is no one book which summarises the field, but for an excellent circular on reading material, including a list of visual aids, write to the Mahabodhi Society. Reading lists will also be supplied by the other main London organisations, but these vary in content. Regular journals are produced by The Buddhist Society, The Friends of the Western Buddhist Order and the Buddhapadipa Temple. In addition, regular news-sheets are put out by the other main groups.

Founded in 1924, *The Buddhist Society* can claim to be the oldest and best established of British Buddhist groups. Its essential teaching revolves around meditation, and includes regular lectures and discussions. Membership of the Society tended, until recently, to be largely middle-aged, and the approach was basically intellectual. But an increased interest in Buddhism from the young has changed the Society, and it is now more difficult to define its approach precisely. Although it adheres to no single school of Buddhism, the Society is probably closest to the Mahayana school.

Facilities at the Society's premises in Eccleston Square include a large meeting room, library and reading room, bookstall, meditation room, general office and enquiry room. The premises are open every weekday, from 2 p.m. to 6 p.m., and are well worth a visit. The library contains over five thousand books on Buddhism and allied subjects, and is open to non-members at a fee of £2 per year. Most of the more valuable books are kept in the reference library, but the contents of the lending library are available in a limited postal lending scheme for members in the U.K.

Free meetings for non-members are held regularly, and these are followed by more detailed courses on topics such as Zen Buddhism, meditation and other aspects of the teaching. The more advanced courses are only open to members, and full programme details are available from the Secretary. There is no fixed code of behaviour, and the Society lays down no rules or advice, such as requiring its members to be vegetarian. If you are interested, begin by attending the introductory lectures, after which you can go on to the basic meditation class. Here you will learn simple forms of meditation based upon breath control. This is designed to stop mental chatter. Once you have gained a basic grounding in Buddhist belief and practices, the path widens to offer a greater variety of meditation techniques and teachings. Zen, especially, has become increasingly popular recently. The Society provides a basic teaching in Buddhism, but you will find some aspects become more attractive and appeal to you more than others. Although the introductory course is easy to follow and requires little sacrifice, extensive progress comes only after extensive effort. If, therefore, you are looking for dynamic results, you should be prepared to work hard at the teachings, in whichever form you prefer, over a number of years. The Buddhist Society places little emphasis on the devotional aspects of Buddhism, and Buddha himself is regarded strictly as a teacher.

The Society has an international membership, and terms of entry are easy. Anyone who signs the application form and undertakes to support the aims of the Society ('To publish and make known the principles of Buddhism, and to encourage the study and practice of these principles') is eligible to join. Details of membership, including an introductory leaflet and programme of activities, can be obtained from the Secretary at the London headquarters. The Society's magazine is called *The Middle Way*.

The Friends of the Western Buddhist Order are probably the most active and youthful of the Buddhist groups. The group was started by an English traveller in India, the Venerable Maha Sthavira Sangharakshita, who first went East when he was conscripted into the Royal Corps of Signals in 1943. He served in India, Ceylon and Singapore, and came into contact with a number of prominent spiritual figures, both Buddhist and Hindu. These meetings persuaded him to become a vegetarian and to take up the practice of meditation. Sangharakshita began to write and lecture on Buddhism, and after leaving the army in 1946 he adopted the name of Dharmapriya, 'Lover of Doctrine'. For more than two years he wandered around southern India, living the life of an ascetic. During this period he sat at the feet of such well known gurus and holy men as Ramana Maharishi, Swami Ramdas and Anandamayi Ma, as well as meditating in the solitude of isolated hermitages and remote mountain caves.

Then in 1949 he travelled north and received the lower form of ordination into the Buddhist religion from U Chandramani Maha Thera, the most senior monk in the Thervada Order in India. It was then that he was given the name Sangharakshita, 'Protector of the Order', and continued his way north. Travelling by foot, begging his way from village to village in the traditional manner of Indian spiritual pilgrims, he reached Nepal and lived for a month in a Buddhist monastery. From then on he claims to have progressed in his spiritual understanding, and he has held many posts of importance in Indian Buddhism, most notably editor of the *Maha Bodhi Journal,* an important monthly journal of the Maha Bodhi Society of India. Later he was initiated into Mahayana Buddhism by Dhardo Rimpoche.

Finally, in 1964, Sangharakshita visited England. He intended to stay for four months, but his visit lasted two years, during which he decided that the appeal of Buddhism to the West was too large to overlook. After a farewell tour of India, during which he addressed gatherings of more than a quarter of a million people in Nagpur, he returned to England to found The Friends in April 1967.

While in England Sangharakshita has initiated many Westerners into lay ordination, although his eagerness to spread the message of Buddhism has sometimes made his selection of aspirants the object of criticism. In fact, his whole approach and methods have come under fire from many older and more respectable British Buddhists, but he has undoubtedly succeeded in his main objective of starting a strong *sangha* (spiritual community) in England. Ordination by him is now much more difficult to obtain.

The Friends have drawn most of their support from young people, and even today they tend to be long-haired and more casually dressed than other Buddhist groups. They do not place much importance on rules, but stress instead 'the act of taking refuge'. This is the strength of commitment to the *sangha* itself, a concept which is central to their beliefs. The Friends regard themselves as a spiritual community or fellowship which reaches beyond religion. They organise celebrations of various Buddhist festivals, poetry readings, karate classes, and hatha yoga classes, as well as classes in which communication exercises are practised. They are an open, friendly group, and a visit to their centre provides the best introduction to their activities.

The Friends have an introductory course, lasting twelve weeks, which costs about £15. Free beginners' classes, however, are held on Wednesday evenings at 7 p.m., and on Sundays at 5.30 p.m.. and these include basic meditation classes, taped lectures by Sangharakshita, and tea, with an opportunity to ask questions. There is a bookshop at the Archway centre which also offers a postal sales service and stocks a wide variety of works from Hermann Hesse through Buddhist standard works to Krishnamurti. A book list is available on request, as are recommended titles. In addition, taped lectures by Sangharakshita can be bought.

Although The Friends' activities centre on London, there are various provincial centres, whose addresses can be found in the quarterly newsletter or by writing to the Secretary. The Friends are noted for their retreats which are held regularly, and some are specially designed for beginners. For full details, write to the Secretary, giving your age, interests and previous experience with spiritual groups. Prices for retreats vary, depending on where they are held, but a rough guide would be £1 for a day-retreat at the Archway centre, including two vegetarian meals; £3–£4 for a weekend; and £24 for the bi-annual large retreat, which caters for beginners. The two big retreats are at Easter and in August, and individual days may be taken at these at a reduced cost. A wide variety of activities are offered at retreats, including meditation and hatha yoga.

Closely linked with the Archway centre is the *Aryatara Buddhist Community*, which although autonomous, is basically the same in its outlook and association with Sangharakshita. Regular retreats, organised from Archway, are held at the Purley community, as well as separate events.

The *British Mahabodhi Society* (also known as the *London Buddhist Vihara*) is a Hinayana group which evolved from the Buddhist Mission started in London in 1925 by a Sinhalese monk who travelled from Ceylon for the purpose. The Society is now headed by the Venerable Dr H. Saddhatissa, and is fully independent of Ceylon, although it occasionally receives donations from the Mahabodhi Society of Sri Lanka (Ceylon). It possesses a shrine hall in the vihara, and a lecture room containing a library, which is open to all supporters of the vihara. The shrine hall may be used for private meditation and devotions, while the library contains over one thousand volumes, comprising sets of the

Buddhist canon in English and Asian languages, as well as works on Buddhism and related subjects. When this group was researched, their activities were in a state of flux, and for this reason not much detail can be given. If you are interested write for up-to-date information of activities, while enquiries of a more general nature are welcomed and will be answered.

The Society, which attracts all types of people, offers standard training in meditation and devotion of the Thervada school, including breathing awareness and *satipatthana*, or mindfulness of action. It is, however, necessary to understand the essentials of theory before proceeding to meditation itself. The Society's activities are somewhat limited as they have only one monk, but there are plans to get more from Sri Lanka. The resident monk will, wherever possible, arrange to give talks outside the vihara, or to see interested people there, and no charge is made. The leaflet produced by the vihara for schools and colleges interested in studying Buddhism contains a comprehensive reading list, which does not confine itself to Thervada Buddhism.

The *Buddhapadipa Temple* is a Thai Buddhist group, financed by the government of Thailand. It has five resident monks, all sent from Thailand, but the temple is designed to serve the whole Western world, and it is not therefore unusual to find several of them absent at the same time. The monks perform ceremonies and give instruction in the temple, as well as travelling to Europe and North America to give talks.

As a quorum of four monks is required to ordain a novice monk, the Temple is the only place in Britain where ordination takes place. Several English people have applied for this in the past, but as there was nowhere to accommodate them at the London Temple they were assisted to travel to Thailand to be initiated there.

The Lay Buddhist Association at the Buddhapadipa Temple exists to help support the Bikkhus (monks) and to encourage the study, practice and propagation of the Buddha's teachings. They also help and encourage newcomers to the Temple. Membership is £3 a year, including a subscription to the Temple's journal, *The Friendly Way*. The journal is issued quarterly, and includes articles on Buddhism generally, and information and news on the Temple in particular. A small news-sheet is also published from time to time, giving details of forthcoming events.

The best day for a newcomer to attend the Temple is a Sunday. There is a discussion between 4.30 p.m. and 5.30 p.m., which includes a talk on Buddhism when questions will be answered. Then follows an hour-long meditation class and lecture. No charge is made for the sessions; newcomers are always welcome; and no demands whatsoever are made on the casual visitor. The initial techniques of meditation taught by the monks are basic Buddhist ones, revolving around concentration on the breath. More advanced techniques are taught to those who have reached a later stage.

The Temple's activities are made known mainly by word of mouth, and also by means of the visits which the monks pay to universities, colleges, etc. Students and other organised groups may also arrange to visit the Temple itself for talks, and, if desired, individual audiences with a monk may be arranged to discuss more particular problems. The Temple is open seven days a week, until 10 p.m. Apart from the usual classes, more personal and detailed instruction in meditation is available. The financial support of the Thai government means that the Temple is situated in a very beautiful house, where Buddhist ceremonies such as marriages, and those connected with birth and death can take place.

The only Rinzai Zen group operating in Britain at the moment is *London Zen Studies*, although Rinzai meditation itself is also taught at The Buddhist Society. L.Z.S. has twenty to thirty regular members; meetings are held in their homes, and there are no fixed schedules. Thus it is always advisable to check on the time and place of meetings by writing to the Secretary.

Although small and producing no literature, the group is important as it is the only one of its kind. It has no resident teacher, but Dokyu Nakagawa, leader of the Zen group in Jerusalem, pays regular six-week visits to London. The only requirement for membership is a willingness to join in the prescribed activities. These centre round 'Zazen', a particular form of meditation which involves sitting silently for periods of up to two hours, with breaks every twenty-five minutes. Sometimes these sessions (*sesshins*) extend for several days at country retreats.

Zen has a distinctive, strong flavour of its own, which is often difficult for the Western mind to come to terms with. Nakagawa does not give lectures, and *sesshins* are not really concerned with the answering of specific questions. Zen is not taught here as a philosophy, but rather as a form of self-awareness. You are your own teacher, for only you know your own circumstances, and it is claimed that through the practice of self-awareness perfection is attained.

Nakagawa claims that there are three parts to Zen – Great Doubt, Great Delusion, and Great Faith. The practice of meditation leads from the first to the last of these stages, and there are no intellectual shortcuts. The only basic rule, by which the Master himself lives, is 'Be kind to your own true nature'.

To find out about London Zen Studies, its Master and its meditation, it is necessary to go along and experience it first-hand. Nakagawa said that despite its smallness, L.Z.S. is not an isolated group – 'There are no gaps between Buddhist groups, just overlaps'.

When this book was being researched a new group, the *British Buddhist*

Association, had just held its inaugural meeting. The Association grew from an extra-mural course run at the Working Men's College in London, and was founded to provide systematic instruction in Buddhism for individuals, taking into account their degree of knowledge of the subject. This aim, claim the founders of the Association, makes their organisation unique and of broad appeal. It will try and give a clear and thorough explanation of Buddhism to its students, if necessary before progressing to the practice of meditation. This, says the Association, will provide a 'clear direction and purpose for the practice of mental development'.

The Association will offer facilities for tutorials, informal discussions, 'sutta' (canonical discourses of the Buddha) studies, the teaching of Pali (the language of the Buddhist scriptures), meditation sessions and general Buddhist religious activities. A correspondence course and comprehensive book service should also be available. The Association will be Thervada, although not exclusively so, but it should be borne in mind that the Association is only in its infancy, and may develop in a number of ways. For further information write to the Secretary.

Perhaps the best known Buddhist retreat in the U.K. is the *Samye-Ling Tibetan Centre* in Scotland. The main emphasis here is on the instruction and practice of meditation, and for this reason the retreat was founded well away from city civilisation. The retreat consists of a large, comfortable, twenty-five roomed house, with outbuildings, standing in the middle of twenty-three acres of wooded grounds near the river Esk. The quiet valley in which the centre lies is fifteen miles from the nearest city, 'the surrounding hills and woods provide a perfect environment for study and meditation'. However if you visit Samye-Ling expecting a holiday camp, you will be in for a rude shock! Visitors are expected to work for a few hours a day during their stay, and those who are not genuinely interested in making a contribution to the life of the community are unlikely to stay long.

The Centre is just north of the English border, and takes its name from the first Buddhist monastery to be founded in Tibet. Formerly Johnstone House, the present retreat is administered by a registered charity, the Johnstone Trust. It was started in 1967 by the Venerable Chogyam Trungpa and the Venerable Akong Tarap as a result of the interest shown by Westerners in meditation. Having been very successful for the past seven years, the Centre can now be considered a well-established part of the British Buddhist scene.

Samye-Ling serves three main purposes. Firstly, it is a meditation centre where Tibetan lamas in Britain can teach and study, the emphasis being on the instruction and practice of meditation. Also, those who wish to enter the Tibetan Sangha, or Buddhist Order of lay monks, may receive training. Secondly, it provides a place of quiet retreat for lay people of all religious beliefs and backgrounds, where they can go for periods of regeneration and the practice of meditation. Thirdly, Samye-Ling is where Tibetans in the West can go for religious instruction, thus helping to preserve Tibetan art and culture.

However these are not hard and fast rules. The Centre likes to think of itself as 'a living, changing community, where East and West are learning to unite in spiritual and practical harmony'. Although Samye-Ling is a Tibetan centre, it is important to stress that it is open to all types of Buddhists, and many prominent members of other Buddhist societies regularly visit it.

Meditation is taught at the Centre, and there is a library, containing one thousand books on a variety of religious topics, open for use by visitors. A small charge of about £2 per day is made to visitors for food and accommodation, and it is assumed that those who attend the Centre will show a 'willingness' to sleep on the floor if necessary. In addition to religious pursuits, guests can also take part in craft activities, including pottery, woodblock printing, candlemaking and weaving. Full details of accommodation, vacancies, travel routes, clothing and times of arrival are available by post from the Centre.

The *Kham Tibetan House* was established early in 1973 by a Tibetan refugee, Lama Chime Rimpoche, to enable Westerners to study and practise the oral transmissions of the great Tibetan sage, Milarepa. Lama Chime Rimpoche was born in the eastern Tibetan province of Jyekundo, and was brought up in a Buddhist monastery at Benchen. Having been recognised as a lama, he undertook study and meditation as part of his training for the post of Abbot of the monastery. After completing his formal study, at the age of sixteen he entered a retreat which lasted well over three years. Soon after completing this vigorous preparation for his position as a lama, he was forced to flee from Tibet in the wake of the Chinese invasion. He first journeyed to India, where he learnt English, and in 1956 he arrived in the U.K., initially to study English, but later going on to give lectures on Tibet and Tibetan Buddhism.

From this brief biography it can be seen that Lama Chime Rimpoche is well qualified to be a spiritual teacher, and this is confirmed by the number of pupils he has attracted. He emphasises that his knowledge of the dharma (the Buddhist way) is the result of prolonged study and practice – any Westerner who wishes to acquire such knowledge must fully experience the path that leads to it.

The 'yoga' school of which Lama Chime Rimpoche is a member is based on the Six Doctrines expounded by the four Buddhist saints, Tilopa, Naropa, Marpa and Milarepa. It emphasises the metaphysical aspects of the *sunyata* (unqualified void), or the undifferentiated unity between subject and object, which rests completely in itself.

The school of Milarepa developed a special system of meditation known as Mahamudra meditation, and Lama Rimpoche represents the last generation of Tibetan lamas who have had the opportunity to develop their meditations and studies in a society sympathetic to their efforts. Since arriving in the U.K., Lama Rimpoche has seen his duty to be the instruction of Western pupils in the oral transmissions of which he is the holder, thus ensuring they will not disappear.

The Kham Tibetan House is rather strict in its outlook, welcoming only those 'who are prepared to make a sincere effort to follow the path of liberation unselfishly'. To this end, certain rules operate to ensure visitors are able to practise undisturbed meditation and study. Food at the house is strictly vegetarian, and drugs and alchohol are banned. As the prospectus puts it: 'These rules should not be seen as infringements of personal liberty: rather they create an environment in which a serious and rewarding pursuit of peace and happiness can be sustained'.

The centre is described as small and quiet, with a monastic atmosphere. Individual advice on meditation is given, and fees, which include comfortable accommodation and three meals a day, are about £2 per day. If you intend to visit the Kham House, you are advised to telephone or write first. Please avoid phoning during the meditation hours of 8.15 – 9 a.m.; 11 – 12 a.m.; 5 – 7 p.m. and 8 – 10 p.m.

Another centre which provides a 'retreat-like' atmosphere is *Throssel Hole Priory*, which is essentially a training centre for Zen Buddhists wishing to become priests. It was founded in June 1972 by the Rev. Jiyu Kennett Roshi, Abbess of Shasta Abbey, California. This English lady received her instruction at one of the two head temples of the Soto Zen sect in Japan.

At present the Priory is under the direction of one of her senior disciples, the Rev. Daiji Strathern, who studied at Mount Shasta for some years. Although mainly for trainee priests, Throssel Hole is open to laymen who are prepared to abide by the strict rules.

Soto is one of the two main branches of Zen meditation (the other being Rinzai), and can be roughly described as 'a detached watching of the stream of consciousness'. This takes the form of sitting quietly and observing the thoughts inside the mind. It is the quietest type of meditation, closely equivalent to the Thervada meditation technique of Vipassana. It must be pointed out that Soto is dangerous to practise without a teacher. Although it may sound simple and straightforward, Soto is actually very difficult, the meaning of the word being an untranslatable term.

Those considering visiting Throssel Hole are recommended to read Kennett Roshi's book, *Selling Water by the River: A Manual of Zen Training* (Allen and Unwin, available in paperback from the Priory, price £1.50 incl. p & p). This includes her own writings of Zen training, along with translations from the founders of the Soto School in Japan, and all the important ceremonial of Soto Zen. Once again, the Priory is no holiday camp. Hard physical work, gardening and repairing the building, are considered as important as meditation. With every booking form is issued a list of fifteen rules, which are strict by any definition. As well as the usual instructions regarding smoking and drugs, other rules relate to dress, silence during mealtimes, and the banning of 'idle chatter'. All personal religious practices are strictly forbidden, as is the reading of unassigned material. The Priory is located in eighteen acres of land, twenty miles south west of Hexham in Northumberland, where bad weather conditions can make life very hard. If you feel put off by the lack of normal Western material comforts at the Priory (both mental and physical), details of small Soto groups around Britain are contained in the Priory's bi-monthly newsletter, which costs £2 a year. Included in this fee is a postal advice service for those having problems with their meditations, etc. Subscribers are also given preference with regard to places at retreats. Charges at the Priory are very reasonable.

An unusual Zen school which incorporates karate training into its system is the *Hakurenji Zen Centre*, based in London. The Centre teaches a system known as Kongo Raiden Zen, which is a special form of meditation training developed by the Buddhist Saint Bodhidharma at a Shaolin temple in northern China. It is said that he was noted for his instruction in the art of self-defence, and that he originated many forms of unarmed combat, and in particular the karate-do system. The emphasis in the Kongo Raiden school is on the use of bodily movements as a means of obtaining spiritual experiences. According to literature:

By harmonizing physical and mental concentration a state can be realised which brings Peace, Harmony and Wisdom in its wake. These facets are not, within Kongo Raiden, restricted to endeavours of a spiritual nature but permeate into all parts of one's life.

There are two main aspects to the Kongo Raiden doctrine – Kengyo (outer doctrine) and Mikkyo (esoteric doctrine). Kengyo is the external or formed path which encompasses various physical arts, and in particular karate-do. Mikkyo centres on meditation and devotional practice, and is more mystical, involving both study and introspection. Normally one would not undertake the Mikkyo until some skill at applying the principles of the Kengyo path had been obtained. In addition to the various physically orientated studies, students of Kongo Raiden undertake the study of other ancient arts such as igaku (medicine), eki (divination) and ryorido (dietry therapeutics). They are encouraged to take a broad integrated approach to their spiritual endeavours, rather than

107

concentrating on any one particular area. Intensive study of Buddhist scriptures does not play an important role in the school, although the writings of Bodhidharma are sometimes referred to, and scriptures of other religions may be introduced by teachers to illustrate particular points.

The teacher–pupil relationship is of utmost importance in the Kongo Raiden school, as it is traditionally in most Zen schools. Initial training is a preparation for being accepted by one of the school's teachers as his or her personal student. Formal acknowledgement of this acceptance is given at a special ceremony known as Okan, during which the aspirant is given a new spiritual name. Around the time of Okan the prospective Master gives 'the gift of Threefold Transmission', which means that he accepts the responsibility for the future spiritual welfare of the student and undertakes a commitment to teach him. The accepted student then enters a pupil–teacher relationship in which he is expected to serve his teacher faithfully and be attentive to his teachings.

No teachers of the school are allowed to accept payment, and students are not required to pay any sort of fees for their training. What is demanded is that they attend classes regularly, as well as attending various seminars which are held from time to time. These events are regarded as important within the Kongo Raiden tradition, providing as they do the opportunity for a 'spiritual family reunion'. At them further teachings and meditations will be given to the student, and there will be opportunities to discuss any personal problems which may have arisen.

Mushindo Karate-Do forms an important part of the school's training, but it should be stressed that this is not in any way similar to the 'sport' karate which is widely taught in Britain. First the student undergoes training and hard practice in the mind/body relationships associated with the ancient forms of karate practice – this is known as the Mushindo school. This then leads to the deeper stage, called the Kongojo school, which involves more commitment, and is really only for the serious student. Students who reach this stage will normally go on to learn the deepest aspects of karate, involving much meditation and retreat. The entering of the Kongojo path should be the aim of all Mushindo students, and all Mushindo black belts have to possess a certificate granted by the Order showing that a balanced course of instruction has been completed.

Closely associated with the school is the *Mushindo Karate-Do Association*, which has centres throughout Britain run by teachers under the Masters of Kongo Raiden. Regular residential courses, called Gashaku, are held, and Mushindo students from all over the country come together. There are four grading examinations a year, and in this way the student's progression is clearly marked out. Newcomers are welcome to come along and watch a class in progress, and local clubs run special beginners' classes. For further information about Mushindo Karate-Do and details of your nearest club, write to the national Secretary of the Association enclosing an s.a.e.

3 Esoteric Societies

Theosophy

The movement which, perhaps more than any other, was responsible for
first popularising Eastern and esoteric doctrines in the West was the
Theosophical Society, founded in New York in 1875 by the now legend-
ary Mme Helena Petrovna Blavatsky. Theosophy, meaning 'knowledge
of God or the divine', is a system of thought which has close connections
with Buddhist, Vedic and Brahmanist traditions. Mme Blavatsky claimed
to teach an ancient hidden wisdom ('theosophia'), the central core of all
religions, contained in the 'secret doctrine'. In the early days of the
movement Mme Blavatsky, a woman of great psychic ability, was joined
by another outstanding woman, Mrs Annie Besant, in setting up the
headquarters of the movement in India, where it remains to this day. This
was done in the belief that the continent would be the birthplace of a
great spiritual world revival. In its early days the Society attracted a great
deal of attention from leading intellectual figures of the day, including
Rudolph Steiner (*see* Anthroposophical Society). But the movement was
to experience stormy developments, which would cause splits within it.
Following the death of Mme Blavatsky at the end of the last century,
Mrs Besant finally emerged as the Society's new president, but only a
year later she caused great dissension by 'discovering' a young Indian
child, Jiddhu Krishnamurti, and pronouncing him the new Messiah.
This was too much for many theosophists to take, and the resulting rows
divided the Society. Mrs Besant toured the world with Krishnamurti
until, in 1929, before a large American audience, he announced that he
was no more than an ordinary mortal.

But despite these early dramatic developments, the Theosophical
Society has continued its work, and today exists as a sizable inter-
national organisation, with branches in well over forty countries.
Throughout, its three stated objects have been:

1 To form a nucleus of the universal brotherhood of humanity without
   distinction of race, creed, sex, caste or colour.
2 To investigate unexplained laws of nature and the powers latent in
   man.

3 To encourage the study of comparative religion, philosophy and science.

Theosophists claim its truths stretch back to the beginnings of man himself. Throughout history these truths have been known to small numbers of 'initiated seers', but down the ages the doctrine has been kept largely secret, revealed only to the chosen few.

Only with the beginnings of the Theosophical Society were some parts of this teaching first made public, through the writings of Mme Blavatsky. According to theosophist literature, the truths revealed are 'concerned with the laws of nature and of man's being, physical, mental and spiritual . . . The vast plan of universal origins and the possibilities of man's development are revealed in these writings, and meaning and incentive given to his progress.'

Theosophists believe all great religions and the teachings of wise men throughout history have a certain common body of knowledge, and it is this which is referred to as theosophy. The principle doctrines involved are that existence is a unity governed by certain invariable universal laws. Evolution is a fact of nature, and man himself is part of the evolutionary process, distinct in that he has responsibility for his actions and can direct the course of his future evolution. At the same time, each human life is a part of a total pattern of individual evolution, governed by the natural laws, such as those of rhythm and karma. While the forms in which life expresses itself are transient, the spirit behind them is eternal, and thus when man dies his individualised spirit continues. After a period he is restored to a new body, and so his spirit continues through a number of earthly lives, progressively unfolding his spiritual powers. Individual earthly conditions are determined according to the law of karma.

Throughout, it is stressed that man has the power to free himself from all human limitations, to experience reality directly, and to know God without an intermediary.

A vital part of the liberation process for theosophists is concerned with the practice of meditation, for they believe that as the journey to self-realisation is an internal one, ultimately all methods merge into the practice of meditation. It is only through meditation that man can go beyond his normal limited mind to experience Reality.

These ideas, which are crude simplifications of a few of the concepts contained in theosophical thought, serve only to give something of the flavour of theosophy's teachings. They are not, however, regarded as a creed which must be blindly accepted by followers of the path. They are looked upon rather as facts of existence discovered by generations of students and put forward as hypotheses to be examined by those who wish to know the Truth. Only when an individual develops the powers to examine them himself, does he join the ranks of those described by theosophists as the 'Knowers'. It is always the responsibility of the

111

seeker to discover truth for himself, and the distinction is always drawn between knowing the Truth and knowing *about* the Truth.

Freedom of thought is highly valued within theosophy, and was guaranteed by a resolution passed by the General Council of the Society:

' . . . there is no doctrine, no opinion by whomsoever taught or held that is any way binding on any member of the society . . . Approval of its three objects is the sole condition of membership. No teacher or writer, from H. P. Blavatsky downwards, has any authority to impose his teachings or opinions on members.'

The Theosophical Society is organised into national sections, each of which constitutes a national society, with its members generally organised into branches or lodges. All groups of members, whether local or national, are largely autonomous, with the powers to frame their own rules, elect their own officers etc. Meetings normally take the form of lectures or study and discussion groups, and there are also occasional public lectures. Study groups and guided meditation sessions are held at the Society's London headquarters and in some branches are also open to non-members. Special discussion groups are organised for those who are interested in joining. In addition, large gatherings in conferences, summer schools and camps also take place.

For those interested in finding out more about the Society, there are a large number of books on theosophy, many of which are published by the Society's own Theosophical Publishing House. These are available from many bookshops and libraries, as well as the Theosophical Bookshop in London. The Society has a lending library at its headquarters which is open to members and non-members. For free leaflets, booklets, programmes and details of library membership, write to the Information Department in London.

Details of membership, application forms and the address of your local branch will be sent, on request, by the Society's headquarters. Either write or telephone, or you are welcome to make a personal visit. Application for membership is made through the branch secretary or direct to the General Secretary, but two sponsors who are already members of the Society will be required to endorse your application. If these are not available, the General Secretary will interview you personally, or if you cannot conveniently come to London, you must accompany your application form with a short letter describing your interest, your acquaintance with the Society and any comment you wish to make on its objects. The present membership fee is normally £3 a year, with reductions for the elderly and those under eighteen. The Society publishes its own *Theosophical Journal* which is sent free to members. New members normally receive an introductory course in theosophy.

Anthroposophy

A charge frequently made against spiritual philosophers is that their work has an 'other worldliness' quality which prevents it being applied to the practical aspects of social life. Nothing could be less true about the work of the highly original *Rudolph Steiner*, whose writings and ideas have inspired a wide range of enterprises still flourishing today. His attempts to develop a system linking the world of natural science with the world of the spirit have given birth throughout the world to projects utilising his philosophy, in areas ranging through drama, art, architecture, education and even farming. Although little known to the general public, his ideas have revolutionised the thinking of many doctors, teachers, actors and religious ministers, many of whom have dedicated their efforts to working in special institutions based on his philosophies.

Steiner was the son of a minor railway official and was born on the Austro–Hungarian border in 1861. After studying science at the University of Vienna, he developed a deep interest in the work of the German poet and thinker, Goethe. Steiner had, in his early life, undergone clairvoyant experiences, and outside of his scientific studies had developed a wide knowledge of literature and the arts. It was this combination of scientific and artistic interests which attracted Steiner to Goethe. At the age of twenty-three, he edited some of Goethe's scientific works, and later went to Weimar to work on more writings at the Goethe archives. Some of his major work in this area was on Goethe's 'Theory of Colour', which eventually gave rise to his own development of 'colour therapy', utilising the supposed beneficial effects of colour.

While at Weimar, Steiner undertook the tutoring of a backward child, providing experience which would be significant in the development of his later work. He also elaborated his own philosophies in *Truth and Science* and *The Philosophy of Freedom*, in which he asserted that thought could become an organ with which to perceive the spiritual. Although attracted to the work of the mystics, Steiner maintained that he wanted to experience the source of wisdom through ideas, which he termed 'a mystical experience of thoughts'.

In 1897 Steiner moved to Berlin to edit a literary magazine, and there became involved in drama and the theatre. By this time he had also taken up meditation, which he claimed gave an experience through which one could reach the spiritual world far more than with ideas.

After being invited to lecture on Goethe to a theosophical circle, Steiner began a connection with the theosophical movement which was to last ten years. He even reached the post of General Secretary of the Society's German branch, but in 1909 he broke away because of his opposition to its declarations concerning the divinity of Krishnamurti (see Theosophical Society). At this point Steiner formed his own 'splinter' group, which he called the *Anthroposophical Society*, from the Greek 'anthropos' meaning man and 'sophia' meaning wisdom.

His first two anthroposophical works were *Knowledge of Higher Worlds* and *From the Akashic Record*. The first of these describes the 'path of initiation' for modern Western man, providing exercises for development. The second begins his teaching on the universe and man, claiming that there exists an earth memory, written in an earth aura, which is accessible to a trained clairvoyant. The information contained in this aura, Steiner claimed, could be used to provide new perspectives in the study of man, provided modern scientific discoveries were also taken into account.

During this early period of his work, Steiner also lectured widely on the gospels, although never a Christian in the orthodox sense of the word. In *Christianity as Mystical Fact* he expounded the gospels as esoteric documents which were, he claimed, intended only for the initiated.

Occult Science – An Outline is another work belonging to Steiner's early period, which summarises the philosophy of Anthroposophy, introducing his ideas on the four 'bodies' of man, his soul, life in the spiritual world, the evolution of earth, the seven epochs and seven historical civilisations, and so on. Steiner adopted a strictly monistic view of creation, arguing that everything, including physical material, had its origin in living spirit, with man constituting the highest development in evolution.

During his years with the Theosophical Society, Steiner had travelled on lecture tours throughout Europe, and had studied the art and architecture of each place he visited. He desired strongly to express his spiritual vision through art, and this led him over the years to write four mystery plays, utilising an art of movement to speech and music which he developed, called 'eurythmy'. This art, still enthusiastically pursued by Steiner's followers today, uses movement to express both music and speech. It aims to express in gestures the actual sounds which form the words of speech, and the actual notes and intervals contained in music. Requiring much study, eurythmy captures and expresses, through movements particularly of the hands and arms, the formative power contained in the sound of music and speech.

The project which was possibly to have the widest influence of any of Steiner's work was the establishment, in 1919, of a school in Stuttgart for the children of employees of the Waldorf-Astoria cigarette factory. It was this first 'Waldorf school' which formed the launching pad of an educational movement which has spread throughout the world, and now has about ninety schools educating a total of 40,000 pupils. Among those who approached Steiner for guidance at this time were teachers of backward children, farmers and doctors. The advice which he gave has led to movements in curative education and a school of medicine. In the

114

field of farming, Steiner developed the 'bio-dynamic' approach, which is also pursued today. During his final years, Steiner lectured on subjects ranging through mathematics, astronomy, medicine, economics and many others. He died in 1925.

Followers of Steiner are active across a wide spectrum of practical activities in this country, including schools, homes for children in need of special care, teacher-training centres, eurythmy and artistic therapy centres, a nursing home, a science foundation, an agricultural association, and a company manufacturing and distributing medicinal and toilet preparations. The central body representing Steiner's work in Britain is the *Anthroposophical Society in Great Britain*, whose headquarters are in London. Although the various institutions pursuing Steiner's teachings in particular fields are independent, the Society will be pleased to give information about them, and publishes a booklet, *Practical Activities founded on the work of Rudolph Steiner*, which is available on request for 15p. The Society's headquarters, Rudolph Steiner House, contains a bookshop which stocks all the English translations of Steiner's work, as well as a large selection of related books. A catalogue will be sent on request.

The Secretary's office is open every day from 10 to 5, to answer enquiries about Steiner's philosophy, and also general enquiries about the Society and its work. A full programme of lectures, classes and performances are held at Steiner House, including introductory study groups, classes in artistic activities such as painting, speech and drama, and special events such as performances of eurythmy. A syllabus of activities is available on request. There is a library which contains all Steiner's books and lectures, open for reading and borrowing from 2–6 p.m. on Mondays, Wednesdays, Thursdays and Fridays, and until 7.15 on Tuesdays. Books are available to members free of charge, but non-members may join the library for a small charge. There is a postal service for those unable to call.

The Society produces a large number of publications, including an annual magazine, *The Golden Blade*, and an *Anthroposophical Quarterly*, containing lectures by Steiner plus other articles and reviews. These and publications produced by other Steiner bodies are all available from the Society's bookshop.

Those interested in membership are advised to join the library or attend lectures and classes in order to gain preliminary understanding of Steiner's work. Membership is open to anyone in sympathy with the Society, on the recommendation of two of its members. Intending members should ask for a printed 'Note on Membership', or ask for an interview with the Secretary or Chairman. Groups, local centres and study groups of the Society have been established throughout the country, and the addresses of these are available on request from the Society.

Alice Bailey

Another teacher who worked for a period within the Theosophical Society but later split to form her own group was Alice A. Bailey. The organisation based on her teachings is *The Lucis Trust*, which includes within it the Lucis Press, and the more specialised groups, the *Arcane School, Triangles* and *World Goodwill*.

Alice Bailey was born into respectable, middle-class, Victorian Manchester in 1880, the daughter of an engineer. Although both her parents had died before she reached the age of nine, she was given a typical Victorian young lady's upbringing, which included travelling abroad, as well as attending finishing school at the age of eighteen. It was in 1895 that she underwent her first 'visitation', when she met her Master K. H. (Koot Hoomi). She reports that while sitting alone in her room, a tall man wearing a turban walked in. He told her that there was certain work which was planned for her to do, and that if she attained self-control she would travel all over the world, 'doing (her) Master's work all the time'. It was only years laters, after she had come in contact with the Theosophical Society, that she discovered the man was not Jesus, as she had supposed at the time. He was, in fact, Master K. H., whom she describes as 'a Master who is very close to the Christ, who is on the teaching line and who is an outstanding exponent of the love-wisdom of which the Christ is the full expression'. Later in her life Mrs Bailey was to become one of the senior disciples within Master K. H.'s 'group' or ashram.

Despite her contact with the Master, not to mention other startling and unusual experiences, throughout her early years, Mrs Bailey was to remain a staunch Christian, describing herself as a 'dyed-in-the-wool fundamentalist'. As a worker with the YWCA she became an evangelist, and after working for some time with the British army, she went to India to evangelise British troops and also to run a number of soldiers' homes. But her work there began to take its toll, both physically and mentally, and after falling in love with a British soldier she later travelled to America, where her new husband, Walter Evans, had become a clergyman in the Episcopal Church. The marriage, however, was doomed to failure, and in 1915 her husband left her alone to care for their three young daughters. The split marked the beginning of a period of great hardship for Mrs Bailey, during which she struggled hard to maintain her family, and she was eventually reduced to packing sardines in a canning factory. By this time she had, however, become disillusioned with orthodox Christianity, and had begun to question whether it really represented the only way to salvation.

The process of her changing attitude towards Christianity was aided by her initial introduction to theosophy, which she discovered after meeting two old ladies who were both personal pupils of H. P. Blavatsky (see Theosophy). After spending some time being tutored in theosophy, she finally joined the Society, and began to take classes and teach herself. It was through theosophy that she first came in contact with the teaching that there is a great and divine plan behind creation, and that there exists 'Those who are responsible for the working out of the Plan and who, step by step, have led mankind on down the centuries'. At the head of this hierarchy, claims Mrs Bailey, is the Christ, 'the Master of all Masters and the Teacher alike of angels and men'. Through her work with the Theosophical Society Mrs Bailey met Foster Bailey, who was later to become her husband and co-worker. In 1919 Foster was made general secretary of the Society, while Alice became editor of the Society's magazine, *The Messenger*.

But in the same way that she had become disillusioned with Christianity, so she became critical of the Society and its workings.

In 1919 she came into contact with 'the Tibetan', who was to be the inspiration for the bulk of her later writings and teaching. While walking near her home, she heard a voice which asked her to write certain books for the public. Despite her refusal to do so, on the grounds that she was not a 'darned psychic', three weeks later the voice came to her again, asking her to reconsider. She undertook this time to try for a few weeks, and during this period the first chapters of *Initiation, Human and Solar* were written. Mrs Bailey claimed she was not a practitioner of automatic writing, but while fully conscious would make herself alert and attentive. She would then write down words which she heard and thoughts which dropped into her mind, and would not in any way alter them, except to improve the English. Thus she asserted that the books were not written by her, but by the Tibetan. After a month of writing she became scared and refused to do any more work, but after contacting Master K. H., she was assured there was no danger in what she was doing, and in fact it was he who had suggested to the Tibetan that Alice Bailey should undertake the work. Thus she continued writing, producing books which contained 'new truths which humanity needs.'

In 1921, after continuing struggles within the Theosophical Society over a variety of issues, both Alice and Foster were sacked from their posts. They continued teaching the work of Blavatsky in their own Secret Doctrine class, and at the same time the books of the Tibetan were being published. As a result of the class and the books, they found a great interest in their work, and in order to deal with this formed their own esoteric group, the Arcane School, in 1923. The school, according to Mrs Bailey, was non-doctrinal, non-sectarian, and based on the 'Ageless Wisdom'. Among the teachings was the idea that the work of both Buddha and Christ must achieve fusion. Mrs Bailey claimed there is no divergence between the two Masters, and that while Buddha prepared people for discipleship, Christ prepared them for initiation. She also taught that the hierarchy of Masters are taking the first steps towards coming close to mankind, and to restoring the ancient mysteries. The second advent of Christ is coming, when he and the Masters will return to the earth and be known once again among mankind. The Tibetan also gave new rules for discipleship, which gave much greater individual freedom to the disciple than in the past – something still of great importance within the Arcane School today. No obedience is exacted, and the disciple is regarded as a free and intelligent agent, left to follow the path as he feels best. There is no longer any secrecy surrounding the teachings, and disciples are trained telepathically, rather than through the physical presence of a Master. Instead of stressing personal development, the new teachings stress the needs of humanity, and modern disciples are taught to work in groups.

The *Lucis Trust* is the umbrella organisation for the various activities based on the Bailey teachings, including the Arcane School, World Goodwill and Triangles. It runs the Lucis Press, which publishes her books. A catalogue of these and price list is available on request.

The Arcane School gives a training based on occult meditation, study and service to humanity, and aims to help students to move onto the path of discipleship. The aims of a disciple are given as: (1) To serve humanity; (2) To co-operate with the Plan of the Hierarchy as he sees it and as best he may; (3) To develop the powers of the soul, to expand his consciousness and to follow the guidance of the higher self. The work of the school is carried on entirely by postal correspondence between the student and headquarters. There are no lectures, classes or discussion groups, no examinations or competition. The work is individual and confidential, and each student is expected to search out the truth for himself. The work is regarded as taking place in 'groups', although individual students may never actually meet each other. A free lending library of occult and esoteric books is maintained by the Trust, and books may be borrowed by post. There are no fees charged, and the school is financed by voluntary contributions. The school respects the right of each student to hold his own beliefs, and does not rely on authoritarian presentation of any one particular line.

World Goodwill, founded in 1932, is the organisation basically concerned about dealing with the world's major problems by utilising the constructive power of goodwill. It aims to mobilise this energy, and to educate public opinion in the fundamental causes and solutions of world problems. At the same time, it is involved in 'preparing the ground' for the re-appearance of Christ on earth. It has no formal membership, and does not charge membership fees.

World Goodwill aims to educate public opinion, and mobilise individuals 'to establish goodwill as a keynote of the coming new age civilisation'. It provides advice and assistance to individuals, co-operates with groups and organisations undertaking world service projects, and supports the work of the United Nations, which it believes is the 'main hope for humanity's future'. It also runs a world-wide educational programme, which includes the printing and distribution of pamphlets, study papers, a periodical and other publications. There is an information service, which maintains details about trends in world developments.

As part of the work of establishing the power of international goodwill, *Triangles* links individuals who are able to work constructively together through the setting up of a 'network of light'. Employing the power of constructive thought, groups of three people link together every day for a few minutes of meditation. The members of a triangle need not live in the same locality, but sit quietly every day to link mentally with the others of their group. They 'invoke the energies of light and goodwill', and visualise these as circulating through the three points of a triangle. In this way it is claimed that a network of triangles surrounds the planet. At the same time, individuals repeat the Great Invocation, a universal prayer, which helps 'form a channel for the downpouring of light and love into the body of humanity'. It is not necessary for the members of a triangle to synchronise their activities, and once established, a triangle can be vitalised by any one of its members. Triangles' workers keep in touch with each other by letter, and wherever possible meet, to ensure their triangle continues functioning within the network.

As well as publishing a bulletin, Triangles provides literature and advice for those wishing to form triangles. Membership is open to all, and those concerned are encouraged to interest others in forming their own triangles, in order to strengthen and expand the network.

Universal World Harmony

The *Universal World Harmony* movement employs many of the methods and ideas incorporated in the work of the Lucis Trust. Like World Goodwill, Universal World Harmony (U.W.H.) aims to link people of goodwill throughout the world, and, like Triangles, it attempts to utilise the power of constructive thought in an effort to counteract the negative influence in the world.

The movement began in 1969, when a group of individuals hit upon the idea of a day set aside each year for counteracting the hate and fear being generated in the world. After discussion, it was decided to set the day at 11 November, Armistice Day, which already existed as a day of remembrance, and had within it an element of silence, which the founders of U.W.H. felt had a healing potential. Thus U.W.H. set itself the task of initiating a project which would be international in scope – a world day geared to a time of silent vigil at 11 a.m. It was believed that this silence, observed by individuals throughout the world, would create a 'chain reaction of positive and dynamic thinking', which would work not only nationally and internationally, but also spiritually.

119

U.W.H. sees itself as 'a world-wide organism, linking together the great army of people of goodwill who serve humanity individually and collectively as single units or as groups and organisations'. It seeks to promote any cause which aims to alleviate the ills of humanity and the other kingdoms of nature, believing that man can act as a 'bridge between the material worlds and the spiritual or universal spheres'. Its philosophy stresses the reality of the brotherhood of man. It claims it is no longer feasible to regard ourselves as citizens of one particular country, but instead calls upon individuals to recognise the needs of the entire planet.

The concept of harmony has a very special role within U.W.H. Within the universe is a cosmic and fundamental Law of Balance, which creates harmony within every sphere and at every level of creation. Any disturbance of this law upsets the 'perfect rhythm of the universe', and this in turn results in a number of chain reactions, which continue until the balance is restored. Man, it is claimed, is the prime offender in disturbing this balance and failing to conform to the fundamental law. He chooses to 'disrupt the pattern and interrupt the flow' of creation – something which may be seen both in his unharmonious relationship with nature (note the world's ecological problems) and in his relationships with his fellow man.

After a time it was felt that to meet the increasing needs of the world the original two minute silence should be extended to include an annual period of a week. This 'Week of Harmony' begins at 11 a.m. on 8 November and continues until 14 November, and during it individuals take part in a more concentrated period of spiritual thought. Thus the week is the culmination of the year's efforts, in which all those working for the movement come together. During the week a Remembrance Day conference is also usually held in Britain.

In 1971, U.W.H. decided to provide further strengthening for the effort made during the November period. Meditation and prayer requests were circulated throughout the world, asking people to allocate a portion of their daily prayer and/or meditation to strengthen the work of U.W.H., through the power of positive thought. In this way, 'a vast dynamo of creative energy is produced, which achieves its greatest momentum each year during a Week of Harmony . . . This united exercise . . . will promote a world-wide spiritual and esoteric force capable of upholding humanity.'

Those interested in participating in the work of U.W.H. should write to the Honorary Secretary, who will be pleased to send further information. In addition to the central headquarters in Lancashire, the movement has regional centres in the Isle of Man, Cheltenham, Stockport and Edinburgh. A preliminary course in spiritual and psychic study is also provided for those who come fairly new to the field, under the title 'The Quest'. This is a two-year postal course, drawn from a number of sources, open to anybody who desires to become a 'seeker after Truth'. It consists of four sections with a total of twelve lessons, covering such topics as the nature of religion, the composition of the spiritual hierarchy, the etheric body and the divine laws of the universe. Apart from the postage costs, the course is offered free of charge, and those interested in becoming students should write to the Honorary Secretary.

Gurdjieff

A figure whose work has profoundly affected modern mystical thought, and who stands out as a charismatic giant in the recent history of the esoteric, is the Armenian-born master, *George Ivanovich Gurdjieff*. He was an individual who did much to translate Eastern mystical thinking into a framework comprehensible to the West, while his colourful, romantic life still exerts an influence over those who follow, more than twenty years after his death.

Gurdjieff was born in the 1870s, in the Armenian city of Alexandropol, near the Russian border, to Greek parents. Like many dynamic spiritual figures, the details of his early life are somewhat obscure, but it seems that he spent the first forty years of his life travelling widely.

From early fascination with esotericism, he began visiting local monasteries, and finally set out in search of an ancient brotherhood, which he believed was established in Babylon in 2500 B.C. His travels took him as far afield as Tibet, and he even participated in an expedition to find a hidden city in the Gobi desert. During this period he came into contact with a variety of spiritual and occult schools, including a number of Sufi orders. Some say he also studied secret disciplines originating from pre-Christian times. He finally decided the time was right to pass on his teaching to the world, and some time before the First World War he returned to Moscow. Here he gained a following among the aristocracy, and began to draw his first pupils to him. Around the same time he came into contact with the Russian mathematician and mystical philosopher, P. D. Ouspensky, on whom he was to have a profound influence. With the advent of the Russian Revolution, however, both men fled their native land. While Ouspensky moved to London, Gurdjieff travelled, via Istanbul, to France, where in 1922 he founded a colony of followers at Fontainebleau, near Paris, called the Institute for the Harmonious Development of Man. Except for visits he made to his students in New York and elsewhere, here he was to remain, teaching a continuous stream of disciples, until his death in 1949. By all accounts life with Gurdjieff was anything but dull — it was said that his unconventional behaviour was, as much as anything, to test his followers' seriousness. He wrote one major work, called *All and Everything* — a strange, part allegorical, part autobiographical work in three parts, which were published after his death. However, his work has probably had its major impact through the writings of his disciples, most notably Ouspensky and J. G. Bennett and Dr Maurice Nicoll.

According to Colin Wilson, the key to Gurdjieff's teaching lies in the word 'work'.

From birth until the age of twenty-one we grow physically and in every other sense. Changes take place inside us without our volition. Then it stops . . . and most people slowly ossify. If growth is to continue unusual efforts must be made in order to stimulate the robot into providing 'newness'. This is the core of Gurdjieff's work. Its first aim was to defeat man's natural laziness, his tendency to relax and 'switch off'.

Gurdjieff's 'work' therefore was employed to wake his disciples up and knock them out of their complacency. At the Institute at Fontainebleau his disciples, many of whom were wealthy, aristocratic and cultured, were set to work at the most menial and back-breaking tasks, scrubbing floors, chopping wood, breaking stones and generally involving themselves in farming work. When the pupils had finished their labours they could by no means look forward to a comfortable rest.

However, this otherwise materially drab existence would be punctuated with great feasts, involving ritual toasting, or surprise picnics in the countryside.

Another aspect of the work which Gurdjieff taught at Fontainebleau involved sacred dances choreographed by Gurdjieff and often supervised by the Master himself. Gurdjieff said he collected the 'movements' from a variety of Eastern sources, and they have been described by some as a form of yoga in motion.

Those taking part claimed the dances had the effect of waking them up, and somehow releasing large amounts of energy. Thus we see once again Gurdjieff's efforts to awaken people from their spiritual slumbers, and make them aware of an existence beyond the mundane. He taught that a person's life is a reflection of his level of consciousness, and that the mass of mankind leads a 'robot' existence. People imagine they are free, but in fact they are imprisoned. They believe they have free will, but in reality they are helpless. He claimed man was ruled by his three centres – the emotional, intellectual and physical – and that most people suffer from an imbalance between them. It was his aim to help people achieve a balance, in which each centre could work in harmony with the others.

The path taught by Gurdjieff was known as the 'fourth way'. The other three paths are the way of the fakir (physical discipline), the monk (emotional discipline) and the yogi (intellectual discipline). These were rejected by Gurdjieff, who believed they lead to imbalance. His own way did not involve any form of renunciation or withdrawal from ordinary life or behaviour. Instead, it stressed a change in one's attitude to life rather than in the lifestyle itself.

There exist a number of groups which continue to study and practise the teachings of Gurdjieff, each with their own individual approach and different emphases. They vary greatly in size, some being little more than small study groups, but perhaps the largest group is *The Gurdjieff Society*. This was originally founded in 1955 as 'The Society for Research into the Development of Man', and its stated aim is 'to promote research and investigation into the latent possibilities in man'. In practice, this means members follow the teachings of Gurdjieff, and the Society is linked with similar bodies in Paris, New York and elsewhere across the world. Contacts are also kept up with those who studied personally under the Master, and individuals 'prepared by Gurdjieff personally' are available in London to provide guidance both to the Society and its members.

The Gurdjieff Society is, however, very shy of publicity. It believes the importance of its message might be lost through over-exposure and the consequent trivialisation which all too often ensues. For this reason, it does not advertise its existence, and adopts the attitude that 'only those who themselves make the effort to find a group are likely to be ready to follow it'. It demands serious intent from those who wish to become involved with its work, and is not the type of organisation which welcomes the spiritual tourist.

The Society emphasises group work, and operates a house in London where group meetings and the 'movements' are practised. There is also provision for physical work in a house outside London on weekends. Introductory, basic courses are run for newcomers, but it must be stressed that even to be admitted to these would require some degree of knowledge and commitment. The Society in no sense regards itself as a popular spiritual movement, but rather as existing for the small minority for whom Gurdjieff is suited.

Another Gurdjieff group which until recently has been shy of advertising its existence, *The Dicker*, has now begun to publicise its work in a limited way. The group follows the teachings of both Gurdjieff and Ouspensky, and also of Dr Maurice Nicoll, who had been a leading figure in the Jungian school of psychology in Britain. After studying with Gurdjieff and Ouspensky, he finally founded his own groups, both in London and elsewhere around the country. Following his death in 1953, his pupil and secretary, Beryl Pogson, continued the teaching line by forming groups in Sussex and London, and it was she who purchased a large house as a permanent centre in the Sussex village of Upper Dicker. 'The Dicker', the house from which the group derives its present title, still acts as the group's centre, and following Mrs Pogson's death a few years ago the present head took over its leadership.

The Dicker involves itself with applying the teachings of Gurdjieff and Ouspensky, although the work of both Nicoll and Pogson are studied in the belief that they gave their own formulation of the original teaching, while at the same time maintaining its purity. The work carried out by the Dicker is based largely on Dr Nicoll's books, *Psychological Commen-*

taries on the Teaching of Gurdjieff and Ouspensky. Those interested in the group are recommended to read the first fifty pages of volume one in order to understand the philosophical foundation of the group. The book may be borrowed from the group's library.

The group's work is centred at The Dicker, where members are accomodated on alternate weekends. The rambling house, outhouses and large garden provide the facilities necessary to house the wide range of work carried out. This includes study groups, and the practice of Gurdjieff's movements. Once again, the importance of group work is stressed, and members work together on projects ranging from painting a mural to presenting a play. There are facilities for a number of crafts such as leatherwork and pottery, and simple practical work such as gardening and house maintenance is carried out by members, always as an extension of the psychological work. In addition to the group weekends, weekday meetings are held in London and Brighton and study groups in other parts of Britain.

As with the Gurdjieff Society, The Dicker is only interested in people who are serious in wanting to apply Gurdjieff's ideas, and a degree of commitment is demanded. Those who would like to work with the group should contact the Secretary at The Dicker. You will then be invited to meet the leader.

J. G. Bennett's important contribution to the popularising of Gurdjieff's teachings has already been mentioned. It was he who, in 1946, established the *Institute for the Comparative Study of History, Philosophy and the Sciences*, which set out to examine a variety of techniques of human transformation and methods of self-knowledge. Work at the Institute was based upon Gurdjieff's philosophy and practical techniques. But it also drew upon a number of other sources for inspiration, including Subud, the teachings of the Nepalese saint, the Shivapuri Baba, the insights of Near Eastern dervishes and particularly certain Sufi methods. In addition to testing and studying the various techniques of the past, it has looked into methods derived from modern psychology, trying to keep a balance between Eastern and Western approaches. The Institute has investigated various ways of integrating these forms of knowledge, and in recent years has increasingly devoted its attention to group dynamics, developing its own principles and methods in the fields of communication and education.

The fruition of its work came in 1971, with the setting up of the *International Academy for Continuous Education*, based at Sherborne House, a Victorian mansion in the Cotswolds. Its aim was 'to achieve, in a short space of time, the effective transmission of a whole corpus of practical techniques for self-development and self-liberation, so that people could learn effectively to direct their own inner work and to adapt to the rapid changes in the inner and outer life of man'.

Courses catering for about one hundred people, and lasting ten months, were evolved at the Institute. It was felt these courses were the realisation of Gurdjieff's original vision. The Academy has accommodation for 150, and its facilities include a library, three studios, and a workshop for arts and crafts such as sculpture, pottery, spinning and weaving. It also caters for children, and has its own nursery school, playrooms and studies for older children. The twenty acres of ground include gardens which provide much of the community's naturally grown food.

Admission to the Academy is by no means simple. Candidates, who must be at least eighteen (the average age is thirty-two), are required to undergo a number of tests, be interviewed, and complete what is described as 'a rather formidable self-assessment paper'. It is emphasised that the course makes considerable demands, mentally, physically and emotionally. A student should expect to pay over £600 for dormitory accommodation, and is expected to have earned his fee by his own efforts.

The course itself is intensive, and based on the principle that everyone does everything; thus everyone shares in the practical running of the house and garden. Students learn spiritual and psychological exercises, aimed at 'developing finer perception and states of consciousness', and practise the Gurdjieff 'movements'. They study psychology, art, history, cosmology and linguistics. Meditation is taught, and special methods such as fasting or days of complete silence may be introduced at certain stages during the course. In addition, everyone is expected to develop a practical skill. The aim of all of this, according to the literature, is 'to achieve a balance of bodily, mental and emotional functions and to awaken latent spiritual perceptions. The aim is to make the whole of life significant.'

Although the Sherborne training has now gained something of an international reputation, and has sponsored the launching of a community with its own Academy in America, its future in this country is by no means certain. J. G. Bennett died in December 1974, and all along it had been planned to run the basic training course only five times, with the final one beginning in October 1975. Thus a leading member of the Academy states: 'The Academy itself will not exist, in its present form, for much longer. Nothing is permanent, and adaption will have to be made to the new conditions, internal and external, which will come in the next few years.'

Three or four times a year week-end seminars are held for members of the Institute and friends, and there is also a summer school, lasting two weeks, starting around 20 August, which is open to the public. Details of activities are available from the Registrar. The Academy has links with a number of groups involved with various 'techniques for transformation' around London and the North of England.

Teilhard Centre

Pierre Teilhard de Chardin (1881–1955) was a startlingly original mystical thinker, whose philosophy spanned both the material and spiritual universes, providing a framework in which both could ultimately be seen as inter-related. At once a Jesuit father, prophet, and internationally recognised biologist and paleontologist, it is not surprising that his revolutionary view of creation earned him caustic criticism and isolation both from religious and scientific establishments. In fact his ideas were so disturbing to the church authorities that he was forbidden to publish them, and for this reason it was not until after his death that they first appeared. Yet, as his biographer, Claude Cuenot, points out, 'of the power and extent of Teilhard's continuing influence, there can be no doubt'.

Teilhard's extensive writings (the bibliography in his biography takes up more than seventy pages) present above all else a total view of the universe which encompasses both his spiritual faith as a Jesuit and his fascination with the material world as a scientist. The main theme running through Teilhard's philosophy is that of evolution, which he saw as underlying the universe on every level. He stressed the importance of the evolutionary concept to his thinking when he claimed it was: '. . . a general condition to which all theories, all hypotheses, all systems must bow . . . evolution is a light illuminating all facts, a curve that all lines must follow'.

Teilhard pointed out that the main direction taken by evolution was towards increasing complexity. This can be seen in the process by which sub-atomic particles have developed and evolved through atoms, molecules, living cells, animals and plants to man himself. In other words, merely by looking at life on this planet, we see evolution developing through 'steps' of increasing complexity. As this occurs, there is also an increase in interdependence and interaction between elements which had previously been independent. Thus the new, more complex whole is formed by a process in which individual elements form relationships to create a whole greater than themselves. This is a vital concept in understanding his beliefs about the destiny of creation.

Teilhard also believed that the question of complexity is related to that of consciousness. This is reflected in what followers now call Teilhard's Law of Complexity-Consciousness, which states simply that as complexity increases so, too, does the degree of consciousness. Evolution moves in the direction of greater complexity and consciousness, although as complexity increases, the element of chance present in evolution at its lowest levels becomes increasingly less important. In this way, as life becomes increasingly conscious, it is more and more able to respond to its environment. One of Teilhard's central beliefs was that man was becoming increasingly responsible for guiding his own future –

126

his own evolution and development. What is essential is that man develop a deeply rooted faith in the future, if he is to survive and overcome the crises he is facing at this particular stage of his evolution.

But where did Teilhard himself believe that evolution was going? The answer lies in what he called 'Omega'. His vision was that evolution was moving towards a point of final, complete and total union, and that the whole of the universe was converging on this Omega point. For this reason, man as he is was for Teilhard by no means the last chapter in the saga of evolution, but merely another stage (although a critical one) in the story. Man is not at the pinnacle of the pyramid, as many assume, but is still moving towards that point, and the next stage, Teilhard believed, would be reached through external rather than internal development.

John Newson, editor of the *Teilhard Review*, described Teilhard's vision of man's future development as being towards: '. . . a growing inter-relation between each of us and our human and non-human environment: a psycho-social development in which man becomes corporately capable of physical activity which is beyond his powers as an individual'.

Thus Teilhard taught that the whole of mankind is moving towards the point at which individuals will be united together to form something greater than they are capable of obtaining as independent entities. Indeed, he argued, if it was possible for an individual to reach the peak of his evolution alone, then the efforts of 'earthly organisation' are nothing more than a farce. The alternative vision of the future which he offered was one in which man works 'so that the universe may be raised, in him and through him, to a higher level'. It was this vision, with its ultimate converging of creation at Omega, which Teilhard offered to provide the necessary faith to carry on through what he regarded as a crisis stage in man's evolutionary growth – a stage which is highly creative.

The organisation which promotes the work of Teilhard is the *Teilhard Centre for the Future of Man*, which is based in London, but has around fifty study groups operating throughout the U.K. Some areas, such as Bristol, have more than one group. The Centre fulfils a mainly educational function in encouraging the study of Teilhard's thought. But more than this, it also aims to develop his work further – he himself said: 'If I have a mission to fulfil, it will only be possible to judge whether I have accomplished it by the extent to which others go beyond me.'

The Centre organises special introductory lectures and study groups, arranges conferences and symposia, and involves itself in a range of activities aimed at presenting Teilhard's thought to a wider public. This includes the publication of a journal, *The Teilhard Review*, and a series of books called the 'Teilhard Study Library'. There is a library which is open to anybody interested in Teilhard, and a very wide range of books, both by and about him, are available for sale from the Centre. Membership costs at least £3.50 p.a. for individuals, £1.65 for students. A list of study groups, a book list and other literature is available on application to the Secretary.

Grail Foundation

A group based on the writings of German-born Abd-ru-shin, and in particular on his book, *In the Light of Truth*, is the *Grail Foundation*. Born in 1875 in Saxony (now in East Germany), Oskar Ernst Bernhardt, as he was then known, took up writing after establishing himself as a merchant in Dresden. In 1900 he made his first trip to the Far East, followed by other journeys during which he published a number of travel books, stories and plays. In 1913 he settled in London, but following the outbreak of the First World War was interned on the Isle of Man. During his internment, which was to last until 1919, Bernhardt claimed that he underwent a transition which was to prepare him for the spiritual work he was to undertake. He began to experience the desire to show mankind the way out of its troubles, and once back on native soil he became aware that his mission was 'to open the way to men for a new knowledge of creation'. Bernhardt chose the name Abd-ru-shin (Son of Light) for himself – he claimed this was connected with a former incarnation, when, at the time of Moses, he lived as the prince of an Arabian tribe. In the 1920s he began to hold public lectures, and in 1923 published the first of these as *The Grail Message*. These were followed by others up until 1937. The collection, comprising 168 lectures in three volumes, are now collectively known as *In the Light of Truth*.

In 1928 Abd-ru-shin moved with his family to a house at Vomperberg, in the Austrian Tyrol, where, amid panoramic scenery overlooking the Inn Valley and the Alps, he completed his Grail Message. It was here that the Grail Settlement formed around him, as individuals who read his work and accepted it sought the opportunity to be near the prophet. The Grail Movement came into existence and consisted of readers of the Grail Message who both accepted it and wished to come into contact with other adherents. At first, independent Grail Message reading circles were formed, but in 1932 the organisation became formally registered as the Natural-Philosophic Society of Grail Adherents. But the organisation soon fell foul of the Nazi regime. In 1938 the settlement at Vomperberg was expropriated and Abd-ru-shin was arrested by the state police on the charge that he 'endangers the stability and security of the people and the state through his conduct'. Six months after his arrest, the prophet and his family were exiled in Germany where, under house detention supervised by the Gestapo, he was forbidden to take an active part in the Grail Movement. In December 1941 he died.

Following the end of the war, the settlement was handed back to the Bernhardt family by the Austrian and French military governments. It has since developed as the focus for the Grail Movement's activities, and houses an international community of between sixty and seventy engaged in such things as the management of guest houses, farming and horticulture. The settlement consists of an administration building, private houses, agricultural land, farm buildings and guest houses. There is also a hall of worship, with a capacity of 1,500, and a marble tomb in the form of a pyramid, containing the bodies of Abd-ru-shin, his wife and his son. The leadership of the settlement and the International Grail Movement is now in the hands of the founder's daughter, Irmingard Bernhardt. The Grail Movement is composed of a number of Grail Circles throughout the world. There are a number of publishing houses and associations which deal with the printing and spreading of the works of Abd-ru-shin. International membership is estimated at around 4,000, and so far about 100,000 copies of *In the Light of Truth* in eight languages have been sold. The spiritual high point comes three times a year, when the great Grail festivals, instituted by Abd-ru-shin, are celebrated. These are the Festival of the Holy Dove, the Festival of the Pure Lily (primarily intended for women) and the Festival of the Radiant Star. Hundreds of adherents travel to Vomberberg for these events, which are held in the temple. The occasions are regarded as important, as it is believed that during them great divine powers are poured to the Earth, and these can be experienced by seekers.

The Grail teaching covers a multitude of topics ranging from social and economic subjects through diet and healing to questions of time and eternity. *In the Light of Truth* includes detailed explanations of free will, the soul and the spirit, and clearly lays down a path for man to follow in order to find true happiness. Three Great Laws are revealed, which are said to underly the whole of creation, and throughout it is claimed that the Grail Message 'stands absolutely on the ground of Christ's teaching'. It is argued that the childlike simple belief demanded by Jesus in his time no longer suffices for modern man. Thus the message contains detailed knowledge suited to modern man's intellectual thought, providing the certainty from which the necessary conviction grows.

The Grail Foundation of Great Britain was formed in 1957 by adherents who wished to make the message known in this country. Although autonomous, the group does accept guidance from the Grail administration in the Tyrol. The Foundation is mainly concerned with distributing *In the Light of Truth*, obtainable from the Foundation's London headquarters. Details of other publications are available on request. The Foundation does not undertake regular public meetings or conferences, but adherents meet periodically at a centre in Sidcup. Enquiries should be addressed to the Foundation's London address.

Spiritual Inner Awareness

The Movement of Spiritual Inner Awareness is a relatively small but interesting group, which has at its head an American 'guru-figure', Dr John Roger Hinkins (known affectionately by his followers as John Roger or simply JR). Hinkins, a middle-aged doctor, is described as being a 'metaphysical tramp' for a number of years, until he underwent major surgery and emerged from the experience a transformed person. He founded M.S.I.A. in the States in 1968, and from a series of weekly seminars it spread across the country, until three years later the movement was founded in Britain. It now has three 'ministers' who run the British movement on a part-time basis, although it has not grown to any large extent in this country. There are probably no more than a dozen people who are heavily committed to it, but its weekly seminars in a small London flat have been attended by a number of people who have had varying degrees of contact with it.

M.S.I.A. is based on the teachings of John-Roger, also known as the 'Mystical Traveller'. Followers claim a Mystical Traveller has always been present on Earth, although often he has not made his presence felt directly. Exception to this occurred with Masters such as Jesus. The Traveller is set apart from the rest of mankind in possessing what is described as 'Mystical Traveller Consciousness', described in M.S.I.A. literature as 'existing simultaneously on all levels of consciousness in total awareness'. Thus when John-Roger emerged from his anaesthetic, he found himself to possess this Consciousness. But what is more important, as a Mystical Traveller he has the ability to teach individuals to develop the same attributes themselves. The aim of M.S.I.A. is, therefore, to take individuals from the physical level to consciousness of the soul's perfection.

Although some of the work carried out by M.S.I.A. is done on a group basis, the emphasis is generally laid on individual spiritual progress. The Mystical Traveller, it is claimed, has the ability to work with each person individually, although this only takes place when the person concerned has asked for guidance. Much of this guidance is, followers believe, carried out during sleep, when the individual is taken to other realms of existence, including the Soul Realm.

During these travels the individual is assisted and protected by the Mystical Traveller as he journeys through the 'lower realms of negativity' to the Soul Realm. Followers then concentrate on working to bring these journeys back into their conscious mind, and to this end a 'dream book' is kept as an aid. They believe that much of significance happens in these dreams. They also claim it is eventually possible to travel consciously to other levels at any time, awake or asleep. The important thing stressed is that much of what occurs as a result of

130

accepting the assistance of the Mystical Traveller takes place on subtle levels, and only gradually does an individual develop the ability to bring these events into his conscious mind. At first, experiences during sleep may be recalled as nothing more than dreams, but gradually these 'experiences in the Soul Body' are felt to have more reality than physical experiences.

On a more visible level, M.S.I.A. offers a number of practices to aid students on the path. John-Roger claims to read the karmic records of individuals, and to describe their past action and the 'debts' resulting from these. In addition, he aids an individual to understand his 'karmic responsibilities' and the way these may be fulfilled. Some of this fulfilment takes place in the all-important dreams. Another activity, known as 'aura balancing', may be carried out either by John-Roger himself or by a specially appointed member of his staff. This is said to 'release negative thoughts or actions or patterns that you have experienced and then held within your auric force field'. In this way the aura is 'tuned up', 'much like we would tune up a television set for you, so that you may get better reception'. Aura balancing, said to have an extremely relaxing and re-juvenating effect, is carried out in three sessions. Each of these clears imbalances in the physical, emotional, mental and spiritual auras. The most common way of coming into contact with M.S.I.A. is through seminars – these take place with a group of people listening to a taped talk by John-Roger, although when the Mystical Traveller himself is present these may be live. Quite apart from the overt messages contained in these talks, followers say that simply by listening to them a person may subtly become released from some of his karma. Taped seminars are held at 8 p.m. every Sunday at the Movement's London headquarters, and a nominal charge is made. John-Roger generally visits London for four or five days every year, and at these times may give seminars, aura balancing and light studies. In addition to the activities we have already described, the Movement offers taped talks and 'programmings', a range of publications and home reading discourses, and will be pleased to send speakers to other parts of the country to address yoga groups, etc. Note that M.S.I.A. is planning to move shortly from its present address, but full details about the Movement and its new whereabouts can be obtained by writing to their American address.

Findhorn

A spiritual community trying to demonstrate a 'new age' life-style is the *Findhorn Foundation*. Based at a caravan park near the village of Findhorn in north-east Scotland, it was founded in 1962 by Peter and Eileen Caddy and their young family. The Caddys had been interested in the spiritual life for some years, and were eventually 'led' to park their large caravan in a derelict corner of Findhorn Bay caravan park. At the time, the site was little more than a rubbish tip, overgrown with gorse, brambles and nettles. Some of the first work undertaken by the Caddys was to create a garden out of soil described as 'little more than sand and gravel with an inch or two of turf on top'. From these humble beginnings the community at Findhorn has grown over the years to its present size of over one hundred permanent residents, plus those who maintain a base at the site and go for periodical visits.

The development of Findhorn has been based on the divine guidance received by Eileen Caddy, also known as 'Elixir'. In moments of quiet she claimed to hear God's voice, and it is this which guided the gradual development of Findhorn, providing the source of detailed instructions of projects the community was to undertake. Through the guidance Elixir received, a large office was set up, and a cedar wood sanctuary, which was to become the focal point of the expanding community, was erected. Later, a community centre was built; it comprises a kitchen with catering capacity for 200, and a dining room which will accommodate 150. This is also used to stage concerts, plays and dancing. As the community grew, more accommodation was required, and today there are twenty bungalows and more than forty caravans, contributed by those who either live at Findhorn permanently or just for part of the year. When not occupied by their owners, the accommodation is available to the rest of the community and to visitors. A craft studio has been set up near by, with accommodation for those who work in it. The studio produces pottery, weaving, candles, leather-work and other crafts, and products are sold in shops throughout Scotland, as well as in a shop at the caravan site itself.

In 1971 a house and land adjoining the site were purchased and donated to the Findhorn Foundation, and this is used as a centre for the educational activities of the community, including lectures, discussion groups and conferences. Two years later it became clear that the community centre was too small to meet the needs of the quickly growing community. On Christmas Eve, 1973 Eileen Caddy received guidance that the University Hall was to be built, to house all the educational facilities. This is nearing completion, at a cost of over £100,000. The community has its own fully equipped photographic darkroom, and produces audio-visual presentations. There is also £20,000 worth of printing machinery, producing a large range of booklets, leaflets and other printed material.

One of the most outstanding and unusual achievements of the community is its gardens, which provide much of the produce keeping those at Findhorn going. In an attempt to re-establish an ecological balance, fruit, vegetables and herbs are grown without artificial fertilisers or insecticides. Instead, those working in the gardens try to co-operate with nature, and more particularly with the devas or spirits which are said to be associated with particular plants and flowers.

Findhorn describes itself as a University of Light – 'a training centre for the embodiment of universal consciousness in those who recognise their path is one of world service'. Its members see their main task as discovering the divine potential inherent in each of us, and also, perhaps more importantly, as demonstrating this new vision. Community interests cover a wide range and everyone contributes to the practical needs of the community. At the same time, Findhorn is developing wide cultural interests, and an arts centre is emerging which undertakes work in drama, dance and music. Tapes of new age music and songs, written and performed by members of the community, are already available, and artistic performances are staged, sometimes at day-long festivals. Physical pursuits are also catered for, and an active programme of training involving sports such as climbing, canoeing, hill walking and camping is provided.

As a training centre, Findhorn is both unusual and broad in its approach. While teaching people to co-operate in living with others, it helps them to unfold through lectures, discussions, sports and crafts. Members also learn the mechanics of making a community work, from digging drains to building compost heaps. Throughout, there is an emphasis on the spiritual, and it is this which pervades all the activities undertaken. For those interested in the work at Findhorn, the best course of action is to pay the community a visit. A number of caravans and chalet bungalows are kept available for guests, but because of increasing demand you are advised to give advance notice of your intention to visit. Accommodation with full amenities is provided. Visitors are expected to prepare their own breakfast, and supplies of bread, milk, etc., are available at the community centre stores. Vegetarian lunch and dinner are provided at the Community Centre, but you are free to prepare your own meals in your accommodation. The community shop at the caravan park, as well as providing basic groceries, fruit and vegetables, also stocks a range of other general supplies. Crafts, publications, tapes and photographs are also available at the site.

Visitors are warned that Findhorn is not a holiday camp, and those who come should be prepared to contribute towards the running of the community. Daily and weekly programmes are organised, and include tours of the community, visits to near-by places of interest, lectures and talks, meditation periods, and artistic performances. These take place in the afternoons and evenings, while mornings are devoted to various physical jobs. Costs vary, depending on the type of accommodation and the time of year. During the summer, the cost of a caravan is some £25 per week, while sharing a room in a bungalow costs about £30 per week. These figures are reduced during the rest of the year.

Write to Findhorn for an application form and a copy of 'Information and Programme for Guests', which gives the details a visitor will require. Also available on request are catalogues of books and tapes issued by the

133

Findhorn Foundation. These cover a good range of new age subjects, and describe more fully Findhorn's role. They include a collection of the divine messages received by 'Elixir', the story of the Findhorn Garden, and a variety of lectures. Interested parties are invited to be included on the Foundation's mailing list, to receive leaflets and information on publications, taped lectures and conferences, free of charge. Those who subscribe at least £3 a year will also receive a quarterly magazine with news and information on Findhorn, and articles on the various principles on which the community is based.

Scientology

Few fringe spiritual groups have, in their time, caused more controversy than *Scientology*. An extraordinary blend of psychotherapy and biofeedback, with more than a taste of science fiction about it, it has in recent years attracted a great deal of attention from the press. However, despite the amount of publicity it has received, most people know little about the philosophy and its applications, or realise that far from being a recent fad, Scientology began well over twenty years ago.

The history of Scientology, or 'dianectics' as it was originally known, is closely entangled with the story of its founder, Lafayette Ron Hubbard. Born in Nebraska in 1911, this charismatic leader is regarded by many of his followers as at the very least a remarkable and outstanding thinker, and by some as a modern day Messiah. He claims he first began to develop his thoughts on dianectics while still in his teens, during which time he travelled to many parts of the world with his father, a naval officer. Many of the purported facts concerning his later life have come under severe criticism – his qualifications as a scientist, for example. It seems well established, however, that during the course of his career, Hubbard took part in a number of exploratory expeditions to various parts of the globe, and during the war served as a lieutenant in the U.S. Navy. His literary talents began to assert themselves in the 1930s and he produced a large amount of fiction, including westerns and romances, as well as movie scripts. His big successes in this field came later, when he turned his hand to science fiction, and even today he is recognised by many as a first-rate SF writer.

The first big breakthrough into the public eye came however, in 1950, with the publication of Hubbard's book, *Dianectics: The Modern Science of Mental Health*, which serves as the basic text of Scientology. Heralded as a major landmark in psychotherapy, the book moved quickly into the bestseller list, and overnight Hubbard became a well-known figure. A dianectic craze then swept the country. Basically, the principles of dianectics are extremely simple and bear close resemblance to traditional psychotherapeutic teachings. The mind is divided into two entities – the 'analytic' and the 'reactive'. The first of these is the conscious mind, which under normal circumstances enables the individual to act appropriately in his environment. The reactive mind, parallel to the subconscious, often interferes with the activities of the analytic mind, however, and it is this, Hubbard claims, which leads to neuroses and other psychological disturbances, which he calls 'aberrations'. In times of stress the analytic mind falters, and the reactive mind comes into play, recording details of the unpleasant experience in what are known as 'engrams'. These disturbing engrams are then suppressed when the analytic mind comes back into prominence, but throughout the individual's life they occasionally re-assert themselves. Hubbard goes on to argue that engrams are laid down while we are still in the womb, and with the support of case histories attempts to show how certain instances of disturbed behaviour in adult life are traceable directly back to experiences of individuals when they were no more than a foetus.

In dianectic therapy the 'patient' relaxes on a couch and says whatever comes into his mind, in response to questions by the therapist, known as the 'auditor'. It is the auditor's job, by observing his patient's reactions, to guide him to sensitive areas, and thus confront him with the suppressed disturbing memory. Thus by bringing the troublesome engram into the patient's conscious mind, he is helped to manipulate it and so rid himself of its effects. The technique is still fundamentally the one practised by Scientologists today, with one exception – the introduction of a piece of electronic gadgetry, which more than anything has become the trade mark of Scientology. The 'E-meter', heralded by Hubbard as a major advance in the development of his therapy, is what most people know as a lie detector. By measuring small changes in the electrical conductivity of the skin ('galvanic skin response or simply "gvs" ') it indicates the kind of stress or emotional upsets which are associated with such changes.

In 1955 Hubbard moved the centre of his operations to a Georgian manor house, Saint Hill Manor, near East Grinstead in Sussex. In the same year the first Church of Scientology began operating in Washington, marking an important landmark in the development of the Scientology movement. In its early years dianectics had always been presented as a scientifically-based clinical and therapeutic system. This is testified to by the use of such terms as 'Scientology clinic' by members of the group. However, around the mid-fifties the emphasis began to move from the medical to the religious, and for the first time Scientology was presented as a spiritual philosophy. In this way Scientology ministers and chaplains first made their appearance, auditing sessions became known as 'confessionals', and religious Scientology 'services' were introduced. This change in emphasis was paralleled by the introduction by Hubbard of the philosophically orientated 'Scientology', which was to provide the framework into which the more practical 'dianectics' was to fit. Much of this underlying philosophy was to resolve around the concept of the

135

'Thetan', approximately equivalent to what most of us would recognise as the soul, or the real self. The Thetan is immortal and non-physical, and comes to inhabit a particular human body at the moment of conception.

At the beginning of time it was only Thetans who existed, until they decided to play a game by creating a universe in which they would take part. However, to make things more interesting, they chose to limit their own infinite power and knowledge. Over the course of millions of years they gradually became ensnared in the very universe they had themselves created. Gradually, as they became immersed in their game, they forgot their true status. Today, the Thetan within us all has forgotten his very existence. Thus, Hubbard claimed, it was through Scientology that the Thetan, none other than our true selves, might once again become aware of his potential. It was through this concept that Hubbard explained the neuroses and psychological problems which dog modern man. When the Thetan takes up residence in a particular body, it brings with it all the engrams implanted over the course of millions of years of evolution. Thus an individual undergoing Scientology auditing is not only attempting to rid himself of engrams laid down while he was still in the womb, but also of engrams implanted during previous lives, and even during periods when the Thetan occupied the lowest forms of the evolutionary ladder.

In the jargon which abounds in Scientology, the concepts of 'clear' and 'operating Thetan' are among the most important, representing the ultimate goals of auditing. Within the movement the concept of 'clear' has changed over the years, and in the early days represented something akin to pefection. The claims made for 'clear' are now more modest, and in line with this it is not surprising that the number of individuals who have attained this state are well over 4,000. 'Clear' is the first important goal which any student of Scientology will aim for (and, incidentally, explains why those undergoing more lowly levels of auditing are referred to as 'pre-clear'). According to Scientology literature, 'Clear means calmness and serenity. Clear is certainty of self. Clear is basically you.' The advert goes on to promise that those who reach 'clear' will obtain I.Q.s in excess of 135, creative vitality, deep relaxation, quietness, concentration and revitalised memory. Having achieved this state, the individual can then look forward to pressing on to higher levels, known as 'operating Thetan' (O.T.). A person who reaches this is 'a "clear" who has been familiarised with his environment to a point of total cause over matter, energy, space, time and thought, and who is not on the body level'. Having achieved this level, the keenest Scientologist is still not at the end of his path, for there are still higher levels of O.T. for him to ascend.

This underlines the rigid structure within Scientology, which provides a clearly defined ascending path through a seemingly endless number of grades. At the beginning anybody is invited to become an international member of the organisation, and this entitles you to 'big discounts on books tapes and E-meters. This initial membership is obtainable free for a period of six months by simply writing to the membership officer at Saint Hill. There is no obligation to undertake courses at this point, but if you wish to extend your membership beyond the six months you will be asked to pay some £6 per year. Should you decide to go on and undertake processing courses, you will begin at the lowest level with the 'Hubbard Apprentice Scientologist Course', which is relatively cheap. For the keen student, however, Scientology is undoubtedly an expensive pursuit, and as one moves up the grades the fees increase steeply. For example, a clearing course costs about £400. The prerequisite for undertaking this course is that you are a Grade VI Release, a position which is reached after completing the Saint Hill Special Briefing Course, at a cost of over £300. Other courses can be even more expensive – for example, Power Processing in order to reach Grade V, costs around £500.

Although Scientology began its life very largely as a therapeutic technique, the movement now very definitely presents itself in a religious light. Official literature defines Scientology as 'a religious philosophy containing pastoral counselling procedures intended to assist an individual to attain Spiritual Freedom'. The writings of Hubbard are described as 'religious literature and works', the Thetan is known as 'spirit', and even the E-meter is talked of as being 'a religious artifact, used in the church confessional'.

During the course of its eventful history, Scientology has undergone many trials and tribulations. In 1963 the U.S. Food and Drug Administration raided the movement's headquarters in Washington, and a prosecution ensued. In 1965 an Australian Board of Enquiry into the group produced a report flatly condemning it. In 1967 the Minister of Health attacked Scientology in the House of Commons, and the movement lost its recognition as an educational foundation, with a consequent ban on Scientology students from abroad wishing to enter the country for training. Yet Scientology has survived, claiming in defence that many of the accusations levelled against it still remain to be proved.

Scientology still openly offers its courses and training to the public, operating centres in London, Edinburgh, Manchester and Plymouth. If you are interested in auditing, would like to become an International Member, or simply wish to know more about Scientology, write to Saint Hill Manor. The best introduction to the movement is undoubtedly *Dianectics* by Hubbard, which is available from libraries, some bookshops or from Saint Hill.

Pyramid and Sphinx

There are undoubtedly in this country a large number of groups of individuals concerned with the study of the occult. The word occult itself, although carrying unpleasant connotations for many people, literally means 'kept secret'. Those involved in the occult are concerned with the study of knowledge not openly available, usually concerning matters magical, supernatural, and mystical. It is often claimed that such occult knowledge dates back many centuries to man's earliest cultures.

Obviously, by its very definition, occult knowledge is not publicised. Many occult groups do not advertise their existence at all, and for this reason it would be impossible to include them in this book. Others either declined the offer of inclusion or simply refused to discuss the matter. There were some, however, who were prepared to be mentioned.

A group which describes itself as a 'fraternity engaged in the study and practice of ceremonial magic' is the *Order of the Pyramid and Sphinx*. The Order claims to have access to the unique knowledge of an ancient occult lodge in the Near East, and also to be the custodian of what it describes as 'a hitherto unrevealed tradition which expounds the famous Enochian system of Dr John Dee'. This tradition is said to establish a close communication between man and the angelic kingdom, bringing close contact with the celestial hierarchies.

The Order stresses that newcomers to the occult are not admitted to its membership. Applicants for initiation must already have a good knowledge of occult philosophy in general, and of the Hermetic tradition in particular.

As well as having its own temple, the Order has a library of rare books and manuscripts, although these are only available to advanced students. All teachings are given orally, observing the greatest secrecy. For this reason no printed literature is available. Great emphasis is laid on the kabbalah, an ancient Jewish mystical system centring around the Tree of Life interpreted with reference to the human body. It teaches a system of cosmology which includes methods of interpreting the numerical value of words, and the Order itself teaches detailed interpretation of its symbolism. Other areas studied include Neo-Platonic and Alexandrian philosophy, ancient cosmogony, astronomical mythology, modern freemasonry, and Tarot and Celtic law.

Those applying to the Order must be over the age of thirty, of good moral character and education, teetotallers, non-smokers and strict vegetarians. They must be willing to become Freemasons, if they do not already belong to a lodge. Candidates will be admitted only after a personal interview by officers of the Order, and if accepted will be required to attend meetings of the Lodge once a fortnight. All aspirants are given a thorough training in highly secret esoteric doctrines, but officers of the lodge warn: 'The Order is not for dilettanti or sensationalists, but for those who wish to attain enlightenment . . . The teachings and disciplines of the Fraternity demand dedication and asceticism, and the practical side involves ceremonials, rituals and artistic work.'

The Order does not have branches outside London, neither does it conduct correspondence courses or any other form of postal tuition. No public meetings, conferences or lectures are held, and once again it is stressed that newcomers to the occult are not admitted.

Order of the Cross

A group which concerns itself with a mystical and esoteric interpretation of Christianity is the *Order of the Cross*, founded early this century by J. Todd Ferrier. A Christian minister, Ferrier felt very strongly about the ill-treatment of animals, and eventually gave up the Church to form the Order in 1904. His aim was to link together those who believed in the necessity of vegetarianism, so that they could help each other 'become better equipped to help the world'. He produced a number of books setting out the principles of what followers describe as a 'truly reformed Christian ethic'. These teachings are numerous, and include re-interpretations of the Old and New Testaments. They purport to show the relationship between Christianity and the teachings of the other great world religions, and to present ancient wisdoms in a Christian setting. Books such as *The Message of Ezekiel* re-interpret the words of the Old Testament prophets. Elsewhere, Ferrier virtually re-writes the New Testament, paying particular attention to the Epistles of St Paul, who he believed had a very detrimental effect on Christianity. He claims that the Pauline influence covered over and even changed the nature of Jesus's message, and was largely responsible for the development of an institutionalised Christianity deviating from the true teachings. This is underlined by the fact that Christians through the centuries have shown 'but little reverence for life' by allowing and condoning the exploitation and slaughter of animals. In *The Master: His Life and Teachings*, Ferrier claims to give the inner meaning of Christ's teachings, providing a 'true picture of Him as He was in His life, public and private'. Elsewhere, in *The Logia or Sayings of the Master*, Ferrier claims to present the true, restored words spoken by Christ 'in the form in which they were spoken by Him'. All such re-writings are said to originate from the original 'Divine Source', rather than from any sort of academic authority. Other writings outline the path to realisation, giving in detail the principles of the Order. In addition to his books, Ferrier wrote a number of pamphlets. Again, these cover a wide range of teaching, touching on topics such as food reform, the Second Coming, life after death, and re-interpretations of biblical teachings and stories.

Ferrier himself travelled throughout the country supervising informal groups of the Order, to whom guidance was provided by means of weekly letters. Since his death in 1943, at the age of eighty-seven, members of the Order have continued to spread their founder's teachings and continue his work 'in the spirit which he so nobly exemplified'. The Order teaches that the present time marks the beginning of a spiritual resurrection, in which the individual soul will 'awaken to re-discover its long lost memory of the purpose of life, of its relationship to the living universe'. Man will re-discover his innate powers which have become inert. In particular he will again be able to communicate with 'Watchers and Holy Ones' on higher planes, who through the ages have acted as guardians of mankind. Thus once again 'risen souls' will find the spiritual powers of vision and hearing which will enable them to receive guidance and communication from 'the World Beyond'.

The gradual process of re-awakening will be hastened by the existence of 'pioneer souls', who are already beginning to perceive the Truth. The Order teaches that there are, scattered across the earth, mature souls who are already capable of 'exemplifying the life that should be lived by "Sons and Daughters of God" '. The sun is regarded as playing an important role in this process, pouring out solar energy which is gradually intensifying with the passing of time. This energy has the effect of 'stirring up nations and people for their healing', and in this way the sun acts as a shepherd bringing the planet back to the fold. As souls awaken and individuals' consciousness rises, people are able to absorb increasing amounts of this energy, which affects the inner life of man. He is able to 'bask once again in the realisation of the Eternal Love and Wisdom, and can both give forth and receive that Divine Healing for which mankind waits'.

Ferrier taught that Christ's teachings were never intended to found an earthly Church, but rather to enable man to be restored to the state of illumination of Christhood. Thus the founding statement of the Order gives its aim as to 'attain, by mutual helpfulness, the realisation of the Christ-life, by the path of self-denial, self-sacrifice, and absolute self-abandonment to the Divine will and service'. The three steps necessary to arrive at this state of absolute abandonment are purity of living, of the mind and of the soul. Members of the Order try by example and teaching to win their fellow men to a love of purity, truth and right-doing.

The Order proclaims the brotherhood of man, the essential unity of all religious aspiration, and the unity of all living creatures. In reference to the latter, the moral necessity for a human attitude to all men and creatures is stressed. In line with Ferrier's absolute opposition to meat eating, the Order is committed to working for the abolition of all customs which violate Christ's teachings, especially those involving bloodshed, and more particularly the infliction of cruelty on animals. Members of the Order are opposed to vivisection, and the slaughter of animals for food, fashion and sport. In its place, the universal adoption of a bloodless diet is advocated, along with a return to simple and natural foods. In its own words, the Order is 'an informal Brotherhood and Fellowship, having as its service in life the cultivation of love towards all souls: Helping the weak and defending the defenceless and oppressed . . . Walking in the mystic Way of Life, whose path leads to the realisation of the Christhood; and sending forth the Mystic Teachings to all who may be able to receive them.'

The Order is based in London where requests for information and specific enquiries should be addressed to the Secretary. The headquarters house a sanctuary, where regular meetings are held for worship meditation and the study of Ferrier's teachings. These take place at 11 a.m. on Sundays and 7 p.m. on Wednesdays, throughout the year, except for a vacation period during the Summer, and visitors are welcome. The Order also has a number of provincial groups and reading circles concerned with the study and practice of Ferrier's work. The Order publishes a wide range of writings by their founder, a list of which will be sent on request to the literature secretary in London.

Esoteric Society

The *Esoteric Society* was founded early in 1974 to fulfil the need for an organisation which would simply present a wide range of esoteric studies for those interested in the subject. For this reason the Society is entirely non-affiliated, and does not adhere to or propagate any one particular viewpoint or school of thought. At present most of its activities are concerned with the organisation of fortnightly lectures, held at Caxton Hall in London. Although largely a London-based group, it does have members in other parts of the country who travel down for particular lectures. The majority of seats at these lectures is reserved for members, who pay about 25p per ticket, but seats are available to non-members. The talks are followed by refreshments and discussion with the speakers, who are generally acknowledged experts. Topics cover a wide range of esoteric subjects, including the kabbalah, the Rosicrucians, exorcism, magic, alchemy, Stonehenge, astrology, the Holy Grail, etc. So that members unable to attend particular lectures do not miss out, extracts from the talks are printed in the Society's quarterly newsletter, *Esoterica,* which is sent to all members free. The newsletter also includes details of forthcoming events, book reviews and other relevant news and information.

The Society organises tours to places of interest such as Stonehenge, Avebury and Glastonbury, and some visits go as far afield as Brittany. In addition, each summer a group of members visits an area of interest abroad – in 1974 this was to Bulgaria, with excursions to monasteries and rock tombs in the Rhodope Mountains. Twice a year members are given the opportunity to get together at special parties, which usually also include exhibitions or films of esoteric interest. Membership of the Esoteric Society costs £2 per annum.

Avatar

Avatar is an international order founded by the late John van Ryswyk in 1935 to oppose the 'evil elements' of the age. Its stated aims are to 'challenge atheism and tyranny in any form throughout the world' and 'to defend the sacredness of the individual', while at the same time asserting the spiritual foundation of human existence. Van Ryswyk wished to unite wherever possible with other orders and organisations in order to wage a crusade against what are described as 'debasing and destructive elements'. He also proposed a plan for true government, which advocated the decentralisation of political power, and independence for all people and nations in autonomous states. In addition, a philosophical teaching was given which is said to provide an insight into the great philosophies of the world while providing the individual with a key to his inner potential. This philosophical teaching is available in the form of a series of notes on van Ryswyk's lectures, which will be sent on request.

Although van Ryswyk himself maintained an independent church, which aimed to return to early Christian doctrines, he in no sense opposed other churches or creeds dedicated to the worship of God. For this reason, Avatar members are free to follow their own inclinations so far as the desired form of worship is concerned. Generally, however, they should support the Avatar declaration of faith, which states: 'There is but one Supreme God, one Life created by Him, one Eternal Truth, and one Divine Purpose'.

Those interested in finding out more about the order should write to the registrar at the London headquarters, who will be willing to talk to enquirers by appointment. Otherwise, Avatar holds a number of regular meetings which are open to the public. On the first Monday of each month at 8.30 p.m. an artistic evening is held, at which aspiring poets and musicians submit their work for discussion. On the second Sunday of each month, at 11 a.m., the group holds a service in its own oratory – this consists of a mass with a special liturgy. At 8 p.m. every Tuesday special speakers are invited to talk on a wide range of subjects concerning Britain. In the past, the subjects have ranged from self-sufficiency to English folklore, and they are followed by discussion. All meetings take place at Avatar's London headquarters.

The Emin

The Emin is a highly original esoteric group which until recently did not advertise its existence. It was founded by an individual known simply as 'Leo', who, it is claimed, spent thirty years studying nature and the structure of the human body. During this time he never referred to any books or other teachings. He worked intensively, and arrived at a number of underlying truths and laws purely as a result of his personal investigations and experiences. He then decided to extend his work by drawing to him eight people, with whom he worked in secret for a further two years. It was then decided to 'go public', and since then The Emin have begun to advertise their activities and publish some of their findings, in the form of leaflets covering such topics as reincarnation, will, how to think, and the man/woman mystery. The group has undergone very rapid growth, especially in view of the large amount of commitment which is demanded of members. Membership now stands at more than three hundred, many of whom are under thirty and live in and around London. Those who join The Emin are asked to choose a new name by which they are known to other members. Names chosen vary from the commonplace to the bizarre, but it is claimed that the choice of name by a particular individual represents and reflects the best aspects of him or her. In addition to marking commitment to the group, the name is also said to mark the point at which the individual begins to become responsible for his own actions – an aspect frequently stressed in Emin philosophy.

Teaching, or rather learning within the group, follows the broad pattern laid down by Leo himself. No books are used, and a wide range of subjects are approached through a variety of techniques. Members are encouraged to 'work things out for themselves' rather than rely on any particular knowledgeable individual or written source. Astrology, the tarot, herbalism, sacred dance, massage, theatre, healing are just a few of the studies undertaken by Emin students, who take literally the statement that 'the great university is life itself'. Each member of The Emin studies the whole range of subjects, but it is the development of each person which is paramount throughout. According to Michael McIntyre, one of the group's founder members, 'There are certain underlying natural principles and fundamental laws which apply throughout the subjects we study. It is our aim to make people aware of other ways in which they exist. One has only to go beyond the self and its limitations. Once we are free of our conditioning we learn very fast.'

Group work is very important for Emin students, who adopt the principle that there is strength in union. Each group meets regularly twice a week. There are also group classes led by trained leaders held at weekends, and members hope to get their own permanent centre so that activities can continue all the time. Stressing the importance of group identity within The Emin, members wear special tunics, said to represent their feelings of unity, during their meetings. The colours of these tunics have a special significance.

There are no rules as such within The Emin, although the taking of drugs is banned. The principle of love, honour and respect among members is stressed. The aim of the group, claims Michael McIntyre, is to

143

'develop individuals so they can pay back for the things which they have been given,' their talents, and the gift of life. 'We want to help others to come to the same things we have discovered – to unlock the mysteries of the world and re-pay the planet. The important thing is that this is brought about through their own endeavour. They may gain for themselves some degree of immortality, but this must be earned.' Students of The Emin (which is an Arabic word meaning 'the faithful one') are willing to talk to anyone who is interested in their work, and if after this initial confrontation the enquirer is still interested, and if they are judged acceptable and 'fit', they will be invited to attend meetings. One leaflet promises:

> The Emin will develop you in great and forgotten arts so that you may sidestep the communal deception theatre that we call life and play your part in creation. You will discover the original Tarot and Astrology of the ancients, and learn the mysteries of the civilisations of the past. You will study the hidden teachings of the world's sacred books, the workings of Great Nature and the human body, and arts such as sacred dancing and you will develop natural abilities like clairvoyance and healing skills that man has now lost. And there is much more. You must expect to work hard, that is our first promise, it is the only way.

If you think you would be interested in joining The Emin, write or telephone for further details. The group claim to have archives of work which they have carried out, which would be 'of great benefit to mankind'. They plan to bring out a number of books on such subjects as tarot and astrology.

Axminster Light Centre

There are a large number of small groups and centres throughout the country who concern themselves with the esoteric and spiritual significance of flying saucers. Generally, they share similar attitudes and approaches to U.F.O.s, and typical of them is the *Axminster Light Centre*. This claims to be 'merely one of a world-wide network' of groups who, under a number of titles, share the same aims and receive interrelated communications via sensitives and mediums. Founded in 1970, the group has affiliations and contacts with a number of similar centres, and may therefore be a useful contact point for those wishing to find out more about U.F.O.s and their significance. They also publish a large amount of literature, which typifies the philosophy and beliefs embraced by such groups.

The Axminster Centre describes itself as an information centre 'dedicated to publishing the expanded teachings of Jesus, other World Teachers and Servers, Hierarchical Intelligences and beings on various planes of consciousness'. It claims to be preparing mankind for the coming of the Age of Aquarius, which will include the arrival in large numbers of visitors from other planets. These spacemen are the same as the gods of ancient times, 'like men in form, but nobler'. They are the angels referred to in ancient writings and scriptures, who descended from the skies, but looked, spoke and behaved like men. 'Those who man these craft (U.F.O.s) are our Elder Brothers – not gods. They are like us in many ways, but far ahead in conscious evolution. Through telepathic channels and other E.S.P. communications (including personal contacts) they are bringing messages of comfort and encouragement to those who are ready to receive them.'

The messages received from the spacemen often refer to the threat presented to the world by the atomic bomb, and frequently stress the apocalypse towards which the earth is moving. It is up to man to outlaw war, or, 'the Planetary Armada arranges for a mass evacuation'. It is the task of the spacemen to prevent man destroying himself, and to prepare for the coming of the Golden Age. 'The coming of spaceships to this planet heralds the return – or Second Coming – of the Lord of this Galaxy (Christ to the Christians), who always comes to the planet lowest in evolutionary development prior to a new age. The time of the great harvest is at hand when our elder brothers, at the command of our Lord Himself, will reveal themselves to mankind on earth. Many of them are already among us!'

In addition to a number of pamphlets, the Axminster Centre publishes two main magazines. *Logos* (four times a year) presents exclusively esoteric teachings, channelled from higher intelligences in the astral plane to mediums in meditation. Most of these teachings come from cosmic masters of the 'Unity of the Brotherhood of the Seven Rays'. *Logos Focus* (three times a year) is more concerned with information about and messages received from the spacemen themselves. These messages are also received telepathically and are part of the divine plan for earth, referred to as the 'inter-planetary re-educational programme'.

The Axminster Centre has only two full-time workers, who are unable to enter into lengthy correspondence, or provide callers with food or overnight accommodation. Visitors are welcome, however, but by appointment only. You can write for literature, which is provided free of charge, but you are asked to bear in mind that the Centre has no financial resources and relies on donations from appreciative readers for its income.

Dartington Solar Quest

Another West Country group whose teachings involve U.F.O.s – although they are not central to its philosophy – is *Dartington Solar Quest*. Based at a sixty-five-acre property overlooking the River Dart in Devon,

D.S.Q.'s main task is the spreading of teachings which come from God, via certain Masters and other individuals who exist on 'more subtle planes of existence'. The main theme of the teaching is that after eons of time God has decided to intervene to save Creation and return it to its original perfection. A great battle is being raged between the forces of light and darkness, and those who refuse to turn back to God 'will suffer as never before and be prevented from reincarnating in the world again'. On the other hand, great forces are being brought to bear to bring about the rise of man, and the return of the planet to its rightful place in the solar system. Great beings, from both this and other solar systems, have been directed by God to turn their attention to Earth, and it is man's task to learn to go with these new forces, and dedicate himself to God's service.

Dartington Solar Quest claims to offer a way of life for the coming new age. It is the funnel through which the forces of higher beings are being poured into the planet. Those working with the centre have the task of spreading the new teachings, and have been told that Dartington is one of a number of locations which long ago were designated as 'magnetic centres'. According to the teaching, in the beginning of time the earth was populated by beings known as Ells, who created within the planet powerful electrical forces. These 'magnetic centres and rods' or 'fault lines of power' are said to criss-cross in and over the planet. The Ells are returning to the proximity of the earth, bringing with them their magnetic force. Thus the regeneration of these centres is coming about, and will have a role to play in the restoration of the world. As man becomes more subtle, it is said he is able to tune in to these centres and draw power and strength from them. Man will gradually learn to harness energy given out by the centres, and use it in the same way he uses electricity. Some of the work carried out by members of D.S.Q. is concerned with helping to activate certain rods of power. Guided by the Masters, members visit the locations of the rods, and by utilising their physical vision, the Masters are able to bring about an activation through their eyes.

Regarding U.F.O.s, the Masters teach that flying saucers have indeed landed, and have taken samples of the atmosphere, soil and animal and insect life for testing. Once again, it is said they will be a means of salvation in the face of the atomic threat. Other teachings from the Masters give quite detailed descriptions of intelligent life on other planets, as well as deep beneath the sea.

Dartington Solar Quest publishes its teachings in the form of bimonthly magazines, sent free on request, although you are asked to include the cost of postage. These cover a range of subjects, in addition to those already mentioned: communications concerning healing, Jesus's links with the West of England, meditation, and life after death, are a few of these. As well as messages and thoughts from the Masters, intended as a guide for man's spiritual path, there are communications from individuals who have passed on to higher planes. These include Joseph of Arimathea, Saul, Caesar and lesser known figures such as 'Odin from the North'.

Among practical work undertaken by D.S.Q., healing plays an important role. Absent healing and touch healing are practised, and instruction on both these forms is given to those interested. D.S.Q.'s headquarters has three special healing rooms, mass healing services are held there, and healing groups in other parts of the country are encouraged. Those who require absent healing should send the name, address and age of the person for whom the healing is intended to Dartington, together with a brief description of the ailments. The methods of healing practised were given specifically to D.S.Q. by the Masters, and no charge is made. If you are interested in healing for yourself or someone else, or if you are interested in becoming a healer or starting a group, further details can be obtained from Dartington. D.S.Q. practises and teaches meditation, which is said to enable people to make their own direct communication with God.

Meditation instruction is available by post, and students are welcome to write for guidance. It is stressed that the methods do not depend on the teacher/pupil relationship, but on the student developing his own relationship with 'his higher self, the Masters and to God'.

D.S.Q. is currently trying to expand its movement throughout the country by setting up local groups of 'questors' to practise meditation and healing. Details of these can be obtained from Dartington, where discussion meetings, lectures and demonstrations are held. Speakers to outside groups may also be provided.

Aetherius Society

Another organisation concerned with flying saucers is the *Aetherius Society*, which claims to be 'the largest metaphysical society of its kind now on Earth'. Its members believe that ever since man has been on Earth his progress has been guided by higher intelligences on other planets within this solar system. These intelligences have intervened many times in the past to save man from the consequences of his mistakes. Indeed, say the Aetherians, these are the beings who visit this planet in flying saucers, and they maintain that references to saucer sightings are to be found in such holy books as the Christian and Jewish Bibles, the Hindu scripts and other sacred writings. These intelligences have also sent teachers to this world to instruct its inhabitants on the 'Law which is God' – the ancient Law of Karma.

The Aetherians state that Krishna, Confucius and Buddha were among the 'Cosmic Masters' whose teachings formed the basis for most of the great religions of the world. However, their messages have been debased and distorted by man through the ages, leading to the present confusion concerning all faiths. Now man has 'once again brought himself to the brink of nuclear destruction and the urgency of the Cosmic message is greater than ever'. It is for this reason that 'the Cosmic Masters chose to appoint a new channel for their teachings in this new Age of Aquarius'.

This 'channel' is Dr George King, who was first approached by the spacemen in his Maida Vale flat in May 1954. He heard a voice speaking in English which said: 'Prepare yourself. You are to become the voice of Interplanetary Parliament'. As the Aetherius Society points out, George King knew nothing about flying saucers or the Interplanetary Parliament. But he had spent the previous ten years practising yoga and studying spiritual philosophy. He was also a faith-healer. Eight days after the voice had alerted Dr King, he was sitting alone in his flat when 'a great Master of Yoga walked through the locked door and sat down facing Dr King'. He immediately recognised his visitor as a yogi then living in northern India. This yogi knew of the previous events and instructed Dr King about certain advanced yogic techniques, thereby enabling him to gain telepathic rapport with a being from the planet Venus, who was given the pseudonym 'Aetherius'.

In January 1955, Dr King held his first public meeting at Caxton Hall, London, and he soon attracted a small but faithful band of adherents. They brought out a single-page news-sheet which soon developed into a magazine called *Aetherius Speaks*. In August 1956, Dr King founded the Aetherius Society. The Aetherians state that 'most of the aims of this Society were dictated by Saint Goo-Ling, a member of the Great White Brotherhood, still living on this Earth'. The magazine went through a change of name soon after, when it was altered to *Cosmic Voice*. The next major event in the history of the Society took place on 27 July, 1958 at Holdstone Down in north Devon. It was here that Dr King had a physical meeting with the 'Master' Jesus, or as the Aetherius Society puts it, he was 'overshadowed by Jesus'. In the weeks that followed, Jesus gave 'The Twelve Blessings', described by the Society as 'the Bible of the Aquarian Age'. On 6 June, 1959, Dr King, 'on the advice of space intelligences', sailed to America and began the still-continuing World Mission of the Aetherius Society. Membership of the Society has now spread to many countries throughout the world with active branches operating in the United Kingdom, Australia and Detroit.

The Aetherius Society lists as its main function the propagation of 'vital transmissions from the Master Aetherius, the Master Jesus, Mars Sector 6 and other highly evolved cosmic intelligences'. It is also re-nowned for its operational activities, which take place all round the world. It was after the meeting with the Master Jesus in 1958 that the first of these, Operation Starlight, commenced. This particular operation took Dr King around the world, its purpose being to 'establish a network of mountains charged with spiritual energies by space Intelligences through Dr King as a physical instrument'. Nine of the mountains charged in this three-year operation are in Britain, including Holdstone

Down itself, Ben Hope in Scotland, and Penn-Y-Fan in south Wales. Four more mountains are in the United States, two in Australia, and one each in New Zealand, France, and Switzerland. Mount Kilimanjaro's 19,000 feet were charged by the Masters themselves, because members of the Society had done such a good job in charging the other mountains during frequently arduous assaults.

In 1963, Dr King was directed by space intelligences to perform Operation Bluewater. This lasted for eighteen months, and involved directing energy to certain off-shore psychic centres in the Pacific, off California. Dr King had to design and build instruments to perform this task and had to handle a speedboat in difficult manoeuvres. The Aetherius Society maintains that the success of this mission, among other things, ensured 'the safety of the western seaboard of the United States, at least for the immediate future'.

The next major operation, Operation Sunbeam, began in 1966 and is viewed as one of the most important carried out by the Aetherians. Indeed, unlike most of the other missions, Operation Sunbeam is open only to members of the Society because of its crucial nature. Aetherians regard the Earth as a living organism with its own highly advanced intelligence or 'logos'. The Society believes that man destroyed a planet called Maldek by misuse of atomic power, and that the remains of this planet are what we now call the asteroid belt. It appears that the Cosmic Masters approached the logos of Earth, which in those days was a spiritually attuned and highly advanced organism, and the latter agreed to withold its evolutionary process so that man could grow spiritually. Unfortunately, man proceeded to destroy the civilisations of Lemuria and Atlantis, again by the abuse of atomic power, and so Operation Sunbeam is considered to be of the utmost importance in correcting this imbalance. Practically, it involves the storing of energy collected from the Holy Mountains in spiritual 'batteries' designed by Dr King. This power is radiated 'along an etheric link to Los Angeles and then discharged into a psychic centre of the Earth at sea or on an inland waterway'.

This operation is taking place in conjunction with Operation Prayer Power, which began at Holdstone Down in June 1973. To quote the Aetherius Society once more: 'Dr King has made it possible for ordinary men and women, trained in the sciences of dynamic prayer and mantra, to concentrate energy into a physical battery which can hold several hundred hours worth. This can then be released through special instrumentation to help restore the balance in an area of world suffering, say famine, flood or earthquake, in a matter of hours.'

Before becoming a member of the Aetherius Society one has to agree to certain points of the Society's rules. There is a minimum donation of £3.85 for U.K. residents (£3.50 for those abroad, plus £1.25 airmail fees), and this includes a year's subscription to The Aetherius Society Newsletter. Members have to observe 8 July as the Holiest Day of the year. It marks the date of the Earth's 'primary initiation' in 1964 when the Cosmic Masters, according to the Society, poured a vast amount of energy into the planet. Man must first attain a sufficiently high level of spiritual enlightenment to be able to use this energy for the good of all. The rules concerning the observation of this day are particularly strict and 'failure to observe this condition of membership may result in the termination of membership'. Any prospective member must sign a form saying that he or she 'is not a member of any organisation or group having as its purpose or one of its purposes, the overthrow by force and violence of the Government of the United Kingdom or any of its political subdivisions'.

Viewpoint Aquarius

Viewpoint Aquarius is an organisation based in London but operating world-wide, which attempts to produce a philosophy of life that logically combines flying saucers, esoteric doctrines and the current spiritual 'revolution'. The group take it as gospel that flying saucers exist in great numbers, and that there is a world-wide conspiracy between governments to suppress definite proof of highly advanced civilisations from other galaxies constantly trying to contact us.

Their esoteric doctrines are based mainly on the teachings of Madame Blavatsky (*see* Theosophy). But the group claims not to be exclusive in their attitude to other spiritual movements and philosophies. For instance, in one of their monthly newsletters they recommend the collected lectures of Krishnamurti. The newsletter also runs regular explanations of Madame Blavatsky's beliefs and theories. They state that their convictions are the result of positive knowledge rather than faith or belief. This positive knowledge comes from the flying saucer phenomenon, the theory being that the main stream of visitors from the depths of space have been with us since the alleged existence of the Lemurian civilisation, eighteen million years ago.

The movement's founder, Rex Dutta, has written several books on flying saucers, the latest of which, *Reality of Occult/Yoga/Meditation/Flying Saucers* (published by Pelham Books), is recommended as Viewpoint Aquarius's current basic textbook. It claims to penetrate the underlying cause of things and explain how the 'Powers of the Mind' work. Members who spot saucers are encouraged to send their reports to Mr Dutta, and a dossier of sightings is compiled. Apart from flying saucers, the group interests itself deeply in the study and practice of yoga. The aim is to lift one's consciousness through the seven *chakras*, or planes of consciousness, to Truth. To help this, informative articles appear in the newsletter.

The group was started by Mr Dutta in January 1972 with about twenty-five members. Through a liberal exposure in the media, they have attracted a great deal of response, although Mr Dutta is unwilling to give any indication of the size of their present membership. To be a member you need only apply. The group are looking for hard-working students who have the perseverance and determination to absorb some knowledge of the occult laws, and to take part in saucer hunts. Age, background, intelligence, money, etc., are all irrelevant if you possess the overriding quality of enthusiasm.

Apart from lectures, tapes, broadcasts and public meetings, Viewpoint Aquarius reaches interested members through its monthly newsletter, a foolscap duplicated broadsheet of about thirty pages. An inquiry by letter or telephone to Mr Dutta will inevitably be followed up by a copy of the newsletter through the post, free of charge. Buried in the mass of information it contains will be a small reminder that, despite voluntary labour, the cost of paper, materials and postage is high and continues to rise. If the hint is taken and a donation sent, the newsletter will continue to arrive. If not, it ceases after the second visitation.

Enquiries are welcomed, and there are no 'hard-sell' tactics if you want to discontinue your interest. Only those who express the desire will penetrate to the higher echelons of involvement – and perhaps become a member of the 'Flying Squad', which helps prepare material, give lectures and spot saucers.

The Atlanteans

The Atlanteans are a group who describe themselves as an occult and teaching society, drawing knowledge and spiritual understanding from planes beyond the physical. At regular meetings in London and branches in other parts of the country, speakers from their own organisation, and from other philosophical, scientific and metaphysical groups, give talks aimed at providing the broadest possible understanding of the world. Their approach is described as 'sensitive and compassionate', based on a belief in the existence of an 'ultimate force' and an evolutionary pattern in which the process of spiritual expansion is leading creation back to its source. The Atlantean philosophy is said to be basically without dogma, and members are not obliged to accept any particular set of beliefs.

The Atlanteans was formed in 1957 in London by a small group of people under the direction of their spirit guide, Helio-Arcanophus, formerly a high priestess in the lost continent of Atlantis. Her spirit occupies the body of former actress Jacqueline Murray and speaks through her. At first a dominant interest in the lost continent of Atlantis was common to most members. Since these early days, the society has widened its scope and now concerns itself with all activities covered by the terms 'occult' or 'esoteric'. It also studies past history and present

151

trends in an attempt to formulate a universal philosophy applicable to the contemporary world.

The Atlanteans take the traditional view of Atlantis, believing it was situated between the coasts of Britain and North America and was engulfed by the sea about seven thousand years ago. Although a highly-advanced civilisation in terms of its scientific and occult powers, the continent was unable to withstand the forces of evil which were attacking it. Evil gained the upper hand and, through the operation of laws which modern science has yet to understand, Atlantis was destroyed.

As already mentioned, Helio-Arcanophus is described as a 'guide'. The spirit is the leader of the 'group inspiration' on which the Atlantean philosophy is based. A spirit guide is, according to the society, a discarnate entity that has chosen to work with or through a person incarnate on Earth. In accordance with the capacity and evolution of man, these spirits assist him whenever the need arises. The Atlanteans say the physical and supraphysical universes are interrelated and there is a flow of psychic energy between the two. Occultism is seen as the 'conscious control of thought in all its manifestations' and the practice of occultism is merely the use of thought to control those universal forces which exist and which are in themselves neither good nor evil.

Four festivals are celebrated each year, in spring, summer, autumn and winter: the Festival of Flowers, the Festival of the Ship, the Festival of the Stars and the Festival of Music and Art. Although The Atlanteans is a non-ritualistic society, Helio-Arcanophus says these festivals enact 'a symbolic meeting of spiritual forces with the more dense forces of which (the) material plane is composed'. Helio-Arcanophus describes The Atlanteans as seeking 'to bring Light to this planet by endeavouring to achieve a channel of communication with the gods'.

Jacqueline Murray emphasises the importance of the feminine influence of the world as symbolised especially by the Egyptian goddess Isis. The Atlanteans believe there is a marked lack of the 'feminine ray' on Earth and this is one of the prime reasons for the poor state of the world today. The group claim mankind's problems can be answered in two ways. Firstly, as individuals we must try to live our lives in balance, seeking to understand and love our fellow man and all forms of life around us. Secondly, as a group, we must 'join our thoughts together with the forces of Light in an effort to dispel the fear and hatred that is permeating our planet today'.

Membership of The Atlanteans costs about £3.00 and entitles you to *The Atlantean*, published bi-monthly; the monthly news-sheet, *Atlanteanews*; a diary of events, and notification of all the society's meetings. Tapes of Helio-Arcanophus and other members of the society are available on membership, and there is a library from which members can borrow books at a small charge. Regular meetings and programmes are held throughout the year in Bristol, Bromley, Cheltenham, Ruislip, Slough, Malvern and Ealing.

Great emphasis is also placed on the role of spiritual healing which is given freely at the meetings. Atlantean healing is described as 'the positive application of the power of thought over those imbalances which are the cause of all mental and physical disease'. The Atlantean healer is trained to use his or her mind as a transformer for cosmic forces which exist throughout the universe. Atlantean meditation consists of a series of disciplinary mental and spiritual exercises designed to help the individual to effect a balance and harmony in his life and realise his full potential. Regular classes are available for members at Cheltenham and other branches. There is a printed course in booklet form for those who are unable to attend in person. Details are available from the group's main address in Cheltenham, or from their London branch.

Pyramidology

The Institute of Pyramidology, the only institute of its kind in the world, was founded as a small local group in London in 1940. It developed into an international body in 1941, when *Pyramidology Magazine* was started and pyramid lecturing campaigns began. Its object is to advance knowledge and research into pyramidology and all its branches. It also wishes to make more widely known the 'Divine Revelation' enshrined in the Great Pyramid, in all its aspects – scientific, prophetic and religious.

The basis of pyramidology is, as its name implies, the Great Pyramid of Giza in Egypt, the first and greatest of the Seven Wonders of the ancient world and the only one that remains today. As is well known, nearly all the pyramids in Egypt are the tombs of Pharoahs. But the Great Pyramid has distinctive features not found in any other pyramid and having nothing to do with the dead. This reveals, say the Institute, that this particular pyramid is something more than a mere edifice over a tomb. For example, the Great Pyramid has ventilators, but these do not exist in any other pyramid and, quite obviously, a corpse has no need of air. The base of the pyramid has a unique construction not found elsewhere and this, in a scientific manner, reveals to a second of time, the precise length of the year, both solar and sidereal.

Pyramidologists claim the scientific information revealed in the Great Pyramid is abreast of modern science and in some cases even ahead of it. It is clear that the information and high degree of accuracy exhibited in the Great Pyramid could not possibly have been known by man at the time it was built. Consequently the Great Pyramid is viewed by the members of the Institute as a scientific revelation from the designer of the universe, in the same way that many people regard the Bible as a religious one.

153

Investigations by pyramidologists purport to show that the whole course of human history, past, present and future, is portrayed within the Pyramid itself by the symbolism and measurement used in its construction. Pyramidologists argue it reveals that today we are in a transitional period, not merely between two ages, but between two whole world orders. On its way is a new world order, divinely planned and disclosed in the Great Pyramid which, says the Institute, 'enshrines the Divine blue-print of the plans for our earth'.

According to the Great Pyramid's chronograph, this intervening world turmoil was due to commence in 1914 A.D., while the beginning of the inauguration of the New Age is due to become apparent by 1979 A.D., the date which, in the words of the Secretary of the Institute, Miss G. M. Bourne, 'will go down in history as the greatest turning point in human affairs throughout all ages'.

The Institute of Pyramidology issues a quarterly, *Pyramidology Magazine*, and publishes an up-to-date and fully comprehensive standard five-volume work entitled *Pyramidology* by Adam Rutherford, a founder-member of the Institute. Individual volumes may be obtained separately, directly from the Institute or from libraries and bookshops.

Membership is open to 'anyone who understands that the Great Pyramid is a Divine Revelation represented in stone', and the Institute's activities are carried on entirely through voluntary contributions. While no fixed annual subscription is imposed, the Institute does encourage a regular voluntary subscription since, like most organisations, it would be unable to continue regular work without it.

No meetings are being held at present, but extensive lecture campaigns in England and abroad are arranged from time to time. These will increase when Dr Rutherford completes the fifth and final volume of *Pyramidology*, and resumes his lecture tours.

The Druids

Druidism, the ancient religion of Celtic Britain and Gaul, was finally stamped out by the Romans about 58 A.D. What little we know about it is contained in factual accounts written by the Romans, but these provide only a sketchy picture. In fact many would argue that modern-day druidism dates from the eighteenth century, when the Romantic revival created a renewed interest and new theories about the Druids.

This is hotly disputed, however, by members of current druid bodies, who claim that the original mysteries of the Druids (who were the priesthood) are to be found in their respective orders. To support this claim, they cite evidence of recent archeological discoveries concerning Stonehenge, ley lines, numerology, etc., related to the early Celts.

The two main druid groups operating in Britain at the present time are *The Druid Order* and the *Order of Bards, Ovates and Druids*. The distinctions between them may not appear too obvious to an outsider, yet each claims to be the more authentic of the two.

Dr Thomas Maughan is head of The Druid Order and the present Chief Druid. His counterpart in the O.B.O.D. is Ross Nichols, Chief of the 'reconstituted order'. 'Reconstituted' is the key word behind the dispute concerning authenticity. Ross Nichols says: 'The last key date in the long history of the Order is the autumnal equinox of 1964, when in accordance with druidic organisation elsewhere ... the three grades of Bard, Ovate (Vates) and Druid were again separated.' He asserts that, 'It is the right of any senior body of Druids to declare a separate working,' and claims the bulk of Druids left the Druid Order when he formed his group in 1964. Dr Maughan, however, argues there is no justification for any reconstitution of the Order, since there was never any order to reconstitute. He claims Ross Nichols has no authority to form a druid group.

Today's druidic teaching is similar in many respects to the ancient philosophy, but has been modified by science and education. This is fortunate, because former druidic practices involved human sacrifice, although this element is not much spoken of today. Dr Maughan and his fellow members of the Druid Order believe life is good and find its origin in good, not in original sin. It is a self-rectifying process because man is not very good at living; he possesses a strong tendency to go wrong concerning life and how it should be lived. This results in friction which manifests itself as disease, pain, hunger, separation, loss and indeed discomfort or anguish of any kind. When this occurs, says Dr Maughan, you know some mental adjustment is necessary.

Druidism involves the whole field of human knowledge – the arts, the sciences and the act of living in general. The first job of the ancient Druids was to establish some kind of intellectual light in the early inhabitants of Britain and Gaul and work on that basis. After this, according to Dr Maughan, they reappear and guide intelligence in the right direction, this process gradually giving rise to elements of genius and wisdom. Dr Maughan stresses that we must seek men of individual brilliance today as a means of leading us in a more enlightened way.

Druidic teaching is thought to be more assimilable to a Western mind than the oriental philosophies which are very popular today. The Druids put the rise of Eastern religions down to the fact that there is an absence of a more intelligent Christian mysticism. Perhaps the druidic system is not so complete as oriental philosophies in all fields of learning, but, says the Order, it is more easily understood by a Westerner.

It is important to understand that the Druids are not representative of a faith or cult but consider they transcend, while subsuming, the recognised religions of our day. Truth is viewed as being one, and all religions share a common purpose.

The Druid Order does not proselytise or advertise its existence to the general public. Dr Maughan quotes the words of Jesus at this point: 'Seek and ye shall find'. This is especially significant, since joining the Order is a decision for the individual alone to consider and is viewed as a major step forward for the person concerned. The prospective member is judged on his or her merits and instructed accordingly.

There are three sections in the Druid Order: the Outer Order, which has contact with the public; the Inner Order, which guides and works through the Outer; and the Sanctum, 'of which nothing is said in public'.

The Outer Order has three grades, the first of which is the Gatehouse where anyone can seek admission to the Order through initiation. Next comes the Seven Kings, after a second initiation, where the aspirant begins to tackle the forces at work within him. Finally there is the Ovate Og or Ovydd Og grade. Ovydd is a sapling or any unformed plant and ov means raw. So there is here the idea of a young shoot showing promise. 'It is here that (a man) chooses between the life of selfless service and that of self-aggrandisement.'

The Inner Order also has three sections, and it is here that druid training begins properly. The character of a person must evolve along with the teaching itself, its whole purpose being the refinement of the mind and the ennobling of the emotions. There are no written exams because practice rather than theory is all important. Great stress is laid on the point that druidic teaching is an outward manifestation of the inner light.

Ceremonies are held at Stonehenge at the time of the summer solstice and of the spring and autumn equinoxes. It is at these times that the sun, as it rises, divides into three bars of light when seen from the altar stone at Stonehenge.

Those who are in sympathy with the aims of the Order, but do not wish to take up its studies, may become Friends of the Order. You will then receive notices of meetings, copies of the newsletter, and may take part in public ceremonies. If you wish to be initiated and take up the teaching, you must first become a Companion of the Order. The Order's programme of activities include monthly lectures and meditation and discussion meetings held in London. Details available on request.

P. Ross Nichols, present Chief of the *Order of Bards, Ovates and Druids*, maintains that as a senior Druid it is his right to form a separate body of Druids. The actual reasons for the split in 1964 may never be known to outsiders, but there is some difference between the places used for the ceremonial functions by the O.B.O.D. and the Druid Order. In the O.B.O.D., this involves a mixture of ancient and modern in order to arrive at a satisfactory compromise.

Ross Nichols takes great pains to avoid any possible clash with the Druid Order and arranges his meetings and ceremonies accordingly. The Druid Order uses Tower Hill, Stonehenge and Primrose Hill for its ceremonies, but the O.B.O.D. has ceased to visit Stonehenge because it no longer fulfils the ancient regulations for druid Gorsedds (or meetings) as laid down by Aed Mawr, the founder of the Order. Stonehenge is no longer a green spot because it is 'polluted with gravel', and the former Ministry of Public Building and Works discouraged the general public from attending the ceremonies because of rowdiness – this rather defeated the object of holding public ceremonies.

Stonehenge was constructed to welcome the solstice dawn every year and was the main temple in Britain for the observation of this rite. Now London is the centre of the country and ceremonies must be held with the public in mind.

The approximate dates of O.B.O.D. festivals are based on the times of the ancient solstices of summer and winter and the equinoxes of March and September. The latter are held at Parliament Hill by the stone of Free Speech, the summer solstice at the summit and the winter solstice at a convenient hall in the Westminster area. This may seem odd, but our climate has altered a great deal from the near-Mediterranean type of 2,000 B.C.

There are also four Celtic mystical fire festivals observed by the Order. These are the washing of the Earth's face at Imbolc (Candlemas); the festival of Brighid in early February; and the lightly magical Bealteine (Beltane, on the eve of May Day) carried out on the top of Glastonbury Tor on the nearest weekend date. O.B.O.D. believes it useless under modern conditions to hold ceremonies on days when few can attend. The next observance is Lughnasadh (Lammas) in early August, the high harvest point and beginning of the year's decline, with the rolling of the fire-wheel as the high spot of the ceremony. Lastly there comes the season of the gap between years, when Celtic time was no more and those who had passed on could be contacted. This is Samhuinn ('Sowen') or All-Hallows, in early November.

As in The Druid Order there are initiations to various grades and the aim of the Order of Bards, Ovates and Druids is 'to deepen inner awareness and realisation of the unity surrounding the spiritual basis of the universe'. This involves the idea that there is a central Sun of the cosmos, a guiding intelligence which rules the universe. Once again the emphasis is pragmatic and Ross Nichols fervently hopes the secrets enshrined in druidic lore will not have to remain secret for very much longer. The Order does not accept everybody for immediate initiation. A certain probation is required, partly involving the practice of meditation. Meditation sessions are conducted by Ross Nichols and are seen as a good methods for judging the suitability of applicants. One may also become an Associate member and receive literature and a list of forthcoming events.

[Note: This section was completed before Ross Nichols died in 1975. His successor is John Bryant.]

Torc

In recent years the town of Glastonbury in Somerset has taken on 'spiritual significance' for a large number of people. The Celtic Isle of Avalon; the place of the first Christian church in the British Isles; home of the legends concerning King Arthur; it is all these things and now, in addition, has become a spiritual centre helping to usher in this new Age of Aquarius. All the tales and legends seem to be converging and the old mysteries are coming to light. Young people especially are drawn to the spot, and while calling them the new Glastonbury community would be over-emphasising the point, there is no lack of communal spirit among them.

This spirit is exemplified by Patrick Benham, editor of *Torc* magazine. This is a community journal concerning Glastonbury and all its associations. It is aimed at improving people's knowledge of the area and it sees the town as the spiritual centre of the New Age. The first issue of *Torc* appeared in September 1971, and recently it restated its policy: 'Torc is about Glastonbury and is for people. It doesn't matter which people, but we hope both local people and young visitors and people who haven't been here yet – depending on how well we circulate. We're just trying to inform, communicate and generally help to get things together in this area.'

Patrick sees his role as that of a catalyst, creating interest in the town, contacting groups in other parts of the country through *Torc* magazine and trying to organise pockets of interest in different areas. The magazine itself is about community affairs, ley lines, and a variety of spiritual matters. If you are interested in Glastonbury as a New Age centre, contact *Torc*.

Glastonbury Zodiac

The idea that there exists an area in the Somersetshire countryside which actually represents, by its natural formations, the shapes of the twelve signs of the zodiac is not a new one. The earliest reference to the zodiac existing in this spot is by Dr John Dee, an eminent Elizabethan scholar, mathematician and astronomer. Somehow he had knowledge of a vast zodiac on the ground depicting all the signs that 'lie only on the celestial path of sun, moon and planets'.

There were no further references to the Glastonbury zodiac until this century, when it attracted the attention of Mrs K. E. Maltwood in the 1920s. A scholar of mythology and especially the Grail legends, she was a researcher of medieval manuscripts and ancient documents. She pored over the Ordnance Survey 6 inch to 1 mile maps and things began to fall into place as she examined the various natural hill and rock formations, field boundaries and rivers. Certain signs like Gemini and

Aquarius seemed to stand out in the landscape, but the whole project involved twenty years' research and much hard thought.

Since the signs, if they existed, would be huge in size, Mrs Maltwood thought it best to view the whole area from the air. The zodiac extends ten miles in diameter and has a circumference of thirty, and its immense size is partly the reason why its existence remains in dispute – it is simply too big to be of any use, say the objectors. However, when Mrs Maltwood did finally fly over the site, the experience she had was vivid and indisputable.

Aerial photography was in its infancy at this period, yet the original photographs clearly show a sight which had kept its secret for centuries. At 10,000 feet the whole area was obscured by clouds and observation was impossible. But when the plane was taken to an altitude of 20,000 feet, the sun broke through and Mrs Maltwood could see all the different signs laid out perfectly below her, just as she had always believed. One criticism constantly raised against the zodiac's existence is that one can make a case for zodiacal shapes on any given area of the countryside. This is perhaps true and one can certainly find what seem to be one or two signs at a number of places in Britain. However, Mrs Maltwood says, 'It would be impossible to find a *circular* traditional design of zodiacal and other constellation figures, arranged in their proper order, and corresponding *with their respective stars*, unless they had thus been laid out in sequence, according to plan. Nor could one find thirteen heads designedly turned towards the sunset, with their bodies turning round a central point on which they all pivot!' The odds of this happening anywhere else has been worked out to be 594,000,000 to 1!

Katherine Maltwood's theory has been generally accepted but, as already emphasised, the zodiac's existence is disputed because of its huge size. One has to possess a good knowledge of the area to distinguish any of the signs from the ground, and the figures can really only be viewed properly from the air.

Intergroup Catalysts: Wrekin Trust

Many New Age groups do not adhere to a particular philosophy or set of practices. Instead, they aim to present a range of activities open to all, often in the hope of acting as intergroup catalysts, enabling an exchange of ideas to take place between those of different commitments.

The *Wrekin Trust* grew from the work of its founder, Sir George Trevelyan, for twenty-four years warden of Attingham Park, an adult college offering short residential courses on a wide range of themes. During this time he perceived the need for an enquiry into the spiritual nature of man and his universe, and as a result organised residential courses and conferences on esoteric and spiritual subjects. By his retirement in 1971 these courses had established themselves as something of a tradition, with a mailing list of 1,500. Many people were keen that the work should continue, and to this end they formed the Wrekin Trust as a charitable foundation, with the aim of presenting approaches to spiritual knowledge mainly through short residential courses held in different parts of the country. Since its foundation the Trust has held a large number of conferences, ranging across the entire spectrum of spiritual endeavour. The venues have varied from small New Age centres to universities, involving students from many affiliations and from none. At the same time, interest in the work of the Trust has steadily grown, with the mailing list now in excess of 3,000.

Courses have maintained their breadth of interest – conferences in 1975, for example, cover such topics as transpersonal psychology, anthroposophy, health and healing, astrology, encounter, and Findhorn. In addition to straightforward conferences, the Trust organises events such as experimental workshops employing various techniques, pilgrimages to places of esoteric interest and retreats.

More recently, the Trust has tried to develop and extend itself through encouraging the setting up of small, local groups which meet for discussion, meditation and healing. The local groups also organise one-day events in their locality, attended by the Trust's speakers, including Sir George himself. The long-term aim is to develop a network of local groups across the country concerned with the New Age.

The Trust publishes transcripts of lectures given by its speakers, some of which are also available in tape cassette form – these are often used by local groups. Lists can be obtained on request from the Secretary of the Trust.

In addition to general programmes, which contain full details of the Trust's activities, a newsletter is published containing information about local groups and the latest developments in the Trust and elsewhere. Programmes and newsletters will be sent to anyone who asks to be put on the mailing list, at a cost of 50p per year to cover expenses. Those who wish to support the work of the Trust further may become 'friends' by undertaking to give an annual donation of not less than £3. The money raised in this way helps to support the Trust's work, and to keep course fees down.

Charges for lectures and courses vary from 20p for a single lecture to £1.50 for one-day conferences. Residential conferences can cost from £12 for a weekend conference to over £30. Conferences lasting more than a weekend are still more expensive, although a limited number of bursaries are available. Reductions of up to half the cost of the course may be available to those who write giving details of their interest and circumstances.

Human Development Trust

An organisation which, like the Wrekin Trust, is committed to working for the New Age, although not for any particular practice or philosophy, is the *Human Development Trust*. As its name implies, the Trust is concerned with all aspects of human development, and particularly those involving the mental, moral and spiritual improvement of mankind. Basically it performs an educational function – its stated objective is 'by educational means to assist individuals and groups to apply the principles of creative human development to themselves and society for the general welfare of the human family'.

This work is carried out through specially arranged conferences, meetings, study courses and seminars, and also through the publication of occasional reports, pamphlets and discussion papers.

The theme of the Trust's work is that within man is spirit, which expresses itself through the individual in the search for self-fulfilment and the will to serve. On a collective level this same spiritual impulse is seen by the Trust as a 'drive for constructive progress for the whole human family within a wider planetary destiny'. Many of today's modern problems are caused, claims the Trust, by the fact that man's spirit has outgrown his institutions and conventions. Within the field of education, economics and psychology there is little recognition of the role played by man's spiritual nature. Even the world's religions have little to say on how man's divinity may be expressed in the world.

Thus the Trust adopts a spiritual view of man, which acts not only as a basis for the individual's development towards self-realisation, but also as a framework within which mankind's entire progress towards a better world may be seen. In this way the spirit is not viewed in isolation, but instead an attempt to reach a 'spiritual synthesis' relevant to the modern world is being made, taking into account all fields of man's knowledge and endeavour.

In addition to educational activities, the Trust supports research into questions related to individual and collective human development. This is aimed at eliminating barriers to growth, and producing a transformed and spiritually sensitive consciousness. More particularly, the Trust aims to encourage the formation of specialised working groups in the various fields of human development, in the belief that 'group work will be a characteristic feature of the New Age'. Such groups are entirely autonomous and are in no way subject to control by the Trust. But the Trust does exist to provide back-up services in the form of information, finance and inter-group communication.

These groups, as envisaged by the Trust, combine a professional grasp of a particular field with an ability to deal with new patterns of thought, and translate them into 'practical working concepts and tools'. These 'seed groups', as the Trust refers to them, will pioneer new approaches in many fields, in an attempt to bridge the gap between what life is and what it might be. It was with this in mind that the Trust initiated the 'Seed Group Project', with nine independent and autonomous groups working in their own particular fields, but linked by a common vision and purpose – the transformation of consciousness. It is in relationship to this aim that groups are working in the fields of communication, education, religion, psychology, science, healing, economics, and politics.

The ninth group is called the 'observers group', and their work is concerned with the cleansing of consciousness 'so that reality may be recognised'. Ultimately it is hoped that a tenth group will emerge, representing a synthesis of the others, and attempting to assist the groups in making an impact on society.

For details of meetings, conferences, etc., and also publications of the Human Development Trust, write to the Secretary. If you are interested in taking an active part you should also say which particular area of study interests you.

A recent off-shoot of the Human Development Trust is the *U.K. Advisory Council for Human Development*. The council has a membership of nearly forty New Age groups and centres, many of them discussed in this book. They represent a spectrum of New Age activity, sharing in common a concern with human development and the expansion of consciousness. Although fundamentally a co-operative effort, the groups maintain their autonomy and do not necessarily endorse the activities of other members. They will help and advise each other where possible and inter-group working parties and joint projects will be launched when necessary. The council aims to offer an atmosphere where this sort of inter-group co-operation can take place.

Holonomics

An organisation which acts as a communication network rather than an independent society is the *Holonomics Group* formed by Alan Mayne. The group aims to study in an open-minded and uncommitted way 'the pattern of law of the universe as a whole', utilising experimental and scientific approaches. The basic function of the group is the publication several times a year of a newsletter. These include discussion of scientific advances, outlines of new trends in philosophy and religion, and what are described as 'reports on significant revelation and inspirations'. There are also book reviews, announcements of events, and a correspondence column.

The Holonomics Group has no formal membership as such, but newsletter readers will be encouraged to contact one another and arrange mutual activities. Those interested should write to Alan Mayne, who acts as co-ordinator.

World Congress of Faiths

The *World Congress of Faiths*, as its name implies, is an organisation dedicated to building bridges between the various world faiths, and to combating intolerance and exclusivism. Founded in 1936 by Sir Francis Younghusband, the organisation's stated aim is to '. . . instill a spirit of fellowship among mankind through religion, and . . . to revitalise all that is highest in man's spiritual being'. Basically it works to disseminate more genuine knowledge of the world's religions, while at the same time building up friendly relationships among them. However, the Congress makes no attempts to weld the religions into one syncretic faith, and avoids exalting any one faith against the others. It takes the point of view that all religions have much to teach, and also much to learn from the others.

It believes that inter-religious understanding can best be brought about by encouraging personal contact and frank dialogue, and in its own words, 'exists for all those who believe in spiritual values'. By bringing the various religions together, it tries to promote the universal ethical values common to the great faiths.

The Congress works mainly by arranging lectures, debates, visits to religious centres of various sorts, occasional 'All Faith Services' of united worship, and an annual conference. They provide speakers from various religions to visit schools and colleges to talk about their faith. *World Faiths*, a quarterly journal published by the Congress, contains news of its activities, as well as book reviews and general articles of religious interest.

Lectures on a variety of topics are held on the first and third Tuesday in every month at Congress headquarters in London. These are open to the public, are free, and are generally followed by a short 'social gathering'. A programme of events is available on request.

Membership of the Congress is open to anyone who sympathises with the aims, and the minimum annual subscription is £2. At present there are branches of the W.C.F. in north Kent, Bath and Bristol.

4 Astrology

Astrology is one of the oldest sciences known to man, and for centuries was held in high esteem by both East and West. But the Western world developed its materialistic outlook, with its demands for definite empirical proof, so astrology suffered the fate of many occult ideas, until it virtually fell from the everyday lives of ordinary people.

Yet recent years have seen a growing interest in the subject, among both the general public and the academic community, and once again, people are turning to astrology to re-examine it in the light of the twentieth century to discover whether there is really anything in the old 'myth'.

It is important to distinguish between astrology and astronomy. The latter developed from the original 'Natural Astrology', which dealt solely with the movements of heavenly bodies, whereas the astrology we know today grew from 'Judicial Astronomy', which concerned itself with the effect of these movements on human life and fate.

The traditional method of approaching astrology is to regard it as a literal system in which heavenly bodies are thought of as emanating 'psychic rays', a form of supernatural energy which creates personality at birth and determines subsequent actions. This fundamental approach is shrouded in mystery and unanswered questions, and carries with it an air of fatality and predetermination. It is a universe of supernatural mechanics, beyond our conscious will and understanding. For some quite mysterious reason, what is up there in outer space comes to affect us in 'inner space'.

It is this view which is primarily responsible for bringing astrology into scorn as a spurious pseudo-science, based on tenuous assumptions and making the largest generalisations. But for astrology to be of value it is not essential that we accept this occult view. It may just as rewardingly be treated as a symbolic system, able to provide us with new psychological and philosophical insights. In this sense astrology can be of immense advantage in externalising and focalising conscious and unconscious patterns of behaviour, thereby increasing awareness and self-control. It can highlight positive and negative areas, strengths and weaknesses, outstanding abilities or deep-rooted complexes. It is an aid to personal liberation. Once you lend it an open ear, astrology becomes a sort of mirror that reflects the complex machinations of your personality and your karma.

Astrology is a complicated business, and it is good to know a little about it before having your horoscope done professionally. The first step of an astrologer when dealing with a 'client' is to construct a natal chart. This is a map of the heavens at the exact moment you were born, and to calculate this an astrologer needs to know your exact time, date and place of birth. This is the purely mathematical part of astrology and can be carried out quite safely by a modern computer without any loss in personal inspiration. The true skill of an astrologer comes in the *interpretation* of this map. This is by no means an easy task, for it requires considerable concentration and insight on the part of the astrologer – what Dane Rudhyar calls 'holistic perception' – to uncover a person's psychic patterning: ways to integration, past legacies and future destiny – karma and dharma. To reveal wholeness in another, an astrologer, it is claimed, needs to have reached a certain level of wholeness himself.

The array of information and the possible lines of interpretation afforded by the basic natal chart are vast, and make a mockery of pop astrology – the magazine and newspaper stuff. Most serious astrologers have very little respect for this kind of astrology. What, then, should you expect from an astrologer as the most basic areas of information? A competent interpreter should tell you about the following, and explain what they mean:

1 The positions on your day of birth of the Sun, Moon, and other planets.
2 The positions of the *Ascendant* and *Midheaven*. The Ascendant is the sign rising on the eastern horizon at the moment of birth and represents, in psychological terms, the persona. The Midheaven is, roughly, the overhead point in the sky and represents your aims and orientation in life. This is why an astrologer needs the exact time and place of birth, because without knowing these your Ascendant and Midheaven cannot be calculated.
3 The twelve house divisions. These stand for twelve basic areas of action and environment – e.g., home, finance, career, public relations.
4 The major planetary aspects. These are the angular relationships between the planets, and refer to points of emphasis and counterbalance in the personality.

These are the most basic points an astrologer bears in mind when interpreting a birth chart. Also, you may find mentioned the degree of the zodiac on which the planets fall – this is seen by some astrologers to have an important symbolic value. A good astrologer will not treat all these aspects as separate factors, and read off the attributes of your personality one-by-one like a shopping list. Personality is an organic whole, with each aspect interrelated, and each person basically operates from the centre, as a totality, not as a bundle of isolated facets.

Up to this point, an astrologer will only have dealt with the interpretation of the birth chart as a static seed – your personality in snapshot. But if we consider living as a dynamic process, the personality does not work in suspension, but is always changing. Thus most astrologers will complement their basic interpretation with a *forecast* of how your life will run in the following six to twelve months or even over a period of years. This is the process of unfolding personal tendencies, and may take the astrological form of predictions of specific events – or of more general trends, general psychological currents that you will have to operate with. Here an astrologer refers to what are called 'directions', 'progressions' and 'transits', and one method is to compare the present positions of the planets with those in your natal chart, looking to see where the two sets of readings conflict or harmonise. All this, the basic interpretation and the forecasting, the static and the dynamic, is a very complex business, requiring much study and concentration. For a conscientious astrologer it may mean a week's work, ending in a consultation with the person concerned. For this you can expect to pay anything between £10 and £20, and for the services of a notable astrologer you can well pay between £20 and £30.

You either go to an astrologer to find out about your astrological picture, or you can study astrology yourself, or at least the rudiments of it. The astrology scene is solidly established in Britain, and there are now good opportunities to do either – to study or be studied.

Astrological Lodge

The parent of British astrology is the *Astrological Lodge of the Theosophical Society*. This was founded in 1915 under the guidance of the famous astrologer Alan Leo. A focus of interest for astrologers and those seriously interested in the subject, the Lodge gathered a strong group of members in between the wars, and tended to dedicate itself to the pure and involved study of astrology. There was a concentration upon the esoteric or internal aspects of astrology, and the Lodge's role was mainly a passive and introverted one: it had no policy of broadcasting astrology to the general public, but relied upon drawing people into itself. For many years, Charles Carter, eminent author of many sound text-books of astrology, was the Lodge's president, until Ronald Davison took over. The Lodge produces a quarterly journal, and holds regular meetings on Monday nights at Gloucester Place.

Faculty of Astrological Studies

To cope with the growing interest in astrology and the need to educate people, the Lodge gave birth in 1948 to the *Faculty of Astrological Studies*. Members of the Lodge split off to form a non-profit-making institution which would give British astrology a more public face. The most important thing that the Faculty did was to set up courses in astrology leading to a diploma qualification. There are in the U.K. approximately one hundred diploma holders and thirty abroad. The present president of the Faculty is Julia Parker, a well-known British astrologer.

The Faculty's constitution states their aim as 'to raise the standard of astrological knowledge and practice, to institute courses of tuition, and to organise and promote astrological research and discussion'. Their tuition courses are at two levels: *certificate* and *advanced*. If you live in London, the certificate course is run as three terms of ten lessons, with personal supervision by an experienced tutor, and the cost is £30. Evening classes for the certificate course are now being run in London.

If you live outside London, the course is by correspondence, arranged also in three terms, though students may work at their own pace and begin at any time of the year. Students on the correspondence course receive an astrology text-book, full instructions, tables and calculation forms, along with individual coaching from a Faculty tutor in their locality. The U.K. fee for this course is about £25.

The purpose, says the Faculty, of the London school and correspondence courses is 'to give a full understanding of the basic principles of astrology, to enable a student to calculate a natal chart correctly, and to interpret it in modern and psychological terms'. You don't need to enter for the certificate examination if you don't feel like it: you may prefer to take up astrology purely for your own enjoyment and benefit, enlarging your understanding in a casual way.

If, however, you wish to study astrology more academically and in greater depth, success in the certificate examination, held annually in February, entitles you to move on to the *advanced* course. This provides you with a diploma qualification and the letters D.F.Astrol.S. after your name – assuming you pass the exam – and with automatic membership of the Faculty. The standard of the diploma is rigorous, being generally recognised as the qualification necessary for a practising consultant. Members of the Faculty maintain a strong code of ethics, written and oral, and there is a general abhorrence of pop astrology and astrology practised for financial gain. In order to become a consultant astrologer, a diploma holder must take the Hippocratic oath.

Astrological Association

In 1958 the Astrological Lodge gave birth to its second offspring, the *Astrological Association*, to fulfil a growing need to present astrology with sincerity and integrity to the world and to foster its spread into scientific and professional fields. They act as a back-up organisation to the Faculty, many diploma holders becoming members of the Association, and do not offer courses of tuition, except in small groups. Their

167

membership totals approximately 750, with a hard-core of 450, and costs about £3.30 (half-price for full-time students). The Association is basically a centre of ideas, and the facilities open to members are good: a quarterly magazine, *The Astrological Journal*, and a newsletter, *Transit*, to keep astrologers in touch with the latest news and ideas; a research library at a house in Bromley, Kent, a loan library in Lancashire, and taperecordings of lectures and seminars; regular fortnightly meetings in London and elsewhere, special one-day conferences, and an annual conference held in September at a university college. The Association hopes to attract people with professional disciplines, in particular – psychologists, teachers, social workers, doctors: people who can help them correlate astrological truths with other fields of study and help develop new areas of research. Though they welcome anyone, you are advised to take the certificate course of the Faculty in order to have a basic understanding.

Jeff Mayo

Besides the Faculty of Astrological Studies, there are a few other, smaller, teaching bodies. Jeff Mayo was for many years the Head Tutor of the Faculty, and from 1969–73 its Principal, and is the author of five books on astrology. In 1973 he resigned to found his own school, which he at present operates from Milnthorpe in Westmorland. Tuition is by correspondence only, and the main course is a basic one, comparable to the Faculty's certificate course. The fee at the moment is £24, and, like the Faculty's certificate course, the Mayo basic course offers to teach you the astronomical basis of the birth chart and how to calculate and interpret it 'in terms of potential psychological traits and future trends in life.' You will receive a text-book of astrology, a syllabus of the course, and chart and calculation forms, as well as a copy of your own birth chart; you will also be placed under a tutor who will keep in close touch with you. There is an advanced course leading to a diploma qualification and giving you the title D.M.S.Astrol (Diploma of the Mayo School of Astrology).

John Iwan

Another course is offered by John Iwan. This has a broader perspective in that his one-year course includes a look at Jungian psychology and the history of thought and philosophy. Unlike the other two teaching courses, Mr Iwan does not treat astrology as a separate subject, but tries to relate it to other fields of intellectual endeavour. Mr Iwan read psychology and economics at the University of Wales, where he hopes to research early Celtic religion and, in particular, astrology. The correspondence course he offers takes students to about the certificate level of the

Faculty, though it does have a wider scope of reading. An advanced course is at present in preparation. The cost of the basic course is £20, for which you receive the usual text-book, ephemeris, tables of houses, and chart and calculation forms. Each month you are sent a batch of four tutorial papers covering the four weeks of study. These papers are a complete course in themselves, the text-book providing further reading material, and you can submit your work for correction and comment if you wish.

White Eagle Lodge

A school with a slightly different approach is the *White Eagle Lodge*, which has its base in Hampshire. It is dedicated to spreading the philosophy of the White Eagle, claimed to be a teacher in one of the spirit-worlds, and this philosophy includes astrology. Astrological lectures are given from time to time at the White Eagle Lodge in London and also at the Lodge in Hampshire: details of these activities are available on request to the latter address. They have their own complete system of training for astrologers, which comprises a beginner's course starting from first principles and continuing to a 'delineation' course. The latter deals with the deep analysis of a horoscope from the 'spiritual and karmic angle'. The beginner's course culminates in a certificate examination, and the delineation course in a diploma examination.

Astroscope

If you wish, you can have your birth chart done by computer. The commercial name of the people who do it is *Astroscope* – better known for their work in Dateline, a computer-dating service. The horoscope is stamped out from a magnetic drum containing five million characters, and contains an analysis of your personality and predictions for the following six months. The chart analysis does not deal with the important factors of aspects and house division, nor does it cover the three outer planets, Uranus, Neptune and Pluto, but they are working at including aspects. You get rather a rough, pre-packaged astrological picture of yourself – but it does only cost £2.

There are, of course, many other astrologers who offer themselves for consultancy, but of these perhaps one in particular is worth mentioning, for he is one of the few reliable practitioners of Hindu astrology.

Bhagawan Soaham is sixty-four, Indian, small and smiling, and lives in a tiny house in a seedy area of London under a vow of complete silence. Most of his clients have never seen him, know little or nothing of his one-man campaign for world peace, and do not practise yoga or meditation. They write to him for help in affairs of the heart and with unhappy marriages, for good luck and health, and for success in careers, studies and business. For Soaham is primarily a Hindu astrologer – not to mention palmist, shadow reader and faith healer. His business is conducted by post and through extensive advertisements in carefully chosen magazines and newspapers, and his ability can be judged by an income estimated by friends at over £20,000 a year, for a service that costs 'any amount you wish'. And he also offers a 50 per cent refund to dissatisfied customers.

Soaham's second vocation in life is world peace. That is why he took a vow of complete silence for fifteen years in May 1973. He has also renounced meat, alcohol, drugs, cigarettes, and grains, and has begun to run down his highly profitable astrology business to spend more time in 'penance for peace'. No little sacrifice for the former chain-smoking owner of six cars and four houses!

Bhagawan Soaham was born the son of a wealthy Indian landowner in 1910. Before he became an astrologer, he had several aims in life. One was to be a yogi, a holy man. Another was to be a lawyer or philosopher. But it was not until 1933 that he first learned the tricks of his trade.

In India, astrology is regarded as an exact science, a method of foretelling the future that works as accurately as a compass shows direction. And Soaham has the advantage of studying under Shri Gaurishanker Krishnaram Vyas, one of the country's most respected astrologers. However, until 1947 astrology was only a part of his life. He was imprisoned several times for supporting Gandhi and the Indian independence movement, and tried to become a businessman. But business was bad and he lost all his inheritance, being forced to work in a bank to earn a living. For ten years, from 1937, he was an active politician. And once to show his humility, he worked as a 'shoeshine boy'.

But in 1947 he opened a college of astrology which was an immediate success. The next turning point in his life was 1954, when he decided to see the world and left India for East Africa. From there he travelled to England, arriving in 1961, to set up his present business. He draws customers from all over the world. As an astrologer he requires you to supply him with your date and time of birth, as accurately as possible, and also the exact place of birth. He only asks you to pay as much or as little as you are willing.

5 Psychic and Spiritualist

For all the enormous achievements of science in posting the universe that man inhabits, odd things keep slipping past the sentries. The tap on the shoulder may be fleeting, the brush across the cheek gone sooner than it is felt, but the momentary effect is unmistakable: an unwilling suspension of belief in the rational.

Hardly a person lives who can deny some such experience, some such seeming visitation from across the psychic frontier.

These words, taken from the cover story of *Time Magazine* entitled 'Boom Times on the Psychic Frontier', sum up well what 'the psychic' is all about. It is concerned with phenomena which are beyond the range of normal experience, and appear to be outside the region of physical laws.

From the very beginning of history, mankind has recorded psychic phenomena of one sort or another, either directly or through the means of myths and legends. Clairvoyance, E.S.P. premonitions and communication with spirits, these and many other phenomena, which are today collectively called 'psi', are by no means new. The experience of the 'paranormal' seems to have been with man since the dawn of his consciousness, and during the course of the past hundred years or thereabouts, two important developments have taken place. First, there has developed a religion known as 'spiritualism' which takes as its foundation the psychic experience, and more particularly the ability of 'mediumship' and communication with the spirits of the deceased. Second, there has been a slowly intensifying scientific and systematic investigation of psychic phenomena. Psychic research has grown over the years, not only in the amount of energy, talent and resources applied to it, but also in its scope. The type of investigation now being carried out is very sophisticated compared to the early beginnings, and for the first time the walls between science and para-science show signs of crumbling.

It is important to recognise the distinction which exists between spiritualist groups and psychic groups, the former concerned with the religious aspect and the latter with the research aspect. This does not necessarily imply that such a hard and fast division actually exists, and quite obviously the two overlap in many ways. There are those who follow the spiritualist religion and have no particular inclination or interest in the findings of objective research, while it is certainly true to say that many of those interested in psychic research are not Spiritualists. Today psychical research is enjoying a widespread interest, both among the public and among a growing section of the scientific community, which might not have been predictable from its somewhat humbler beginnings some hundred years ago. Before psychical research got underway, the psychic experience was either blurred into a broader religious framework by 'believers', or dismissed outright as 'poppycock' by the unbelievers.

Fear and superstition are powerful forces which have caused confusion in regard to psychic phenomena, and the confusion still persists today, albeit in a more sophisticated form. Thus the pioneers of psychical research were forced to run the gauntlet of severe criticism and ridicule from the bulk of the scientific establishment. Yet there is a much more hopeful picture emerging, as more and more bona fide scientists harness the methods and discoveries of modern science to an investigation of the paranormal.

That ordinary people are showing an interest is reflected in the enormous amount of attention paid to Uri Geller, perhaps the world's most famous psychic. After his controversial appearances on British television, he was a common topic of conversation for millions. As a result, stories flooded in of 'unusual occurrences' and many local newspapers carried articles of 'schoolchild spoonbenders' for weeks afterwards. The impact which the twenty-seven-year-old Israeli former nightclub magician had on the public was intense, reflecting an interest manifested in many forms, including the many books which are now being published on parapsychological topics. And in this respect, the interest being shown by the American public causes our own to pale into insignificance!

Interest is no less to be found in the scientific community. A readers' poll run by the *New Scientist* found that 70 per cent of those who replied believed in the possibility of E.S.P. (extra-sensory perception) and in a poll involving mainly scientists and technicians! The amount of scientific research resources now being dedicated to examining psychic phenomena is on the increase, and once again Britain lags behind the field compared to America.

Society of Psychical Research

The largest and most influential body operating in Britain is the *Society for Psychical Research*. Founded in 1882 by scholars and scientists who included such distinguished personages as Professor Henry Sidgwick and Sir William Barrett, it was in at the birth of serious examination into psychic phenomena. Its aim was to make a systematic examination 'of certain phenomena which appeared to be inexplicable on any generally recognised hypothesis', ie. the paranormal. Its activities were greeted with total derision from colleagues outside the field, and not, one is forced to say, without cause. The beginnings of psychical research were dogged with a large number of frauds, and the apparent gullibility of these early pioneers did little to develop a serious image.

In fact the Society is beginning to feel the effects of a slight conflict of attitude between the past and the present. Older members tend to take, not unpredictably, the traditional view of research, and such attitudes do not always match with the more exacting and sophisticated demands of younger members.

The Society does not undertake its own research work, and by the same token does not express a corporate view. It does have a number of research committees which look into various aspects of 'spontaneous phenomena', but the bulk of research work is done by individual members who have facilities at their disposal through their normal work. Modern psychic research, unlike the past, now requires highly specialised knowledge, and in the case of such research areas as Kirlian photography ('aura' photography), highly specialised equipment is used. In studies of E.S.P., for example, sophisticated random decay of strontium 90 as well as the most up-to-date electronic switching devices – quite a contrast to the sort of studies being carried out even twenty years ago. The Society is, therefore, a central body which correlates information supplied by its individual members rather than actually initiating and maintaining research. It acts as a sort of clearing house for members' research, maintaining archives and trying to co-ordinate information.

Frequent meetings of the Society are held at which papers are read and discussed by members, and there are also occasional public meetings. The Society publishes a quarterly *Journal*, which contains reports of experiments, texts of papers read at meetings, reviews of related books, etc. *Proceedings* is also published by the Society, in parts as and when suitable material becomes available, and is devoted to major pieces of research, presidential addresses, and papers of theoretical or analytical nature. The Society maintains a library of books, pamphlets and periodicals which is quite unique, and contains material not only on psychical topics but also on related fields such as psychology and mysticism. Members have full use of the archives.

People join the Society because they are interested in the field and want to know how and where they can become involved in research. If the new member is interested in a particular area of research (as most new members tend to be), he is put in touch with the chairman of the research committee which is interested in relevant phenomena. Otherwise, advice about reading can be given, and individuals may be put in contact with other centres which are carrying out research work. Members may be advised on how to carry out their own work, which usually involves the study of spontaneous phenomena. The Society is presently considering financing suitably equipped university departments which have students who want to do a higher degree with a parapsychological content.

With around 1,300 members spread throughout the country, the organisation itself is entirely London-based. There is a number of members in the provinces who organise local events, and the Society's headquarters put members in touch with local organisers where they exist. The Society stresses it is a non-religious body, and the increasing proportion of young scientists who are joining tends to reinforce this. Membership does not imply acceptance of particular explanations of the phenomena investigated, or a belief in the operation of forces in the physical world other than those recognised by physical science. All members are elected by the council, and candidates must either be proposed and seconded by two members, or supply the names and addresses of two responsible people willing to support their application. Membership subscription is about £4 per annum, and students under twenty-five can become student associates for £2 per annum. Members receive the *Journal* and the *Proceedings* free-of-charge, may use the library or borrow books by post if necessary, and receive encouragement and advice from members of the Society for any research work they carry out.

College of Psychic Studies

Somewhere between the strictly scientific approach of the S.P.R. and the more straightforward 'religious' attitude of the spiritualist groups comes the *College of Psychic Studies*. This states its objects as to 'offer both to newcomers and to seasoned investigators the opportunity for experience, experiment and intelligent discussion in the field of psychical phenomena'.

It is the emphasis on 'experience' which sets the College apart from the S.P.R. Whereas it is objectivity and quantification which concerns the scientist, the College is prepared to admit the subjective experience factor into consideration. Thus the college believes personal experience of phenomena is at least admissible, and perhaps even more vital than objective evidence. One should not get the impression, however, that the College is prejudiced against any particular approaches to the subject. Like the S.P.R., it expresses no corporate opinions, and is at pains to stress that it is non-religious, and does not aim to pressurise people into accepting any particular belief.

It takes as its premise the fact that the accumulation of evidence, although not amounting to a scientific proof, justifies a belief in survival after death. It adopts this belief as a working hypothesis, but members are free to accept or reject this as they see fit. The College also claims that the evidence for E.S.P. merits further study, and is a factor to be taken into account when considering the evidence for survival.

The term researcher is applied to all those who come to the College,

174

irrespective of whether their interest is scientific, religious or emotional. The term reflects, however, the College's desire to keep its atmosphere free from pressure on the individual to make up his mind about survival in a particular direction.

There are a number of sensitives (or mediums) attached to the College who are available for personal sittings in private rooms at the College's headquarters. No guarantee is given that the sensitive will go into a trance, but after an initial chat he or she will most probably start giving what is described as 'evidential information'. This might include revelations of 'insight' into your situation, and possibly even messages from the 'other side'. Stress is laid on the requirement that you come along with an open mind, but the firm intention of not being deceived is regarded as completely healthy, and much preferable to emotional gullibility. As well as private sittings, the College offers group and open demonstrations of clairvoyance. Because of its aim in providing evidence of survival, it tries to offer mediumship of a high standard, but once again no results are guaranteed, and it is left to the individual to draw his own conclusions.

Another important aspect of the work carried out by the College is its 'psychological counselling', which it is currently trying to expand and develop. Confidential and sympathetic advice and guidance is always available, both for personal problems and those related more directly to individual research and experimentation. 'It offers help to those who are making their first approach, and who perhaps feel a certain nervousness, and would welcome the protection and aid of those who already have a practical working knowledge of the field. Many are uncertain how best to set about the matter, and the College is available to help them through the early steps and beyond.'

The majority of the 780 members tends to be middle-aged or elderly, but, as elsewhere in the field, there has been a recent intake of the young (18–28 years), and the College now organises occasional youth forums. Another development is that the College's approach is broadening out from the strictly spiritualist to a wider spiritual field. Having accepted the evidence for survival which the College provides, facilities are offered for those who wish to take the next step and become more deeply involved. Messages and guidance from mentors 'on the other side' are, the College claims, concerned little with the outer personality on earth, and more with the soul or psyche, and for some members it is this spiritual side of communication which is more important than the search for evidence. The College offers courses and lectures in relaxation and meditation which, it is claimed, 'is a very useful method of learning how to listen for and become obedient to a wiser inner self within'. Spiritual healing is another area where the College tries to offer facilities to develop along the spiritual path, and members are invited to assist in the simple forms of healing which are practised at the College. Eventually, some people will wish to take the plunge and trust the reality of discarnate helpers and their own spiritual resources. For many this leads to the brink of mystical experience. The College tries to provide, wherever possible, facilities and classes concerned with the more esoteric and deeper aspect of the subject.

Membership of the College is open to all, and may be taken up at any time. Annual fees at time of writing are: fellowship £5.50, full members £4.50, associates £3.40, junior members £1.15, joint members £6.80. There are regular weekly lectures held on Wednesday evenings. These are also open to the public, but members pay a reduced entrance fee and certain classes of members are admitted free. The lectures cover a wide range of subjects, including such topics as E.S.P., altered states of consciousness, dreams, healing, etc. There are also evening courses of study, one-day conferences and annual residential conferences, and these often include meditation groups, consciousness-training workshops and meetings on how to sit with sensitives.

The College library contains around 10,000 books on psychical and related topics, and books may be borrowed by members either personally or by post. A reference library containing rarer books may be consulted on the College premises. *Light* is the quarterly College journal, annual subscription £1.30, and members receive it free. In addition, papers are printed twice yearly and sent free to members.

Although centred in London, the College has members all over the country; they are open to the idea of provincial groups, and have begun to experiment with one or two pilot groups. All communications to the College, either by telephone or post, will be given individual treatment, and psychological help is always available.

We now come to examine some organisations concerned with the religious aspect of the psychic phenomena, known as spiritualism. It is spiritualism, a relatively recent religion dating back some one hundred years, which created the image of psychic phenomena which is widely held by the public, an image which does little credit to serious spiritualism as it is today.

The early days of spiritualism are largely responsible for creating the 'cranky' image with its darkened rooms, circular tables, old ladies sitting round holding hands, and mysterious voices speaking from nowhere. The many proven cases of fraud which dogged spiritualism's early start did little to create an image which could be taken seriously by the public at large, and right up to the present time self-confessed Spiritualists labour under a generally hostile public atmosphere.

The fact that the religion has come to be connected in the minds of many with little old widows does little to improve things. But it is not surprising to find that it is the bereaved who turn to a religion which offers evidence of existence after death, and that these people should tend to be elderly. The time is long passed, however, when spiritualism was the sole perogative of the elderly and dying, and today, more than ever before, the young are showing interest in the field. Almost all the groups interviewed for this book reported that young people were coming into the psychic and spiritualist field in relatively large numbers, and many were making special facilities available for them. The effect of this seems to be one of revitalisation, and a religion which might otherwise have died along with its elderly exponents is probably more healthy now than ever before.

Before looking at the individual spiritualist groups, it would be useful first to establish more precisely what spiritualism is and what it believes. This is well summed up in the seven principles to which most Spiritualists adhere. These are: The fatherhood of God; the brotherhood of man; the communion of spirits and the ministry of angels; the continuous existence of the human soul; personal responsibility; compensation and retribution hereafter for all good and evil acts done on earth; and eternal progress open to every human soul. Although these principles are a good guide, most Spiritualists cannot and would not wish to be bound by any formal statement of beliefs or dogma.

Spiritualists are primarily concerned with proving that the human personality survives death, which they regard as the doorway to another life. They believe all human beings have two bodies, the visible physical body, and the invisible spiritual body, which is its counterpart. These bodies are linked by a cord; at death this cord is cut, the physical body returns to the earth, while the spiritual body takes off for the 'other side'. This spiritual body is regarded as the vehicle of the soul, and Spiritualists believe character and individuality pass with it into the next world. The experience which awaits the soul when it awakes from death depends on the individual's actions and life on earth. The belief 'as you sow, so you shall reap' adheres as something akin to the Eastern notion of karma. If you have led a good and selfless life, honestly trying to do the best you can, then you have nothing to worry about . . . you will be reunited with your loved ones, and will have an even better, happier life. If, on the other hand, selfishness has outweighed goodness, when your day of reckoning arrives, Spiritualists state somewhat ominously that you will 'pay the price'. Spiritualists do not, however, believe in 'hell' in the normal sense. As one spiritualist pamphlet puts it: 'There is no hell in which its inhabitants are condemned for eternity. Once self-realisation dawns and the soul is ready to advance, there are enlightened spiritual beings who will show the way to progress . . . heaven and hell are really states of mind, not geographical locations.'

One of the most important claims that spiritualism makes is not that there is another world beyond death, but rather that communication with individuals in that world is a practical possibility. Just as a radio can receive signals which are beyond the normal range of our physical senses, so Spiritualists believe there are sensitive individuals who have developed their innate psychic faculties to enable them to tune into the spiritual world. These are the individuals known as 'psychics', 'sensitives', and 'mediums', and it is this ability to communicate which is the departure point of spiritualism from the mainstream of most of the world's religions.

'Whereas most religions preach an after-life as a hope, faith, or belief, we maintain that any reasonable person can prove it for himself.'

Spiritualist Association

The spiritualist group which claims to be the oldest and largest in the world is the *Spiritualist Association of Great Britain*, whose high-class premises provide an ironic setting for a group which had somewhat humbler beginnings in 1872, when it was known as the Marylebone Spiritualist Association.

The M.S.A., which was by no means the capital's first spiritualist society, was set up at a meeting of a few interested friends, whose aim was to 'propagate spiritual truths in the Marylebone area of London'. Their early work was dogged with difficulties, and public prejudice was so great that for a period of several years the group had to change its name to The Spiritual Evidence Society, in order to make it easier to hire halls for meetings.

The history of the S.A.G.B. is an interesting and distinguished one, and an S.A.G.B. publication, 'One Hundred Years of Spiritualism', reflects the relish which so many Spiritualists exhibit for the history of their religion. According to the booklet, 'Queen Victoria held many seances after the death of the Prince Consort,' and even more surprisingly, 'Abraham Lincoln was also attending seances at this time'. Spiritualists are also very proud of the many eminent scientists who grace the pages of their past. Another interesting early supporter of spiritualism was Sir Arthur Conan Doyle, author of the classic Sherlock Holmes stories. Doyle appeared on platforms in a number of countries to argue in favour of spiritualism and such was his interest that he even went as far as writing a history of the religion.

Despite widespread public opposition, spiritualism flourished even through often difficult and trying times. A major breakthrough came in 1951, when the Witchcraft Act was repealed and replaced by the Fraudulent Mediums Act. Until its repeal, the Witchcraft Act of 1735 made most activities of spiritualist individuals and bodies illegal, and was occasionally invoked by the police to arrest the odd unsuspecting medium. The new Act which replaced it made a clear distinction between bogus and psychic powers, and its introduction was a big victory for concerned action by British Spiritualists.

It was only four years after the repeal of the Witchcraft Act that the

S.A.G.B. finally moved to its present premises in Belgrave Square, where it has continued to expand ever since. In 1960, the title the Spiritualist Association of Great Britain was adopted to replace the long outgrown and anachronistic Marylebone Spiritualist Association. The activities of the S.A.G.B. are centred in its headquarters, and it is difficult to overlook the atmosphere of activity which pervades the building. There are often large numbers of people around, even during the middle of the day, but it is in the evenings and at weekends that the place really fills to capacity. An estimated 150,000 people pass through the doors of Belgrave Square each year, and the Association has about 7,000 full members, as well as a large number of day members.

The large, spacious, entrance hall houses a reception desk dealing with membership enquiries and bookings for sittings, lectures etc., and also a bookshop with quite a good selection of psychic books. Also on the ground floor is the 'Sir Arthur Conan Doyle Hall', which seats up to seventy-five people, and an extension known as the 'Dowding Wing', which contains six seance rooms. The basement contains a large restaurant and an absent healing room, where a healing circle meets three times a week. So active is this aspect of the Association's work, that a full-time secretary is employed just to deal with absent healing correspondence. On the first floor is another lecture hall, the 'Sir Oliver Lodge Hall', and also the 'William Crookes Library', which contains more than 4,000 books. About 3,500 of these may be borrowed by subscribing members, while the rest fall into the category of 'rare and valuable', available for reference only. On the second floor is the chapel, described as the 'heart of the Association'. It is open for members to use for prayer and meditation throughout the opening times of the main building. The third floor is devoted entirely to spiritual healing, with ten healing cubicles for individual treatment in an area rather resembling the casualty ward of a small hospital. A receptionist is on duty, as are a number of white-coated healers, seven days a week. Some six hundred patients are seen every week by the seventy to eighty voluntary healers, and the service is free of charge to members and non-members alike. The top floor consists of rooms used for private appointments, psychic development classes and group seances. The building is regarded as 'a service to the public', and visitors are always welcome to drop in. In fact a visit to Belgrave Square is probably the best way to get the feel of the Association. There is always something going on: lectures on psychic topics, classes for the development of mediumship, demonstrations of clairvoyance etc., and *Service*, the quarterly syllabus of the Association, contains more than thirty pages covering the Association's activities over the three-month period. There are also some forty mediums available at Belgrave Square for private consultation seven days a week.

The Association, as well as providing a packed programme of activities for its members, has a research council which attempts to employ psychologists, doctors and other professionals in establishing the existence of two distinct personalities in mediums.

In 1971 the Association officially recognised the growing interest of the young in spiritualism, when the Young Spiritualist Association was formed. This was set up to meet the needs of the growing numbers of young people who were attending events at Belgrave Square, and also contacting the Association for speakers to address their meetings. The youth group is currently about one hundred strong, has its own committee, and supplies its own lecturers and speakers to outside bodies. Like its parent body, it is growing in numbers, and this growth is reflected by the fact that the Association 'is today in a healthier financial position than it has been for a long time'.

The S.A.G.B. has what it terms 'a commonwealth of churches' throughout the country, which, although self-governing, are linked with the S.A.G.B. Members and friends of the Association are advised to attend the meetings and functions of their local churches. These have a similar function to local branches, and are found as far apart as Glasgow and the Isle of Wight. Interested individuals who write to S.A.G.B. headquarters will be put in touch with their local spiritualist church. Full membership entitles you to receive both *Service* and *The Spiritualist* quarterly. Members can also enrol for psychic development classes, and are entitled to reduced rates for private sittings wih psychics (about £2). Day members pay nearly £3 for a sitting, and in the long run it probably works out a lot cheaper and easier to take out a yearly membership. Life membership costs £15.

Spiritualists' National Union

A large and important organisation in British spiritualism, which includes in its membership spiritualist churches and groups as well as individuals, is the *Spiritualists' National Union*. The Union began in 1890, when a number of prominent Spiritualists in Manchester founded the Spiritualists' National Federation. At first the Federation was little more than a movable annual conference, at which delegates from spiritualist societies and individual Spiritualists could discuss problems of common interest. It was later felt that the field of co-operation could be widened if the Federation obtained the legal status of a corporation, and in 1901 the Spiritualists' National Union was incorporated under the Companies Act as a limited company.

The primary object of the Union is to promote the spiritualist religion, on the basis of the seven principles set out earlier. It also acts as a 'trade' union, in so far as it aims to unite all spiritualist churches into a spiritualist brotherhood, securing for them full recognition as religious bodies. The Union undertakes missionary work, publishes spiritualist literature, and acts as a sort of governing body, issuing certification for lecturers, exponents and teachers of spiritualism. In 1948 the British Spiritualists' Lyceum Union amalgamated with the Spiritualists' National Union, and its work for the spiritual education of children and young people is now carried on as part of the regular work of the Union. Administration of the Union is controlled by a democratically elected council through a number of committees. Each committee concerns itself with a particular aspect of the Union's work, such as education, and healing.

Nearly 450 spiritualist churches, up and down the country, are affiliated to the Union, which delegates the running of local affairs to thirteen district councils. The churches obviously differ a great deal in their size, but wherever you live there will be a spiritualist church of some description nearby. The addresses are listed in the diary which the Union publishes, but if you write or telephone the Union's head office they will be pleased to tell you where your nearest church is. The programme of activities varies from place to place, but normally larger churches hold a number of different meetings each week. These might include healing meetings, discussion groups, lectures, psychic development circles, and even flower meetings, ladies' meetings and whist drives. There are also likely to be devotional services of one sort or another, involving demonstrations of clairvoyance, sometimes with singing and prayers. There is no set form of service, but newcomers are generally welcome . . . it is possible to sit at the back and observe without fearing anything too weird! Spiritualists will be happy to talk with you and asnwer your questions, and some churches even run special courses of instruction for beginners. It might be worth having a look at the events column of your local paper, where many spiritualist churches advertise their programme of events for the coming week and announce any special speakers or events.

Most spiritualist churches do not have resident ministers or pastors, but are served by different exponents from week to week. The Union does not interfere with the discretion or autonomy of churches in these matters, but it does compile a list of recognised bonafide exponents, and from these selects a number for appointment as National Spiritualist Ministers. The Union, in fact, runs a complicated system of training courses through its Education and Exponents Committee. The course consists of postal tuition allied to local practical experience, and self-instruction by means of guided reading. Courses are reinforced by exhibitions, demonstrations and lectures held at the Union's headquarters, and group study is also encouraged where possible. A Certificate of Recognition is awarded to those speakers and/or demonstrators who satisfy the Committee that they possess a reasonable standard of speaking ability and/or mediumship. Oral and practical tests have to be taken, and information about services and work done locally is considered. The Committee also issues diplomas for those who pass examinations in speaking, platform work, healing and church management. Fellowship of the Union is awarded to those who satisfactorily submit

181

a thesis on a topic allied to spiritualism, thus illustrating their high standard of knowledge. At the 'top of the tree' comes ministership of the Union, which is not an award but an appointment by invitation only. Ministers have to demonstrate a very high level of work and service, and are examined by a special assessment committee. By offering this system of accreditation, the Union gives individuals the opportunity to educate themselves, while at the same time maintaining a high standard of ability and integrity among its churches.

Arthur Findlay College

The Spiritualists' National Union administers the *Arthur Findlay College*, a large residential centre where students can attend courses on spiritualist philosophy and religious practice, spiritual healing and related topics. The College, which is set in fifteen acres of grounds, offers 'comfortable rooms, attractive meals, and very pleasant surroundings'. Most courses last a week, and cover a wide range of subjects – acupuncture, Taoism, radionics, meditation, relaxation, colour therapy etc. There are also courses on more obvious spiritualist interests such as mediumship, and many courses are designed on a workshop or training basis. In addition to week-long courses, there are the occasional weekend courses. Full board is just over £3 per day, but this is subject to review. For full programme details, write for a brochure and terms to the Manager of the College.

The Greater World Christian Spiritualist League

As its name implies, this is an organisation combining the practices of spiritualism with Christian and biblical ideas. The League was set up in 1931, and is based on the spiritual mediumship of Miss Winifred Moyes, and more particularly on teachings received from a personality in the spirit world known as 'Zodiac'.

It was 'in an upper room in the south of London', back in the early 20s, that Miss Moyes first began to receive spirit communications from Zodiac, who claimed to be a temple scribe at the time of Christ. He gave a number of messages consisting of spiritual teachings on a wide range of subjects, and these messages were later transcribed and distributed to interested parties. It is from this small original 'Zodiac Circle', held every Sunday evening, that the League has grown. It now claims a membership of 20,000 in this country, with about 120 Greater World Churches throughout the country.

Although the League's teachings are based upon the Bible, the latter-day teachings of Zodiac are regarded as very important. The tenets of the League are summed up in their eight beliefs and pledge: '(1) I believe in One God who is Love; (2) I accept the leadership of Jesus Christ;

(3) I believe that God manifests through the illimitable power of the Holy Spirit; (4) I believe in the survival of the human soul and its individuality after physical death; (5) I believe in the communion with God, with his angelic ministers, and with the soul functioning in conditions other than the earth life; (6) I believe that all forms of life created by God intermingle, are interdependent and evolve until perfection is attained; (7) I believe in the perfect justice of the divine laws governing all life; (8) I believe that sins committed can only be rectified by the sinner himself, through the redemptive power of Jesus Christ, by repentance and service to others; and the pledge, I will at all times endeavour to be guided in my thoughts, words and deeds by the teaching and example of Jesus Christ'.

It can be seen that for members of the League the Bible and the teachings of Christ in no way conflict with spiritualist teachings. In fact, according to one of the many pamphlets issued by the League, they regard with puzzlement those Christians who repudiate spiritualism. According to members of the League, the composition of the Bible is based upon supernatural occurrences – gifts of healing, contact with spirits etc. – and such occurrences did not end with the Bible. Unlike many Spiritualists, however, the League maintains that Christ was more than just a medium of outstanding ability. 'The Christian Spiritualist . . . regards Christ as the only means by which we can get to know what God is like. Christ represents that accessible, understandable aspect of the father that can be loved . . . an ideal that can be striven for.'

One of the main purposes of setting up the League was to enable the Zodiac teachings to be spread. These are numerous, and cover a diverse range of subjects from 'How World Catastrophes can be avoided' to 'Where is the Spirit World and what is it like?'. They were all given through the mediumship of Miss Moyes, over the course of some thirty years, by Zodiac, sixty-nine of whose most outstanding and important addresses have been collected together in one volume, *The Zodiac Messages*. 'The teachings are the foundation of the League,' said Mr H. Cox, Secretary of Greater World. 'We study them and find a relationship between them and life. They are not rigid, but profound, and help us to live our lives.'

The League publishes a weekly paper, *The Greater World*, which is 'the only spiritualist weekly based on the Christ teaching'. The paper is printed at the League's headquarters, on their own press, as are the large number of books and pamphlets they also publish. The League undertakes some philanthropic work, but its objects are 'to spread in all directions the truth of survival after death, of spirit communion, of healing by the power of the Holy Spirit; to teach and demonstrate the exercise of psychic gifts, to disseminate the teachings received from highly evolved spirit messengers'. The headquarters in London include a sanctuary, consisting of a church with accommodation for 100–150 people. Services, healing meetings, circles and lectures are all regularly held at the headquarters.

Outside London, the Greater World consists of a network of churches, each affiliated to the League but independent regarding their internal working, constitution and conduct. If a group of Christian Spiritualists wish to form a church, or already have a church which they wish to affiliate, they may apply to head office to do so. Churches may consist of actual physical churches, special halls set aside for worship, or they may be a collection of individuals meeting in a private house or hired hall. Services at these churches, as indeed in all spiritualist churches, roughly follow the service of a non-conformist church. There may be hymns, silent prayer, invocation, an address by a preacher or speaker, and then perhaps a demonstration of clairvoyance. There are also healing services, held both at the main sanctuary and in the other churches, and there are absent healing services for those who send requests by letter. The League has a special Greater World Healing Fellowship, devoted entirely to the practice of spiritual healing, which is composed of practising healers. Every church has at least one medium, and he or she will pass on any messages received from the spirit world. In order to maintain a high quality of mediumship in its churches, the Greater World League offers a diploma for mediums. These are regarded as official recognition of the mediumship of an individual, and are also given as a reward for long-standing service to the League.

Those living in or near London who are interested in knowing more about the League are welcome to visit its headquarters, where they can attend services, and chat with staff . . . 'no one is ever turned away'. Those living in the provinces can be put into contact with their nearest church via head office.

White Eagle Lodge

Another organisation whose spiritualist teachings are based on communications from a spirit 'on the other side' is the *White Eagle Lodge*. In this instance, the spirit concerned is a Red Indian, White Eagle, who speaks through the mediumship of Grace Cooke, and, like Zodiac, has supplied a wide ranging set of teachings which form the basis of the group's beliefs and practices. The methods of the Lodge are rather distinct from those practised by most other spiritualists, with a stress on communion with God through the means of meditation, as taught by White Eagle himself.

For members of the Lodge, the path is a three-fold one, incorporating teaching, healing and communion. Teaching involves study of the White Eagle philosophy, which is contained in books, leaflets, records and tapes, all issued by the Lodge. There is a White Eagle Publishing Trust, whose books consist mainly of transcripts of White Eagle communications, covering such topics as 'the nature of life beyond, and how man, while on earth, can build a bridge between the two worlds so that death cannot separate him from those he loves'. There are also a number of books written by Grace Cooke, the founder of the Lodge, on topics such as meditation and clairvoyance.

The teachings of White Eagle offer 'a way of life which is gentle and in harmony with the laws of life'. The Lodge teaches that 'God, the eternal spirit, is both Father and Mother, and that the Son – the Cosmic Christ – is also the light which shines in every human heart'. It is because of the divine Son within us all that we become brothers and sisters, a unity which the Lodge believes runs through all life, both visible and invisible, including the 'fairy and angelic kingdom'. Awareness of the invisible is an important part of the teaching, as it is for all Spiritualists, and a realisation of this is responsible for bridging the separation of death and revealing the eternal unity of life.

White Eagle teaches that life is governed by five cosmic laws:

1 Reincarnation; the soul must return many times to earth until it has mastered all the lessons it must learn.
2 Cause and effect: this is the belief in the Law of Karma, i.e., 'as you sow, so you will reap'.
3 Opportunity: every experience which occurs in life is an opportunity for an individual to become more God-like. Every person is placed in exactly the right conditions he needs 'to learn lessons and give service'.
4 Correspondence: this is the belief that 'as above, so below'. The microcosm is part of the macrocosm. We are cells of the cosmos, just as our bodies, in turn, are made up of cells, with the same laws applying at all levels.
5 Equilibrium and balance: this is a law which is believed to be connected to karma, described by White Eagle as 'the Law of Compensation'. It is the belief that no action can continue indefinitely, but will travel just so far before a reaction pulls things back to normal. Applied to humans, joy and sorrow are supposed to follow this law, i.e., extremes of emotion will eventually cause a reaction which pulls the soul back to normal.

The Lodge teaches that the ultimate goal of mankind is the 'Christing' of man – this is the point at which the inner light becomes so strong that even the cells of the physical body are transmitted into a finer and immortal substance.

Healing is another very important part of the teachings of White Eagle: 'White Eagle teaches us how to contact the power of God, the Christ within our own hearts, and to use that power to comfort and to heal others. All sickness and disease is caused by inharmony, and all inharmony can be cured by the power Christ'.

In true spiritualist tradition, the physical body is regarded as the outer garment of the soul. The subtler bodies, corresponding to feelings, emotions and thoughts, are known as the soul. It is the spirit which lies in the heart of the soul which is known as the Christ Spirit, the 'real self'. Because the various bodies interpenetrate each other, thoughts, emotions and fears all effect the physical body. Disease is regarded as a disharmony at some level, a state which can be avoided if the individual is living a harmonious spiritual life.

Spiritual healing is the process of concentrating 'Divine power' on the soul of the sick individual, in order to soothe the disharmony at the root of the complaint. Three types of healing are practised by members of the Lodge. Absent healing: this involves six healers who sit as a group, and send out 'rays of spiritual light, the colours being carefully selected for each individual patient'. As well as being useful for the sick person, this practice is regarded as being helpful for the healers themselves, in unfolding their spiritual qualities. Lone healing: this is a similar practice, involving thirty-six healers working individually from their own homes. Contact healing: this is similar to the standard 'laying on of hands' methods of healing. It is carried on in the Lodge at special services.

The third aspect of the White Eagle path involves 'spiritual communion' or meditation, regarded as the most sacred and important part of the Lodge's work. It provides the practical experience forming the base of the Lodge's beliefs, and gives an individual an opportunity to commune directly with God, and also with loved ones in the spirit world. Stress is laid on the belief that meditation involves the highest parts of a human being's spiritual existence – 'This is why it is so necessary to aspire first and foremost to God, and to rise above all the mental and emotional links which try to keep us to the lower planes of life.' Spiritual communion is part of every service held in the White Eagle Lodge, and is regarded as the most beautiful and rewarding aspect of the Lodge's work.

Anyone interested in the work of the Lodge who wishes to become involved with it, must pass through three stages, first becoming a member, then an Outer Brother, and finally an Inner Brother. At each stage along the way the individual progresses along the spiritual path as his spiritual knowledge and understanding slowly develop. Membership is open to those who have studied the aims and teachings of White Eagle, and wish to share in the work and is very reasonable. As a member you will receive training in absent healing and contact healing, and will be able to take part in healing services, both at the lodges or as a lone healer. You may also attend meditation classes and certain special services and groups, but it should be noted that attendance at one of the lodges, although beneficial, is not considered essential for membership.

If you have served as a member of the Lodge for more than one year, and wish to dedicate yourself further to its work, you can then apply to become a member of the Outer Brotherhood. This involves a greater degree of self-discipline and dedication, and you will be asked to devote a certain period each week to the 'projection of the Christ Star'. This is a technique taught by White Eagle for the healing of nations and the healing of the 'soul of the world'.

It is believed that the individual undergoes an initiation ceremony on the inner planes, which brings him 'under the ray' of the Star Brotherhood of the invisible world. After a period of waiting, which may amount to many years, and after 'due test and trial', individuals may be initiated into the Inner Brotherhood. This is regarded as a very serious step, at which the soul enters a stage akin to discipleship. A high degree of obedience and devotion to White Eagle are required – 'Love for and trust in our teacher, White Eagle, and dedication to his methods of service and healing are essential to this work.' The Inner Brother is regarded as a channel for both White Eagle himself and for the Star Brotherhood in the heavens. It is the purity of heart and selfless devotion of these Inner Brothers which will determine the coming of the Golden Age.

The Lodge publishes a bi-monthly magazine, *Stella Polaris*, which contains White Eagle's latest teachings, an open letter from Grace Cooke, answering readers' questions and problems, and general articles on such subjects as healing, meditation, life-after-death etc. All correspondence and enquiries should be made to the New Lands Lodge, which will be pleased to send a book list, list of activities and other literature. Callers are welcome, either at New Lands or the Lodge in London, but only between 2.30 – 5.30, Monday to Thursday.

Psychic Press

One of the most influential publications in the spiritualist field is *Psychic News*, founded in 1932 by journalist Hannen Swaffer and Maurice Barbanell, who still edits the paper today. It claims to be the world's only weekly spiritualist paper, with a circulation of 100,000, and is run along independent lines. All its directors are trustees of the Spiritual Truth Foundation which owns an overwhelming majority of the paper's shares, and in this way the independence of the paper is ensured.

The Psychic Press, which publishes the paper, occasionally publishes new books which it considers important, and also publishes psychic classics to ensure that they do not go out of print. On the ground floor of its editorial buildings in London is a bookshop, but the vast majority of its book trade is done by post.

Associated with *Psychic News* is its monthly magazine *Two Worlds*, published since 1886 and now edited by Maurice Barbanell, himself a spiritualist minister. Both *Psychic News* and *Two Worlds* are useful for gaining an overall view of what is happening in the spiritualist field. For free specimen copies, write to the Psychic Press in London. Copies are also available from local spiritualist churches or through some newsagents.

Confraternity of Faithists

The Confraternity of Faithists is a fundamentally spiritualistic group, first founded in this country in 1904 to put into practice the teachings contained in a book entitled *Oahspe*. This book, originally published in America nearly a century ago, was written by Dr J. B. Newbrough, a dentist and accomplished medium, who is said to have possessed 'the most remarkable powers of inspiration and clairvoyance'. While sitting in a spiritualist circle he discovered his hands would frequently fly off into what he described as 'tantrums', when they would often write messages. After a number of years' involvement he became a firmly convinced spiritualist, but remained dissatisfied with the type of communication he received. He decided that the angels with whom he had been in contact would commune with him better if he purified himself physically and spiritually. To this end Dr Newbrough gave up eating meat, fish, milk and butter, and began rising each day before the sun was up. He bathed twice a day, and before sunrise would sit alone in his small room for half an hour in prayer. After following this strict regime for six years, he reported a change in his contacts with angels. Instead of taking hold of his hands, they held their hands above his head, and for the first time he was able physically to see them. He claimed that a light fell on his hands as they lay on the table, and he was able to hear audible angel voices which instructed him to obtain a special typewriter. After some two years, a regular form of communication began to develop. Each morning, for fifty weeks, a light would fall on Newbrough's hands shortly before sunrise, and he would go to his typewriter and work vigorously for half an hour. Each day he would put what had been written away, without having any idea of what it said, until he was told to read and publish what had been given to him . . . the book *Oahspe*. It also contained a number of strange drawings which were communicated to Newbrough in a similar way.

According to Faithist literature, the book contains 'detailed teachings regarding the Creator and His relation to Man and his Universe; the history of the earth and its heavens for the past 24,000 years; the principles of cosmogony and cosmology, embracing a completely revolutionary conception of physics; the nature of the angelic worlds and their relation to the earth; the origin of man and his path onwards and upwards during life after death towards emancipation; the principles of an enlightened morality; the lost keys to all the different religious doctrines and symbols in the world; the history of the great teachers who have been sent to humanity in different cycles; the character of the civilisation which will supercede that in which we are at present living; and a mass of remarkable teachings regarding metaphysics, rites and ceremonies, magic prophecy and the like'.

Although the Confraternity of Faithists uses *Oahspe* as its source book of instruction, it also claims to maintain its own contact with the angelic worlds. The group believes that mankind is now entering the 'Kosmon era', the new age in which light is breaking. It is based upon the principles of worship of the Creator only, belief in life after death and the eternal progression of the soul, and communion with the angels who are aiding humanity. Those who accept these principles are known as Faithists.

Until a few years ago, the Confraternity operated its own Kosmon Church in London, where regular rites were held. These included such rituals as the Rite of Kosmon Unity ('to send out a spiritual call for universal brotherhood and peace') and the Essora Rite ('for communion with angels'). The church has now closed down, however, and the group is mainly concerned with keeping *Oahspe* in print and distributing it – a function carried out by the Kosmon Press. Although the Confraternity encourages the formation of small local groups, the vast majority of its contacts in this country is maintained by post. A group of Faithists living in Surrey do also run a small church, which holds monthly meetings where enquirers can be introduced to some of the Kosmon Church's practices. Those who would like to know more about the Confraternity and its activities, and would like to receive a list of its publications, including, of course, *Oahspe*, should write to the Confraternity in London.

6 Fringe Medicine

The field of 'fringe medicine' has been growing steadily since the last war, with many groups reporting a spurt of interest during the past five years. The range of groups coming under the umbrella of 'alternative healing' is broad and diverse, and it is not easy to generalise about them. But despite this, they are united by the simple fact that, as yet, they have received no official recognition from the bulk of the medical profession or the institutions associated with them. This is not to imply that forms of alternative healing have found no favour among medical practitioners. Homeopathy, for example, is practised only by those who have first received a traditional medical grounding. Yet even this most respectable of fringe practices has far to go before it is totally acceptable within the state medical system. Thus groups discussed here have sprung up and are growing round the edge of the National Health garden.

Perhaps one of the most powerful reasons for the growth in alternative medicine is the widespread and growing disillusionment with traditional medicine. Many are beginning to believe that there is more than one official way to approach healing, and faith in the methods of conventional state medicine – namely that of chemical warfare – is waning.

The medical profession itself seems to be reluctant to change and adapt itself to new ideas and approaches, and this has pushed many alternative methods to the fringe. At the same time, the fringe offers those who feel they have healing ability, but do not have the time, inclination or qualifications to do a standard medical course, the opportunity to develop their skills. In this way healing is taken out of the hands of an exclusive profession, and placed within the reach of ordinary people.

'Allopathy' is the name given to the traditional system of modern medicine used by doctors in this country and in the Western world in general. Unlike homeopathy, where 'like cures like', allopathy uses the principle of counteraction. Where the body deviates from the normal state of health and harmony, a counteracting force should be applied: fevers should be cooled, headaches soothed. Allopathy also has its own drug problem. The use of synthetic drugs to cure disease has become a somewhat sordid and commercialised matter, with new drugs being marketed and old ones removed each year. Sometimes, as in the thalidomide case, the drugs are inadequately tested, and since the precise side-effects are difficult to predict, it is human beings that turn out to be the guinea-pigs. But there are deeper arguments against drugs being used as the main form of treatment in disease. 'Anti-biotic' literally means 'tending to destroy life' – a paradoxical label for one of the most frequently used types of drugs. The problem is that the drug may be destroying not only germs and bacilli but also negating the body's own natural powers of recuperation. There are viruses which have become drug-resistant, and the body, too, viewing the drug itself as an intruder, may build up an immunity to it or react against it.

After three generations of modern allopathy, with the impersonal diseases eradicated or controlled, our diseases in the West are of the mind and personality. In a society increasingly plagued by neurosis and anxiety, the big disease is cancer, symbol of inner decay – a disease of mysterious origin. Many are beginning to realise that illness is much more connected with the individual mind and personality – the way we live, our feelings and reactions, whether we worry or can relax, what we eat and the way we sleep. Psychiatric cases occupy a large percentage of hospital beds (over 40 per cent in 1960), but your local G.P. does not usually tell you about your mind – his training does not involve psychiatry. Instead he prescribes you barbiturates and tranquillisers. Seen from the point of view of many of the alternative forms of healing, allopathy is barking up the wrong tree and appears very narrow in its approach to disease and healing. Allopathic medicine is curative, not preventive. It has established itself as 'medicine' – that is, as a branch of science divorced from other sciences and areas of knowledge: psychology, diet, yoga, religion, art and social values. Thus it is argued that splitting off like this, an allopathic doctor, no matter how humane and loving he may be, can only have a restricted understanding of his patient and, therefore, of how to heal.

Rarely does a doctor put the responsibility of the illness onto the patient. It would come as a shock to many people to think they are the commissioners of their own disease. Yet this is one of the fundamental principles of the fringe philosophy: the disease does not attack you from outside, you allow it into yourself. At a subtle level, you bring it upon yourself, and therefore must be responsible for your own health, which is the register for your whole state of existence. Clearly, this is difficult to prove as a general thesis, but the point being made is that disease is a direct expression of the accumulated actions of our life, the results of which we must inevitably reap.

Many fringe practices claim to 'treat the whole person', a phrase which could really be the motto of fringe medicine. Allopathic medicine still takes a materialistic view of the nature of man and thus gives correspondingly physical treatment. But in fringe medicine, the physical is seen as just one aspect of man's total make-up, although to different groups 'the whole person' means slightly different things. Among the groups practising 'natural therapeutics', the whole person is generally thought of as being a composite of his material self, environment, way of life, and mental and emotional patterns. Sickness is seen as a disharmony in some or all of the relationships between these aspects. It is not until we reach the psychic and spiritual side of fringe medicine that we come upon the full, occult picture of man. Here he is described as in essence a soul, a cell of the Divine, around which are formed various interpenetrating bodies or fields of energy – the mental, astral, etheric, and physical. Disease is a vibration that begins in one of the subtler bodies and works its way, after a period of time, into the physical.

The occult picture of man introduces some interesting possibilities. Is it possible to heal through the subtle bodies, seeing that it is there that disease has its roots? That is the basis of many of the more occult fringe practices. Acupuncture, for instance, tries to readjust and balance the flow in the subtle lines of energy that circuit the physical body. Radionics sends one vibrations that will harmonise one's subtle bodies. The somatographer Bryn Jones 'massages the aura'. And spiritual healers transmit a healing energy to the part of the body or mind that is lacking.

What is happening in these cases does not fit into a physical explanation. In true occult medicine there is no such thing as a purely physical illness. But this principle and the unconventional methods it produces have only helped to alienate the fringe from the main currents of society.

We have talked of *the* fringe, but in fact it is not a coherent movement. The fringe scene is divided, possessing its own orthodoxy and its own sub-fringe, with the more occult practices on the outer limits. So the term 'fringe medicine' in reality only means all those healing practices which lie outside the National Health system.

For the purposes of this book the healing groups have been ordered into sub-sections. The first deals with a selection of groups using natural therapeutic methods. The Vegetarian Society and the Vegan Society are also mentioned among these as part of the general drive towards higher body-consciousness and awareness of man's relationship with nature. The obvious link between these groups is that they use naturopathic techniques – forms of treatment that are purely natural to the body and cause no harmful effects. But it should be borne in mind that it is a gross over-simplification to lump systems such as homeopathy or herbalism under any one heading, when they are both vast and complicated systems in their own right.

The second section is one step into the supernormal. These are the practices that use an E.S.P. faculty, or some other type of psychic energy to help diagnose and treat the patient.

The third section covers spiritual healing, which is sometimes called 'faith healing' (the terms are not strictly interchangeable). Spiritual healing credits its power to a higher superhuman source, namely God. The healer thus acts as a medium for an energy that flows from above. It is the grace of God that heals, so long as the patient – or the healer – has enough 'faith'.

Lastly, we mention a few healing centres, trusts or organisations that do not stick to any one type of healing practice, or that operate activities such as yoga classes for the health of the whole being.

Naturopathy and Nature Cure

This section deals with practices that may not be very spiritually or supernaturally inclined, but which give completely natural methods of cure. 'Natural therapeutics' assist the patient's own natural resources with natural techniques. The principle is that all living organisms have inbuilt powers of self-healing, and that through natural techniques these powers can be aided or stimulated. Harmful side-effects from dangerous drugs are therefore avoided, and precedence is given to the prevention of illness by the education in how to be healthy. Diet, fasting, exercise, relaxation, massage, hydrotherapy, colour therapy, heat treatment, and all such approaches are classed as naturopathic methods. Naturopathy is much more a philosophy and way of life, therefore. Be healthy in the first place is its maxim – know how to eat properly, relax wisely, exercise regularly, and generally help the harmonious flow of your body's life-forces.

The *International Federation of Practitioners of Natural Therapeutics (I.F.P.N.T.)* and the *Paramedical Practitioners Committee for Natural Therapeutics (P.P.C.N.T.)* are two independent, but inter-related bodies whose joint aim is to protect and project the various practices of natural therapeutics. Their roles are political, the first at an international and the second at a national level. Both take a hard line against quackery and the notorious 'diploma mills' which issue degrees and diplomas for small sums of money, involving no recognised course of study. *The Guardian* on 2 July 1974 printed a world blacklist of 148 'colleges' that issue bogus degrees. In Britain, however, where the diploma-mill business is thriving, the Department of Education and Science will not publish its own blacklist, and there are no government proposals to introduce legislation to protect the public. Watch out, therefore, that you do not get fooled by these degree mills, or by someone claiming qualifications from them.

The I.F.P.N.T. and the P.P.C.N.T. both want to establish a rigorous standard of practice, and all the bodies represented by the I.F.P.N.T. are good professional groups, including the Society of Osteopaths, the British Osteopathic and Naturopathic Association, the National Institute of Medical Herbalists, the Acupuncture Association, and the Radionics Association. The I.F.P.N.T. is eager to present the naturopathic practitioner as someone with a highly skilled and scientific mind, and to dispel the superstition that still surrounds fringe groups. The Federation would like Britain to follow the West German pattern, where there is now statutory legislation to regulate natural therapeutics, and where many doctors are also naturopaths. In the U.K. fringe medicine is protected by Common Law, which grants to the individual the right to do as he sees fit. It is a tradition that British people are anxious to preserve, but which may well have a hostile reception in the Common Market. Other European countries do not have such a tradition, and some, such as France and Belgium, are hostile to non-establishment medical groups. It is the task of the I.F.P.N.T. to safeguard the interests of its fringe practices in the face of such opposition.

Except for the British Chiropractic Association, all groups in the I.F.P.N.T. are also in the P.P.C.N.T. The latter is an active political force working specifically to gain parliamentary legislation for the statutory practice of natural therapeutics and to enforce a professional code of ethics for its member groups. The key word in its title is 'para-medical'. A dentist and midwife are classed as 'paramedical', whereas nurses and chiropodists and fringe groups are classed as 'auxiliary'. The P.P.C.N.T. want their members to be classed as paramedical, without the denigrating connotations of the word auxiliary.

The I.F.P.N.T. and the P.P.C.N.T. were both set up to protect and further the interest of fringe medicine, and to see that patients receive good treatment for their money. They may, therefore, be useful organisations to contact should you encounter problems with practitioners, or have general enquiries about natural therapeutics.

Homeopathy

Homeopathy was discovered by Samuel Hahnemann in the eighteenth century as a result of his dissatisfaction with the brutality and inefficiency of allopathic medicine. He sought a system which, by contrast, would be gentle, produce no side-effects and be a natural aid to the body. He discovered the amazing fact that quinine both caused *and* cured malaria, and this led him to reformulate the dictum that 'like cures like'. In large doses the medicines he tried produced all the symptoms of the disease. So he used a small dosage to see if he could work a cure. This succeeded, and he discovered that the smaller the dose, the better the result. Even more amazing, he found not only dilution of the medicine but also vigorously shaking it seemed to give the remedy more energy and a greater healing power. This latter process he called 'dynamising' or 'potentising'. To these first two principles of homeopathy, Hahnemann added a third: that each patient had to be treated uniquely, according to the precise context of the symptoms. A headache for you is not the same for me, and has to be treated in its own right. It was the whole symptom-picture that mattered. So a homeopathic doctor asks not just 'Where is your headache', but questions about your diet, sleeping rhythms, mental and emotional states, and so on. The aim was and is to find the perfect remedy for each case.

Because it has such a broad and accurate range of application, homeopathy is favoured by many other fringe groups who incorporate it as part of their practice. To an orthodox mind the idea of a high-potency microdose, minutely diluted and able to cure, is ludicrous. But to the homeopath it is the energy released by the substance and not the substance itself that matters.

Homeopathy was imported into Britain in the early 1800s and in 1844 the Royal London Homeopathic Hospital was founded in Soho, its name deriving from an interest shown in the therapy by the Royal family some of whom are still loyal patients of homeopathy. Today homeopathic treatment is available on the National Health. There are six homeopathic hospitals, and between two and three hundred homeopathic doctors, although there are many more practitioners on the fringe of homeopathy. Yet homeopathy has not flourished in Britain as it has done on the continent and especially in France. It has never really been opened out on a broad scale to the general public, most of whom, even today, have not even heard of homeopathy and remain ignorant of its potential. At present it has failed to become recognised as part of the establishment (doctors only study it as a post-graduate course), and it is too respectable to ever enjoy the freedom of an out-and-out fringe practice.

If you wish to find out more about homeopathy, contact the British Homeopathic Association which has a large and famous library of homeopathic works. The outstanding homeopathic chemist is Nelson's of Duke Street in London. As well as providing a very good service for specific homeopathic remedies, they also sell first-aid sets for the treatment of very general complaints. Homeopathy is particularly good for young children, whose bodies are less chemically contaminated than an adult's and are thus more receptive to the natural remedies of homeopathy.

Herbalism

Like homeopathy, *herbalism* seeks to cure by stimulating the body's natural life-force to fight and overcome the disorder. But in other respects it is very different. Herbalism has very ancient roots. The *Great Herbal of China* was compiled in 3000 B.C., and in the fifth century B.C. the Greek Hippocrates (reputed to be a son of the god of medicine Aesculapius) was himself a herbalist, one of the key founder-figures of the whole of Western medicine. Today herbalism is the only branch of

195

medicine in Britain outside orthodoxy to have been established by an Act of Parliament dating from the reign of Henry VIII.

Herbalism is probably the only form of medicine which can claim to have truly 'natural' origins. The use of herbs and plants to treat illness takes place among primitive people and notably throughout the animal kingdom. The law is: 'living with nature, nature provides'. Led by instinct, primitive man and animals easily find the leaf, stalk or root that the body needs. So through the centuries herbalism has come up very much as a folk medicine, simple to comprehend and ready at hand, not the sole privilege of men of letters and law. Today, however, herbalism is far from being the simple folk medicine it was in medieval times. It is a comprehensive and rationalised system of knowledge, with training, skill and practice needed to make it a success.

In Britain, herbalism survived, particularly in the north, in the form of numbers of small herbal shops whose owners were also practitioners, with consulting rooms adjoining. This bothered some herbalists, who wanted to make herbalism a respectable and professional alternative to orthodox medicine, and in 1864 the *National Institute of Medical Herbalists* (N.I.M.H.) was founded. Since they did not like the idea of shopkeepers as herbalists, they set up a training school with the aim of having only the qualified among their membership. This unfortunately split the movement, because some of the old-style herbalists did not like the idea of an examination. Different ideas arose as to what should be the standards for professional herbalists, and so a second group was formed, the rival *British Herbalists Union*.

Herbalism is a very clean and approachable form of medicine. The remedies are not complicated synthetic drugs, whose names cannot even be pronounced, but are extracts of the field and forest, which are at hand for all to see. Like homeopathic remedies, herbal treatment creates no side-effects, no build-up of resistance, and is a treatment of the whole person. Mental and emotional states, personality and disposition, are taken into account before a remedy can be prescribed. A good herbalist will spend a long time at the first meeting gathering information about the patient's whole medical and psychological history, and trying to find a remedy which hits at the real root of the illness. Like homeopathy, herbalism can treat mental as well as physical illnesses.

The *National Institute of Medical Herbalists* claims to be the 'oldest established healing institute of herbal medication in the world'. It is a professional body designed to make the herbalist into a specialist. At present, it operates a four-year correspondence course for those wishing to learn herbalism, which includes practical experience at their clinic, and exams all the way through, leading up to a four-day exam at the end. The course is rigorous, and many people fail or do not complete it. Ethical standards are also high. The cost of this course is about £200, and one needs a lot of spare time. There are in Britain two or three hundred practising herbalists who have the N.I.M.H.'s diploma. Because of the high cost of premises, there are not many herbalists in London. A number of N.I.M.H.'s herbalists are gathered in the Midlands and in Coventry in particular, and it is here that they plan to build a new clinic and educational college, where they will run a full-time training course.

The Society of Herbalists is a lay-body formed in 1941 to secure social standing for herbalism, when a parliamentary act was being passed that threatened to make illegal fringe medicine. It has three hundred members all over the world, many of whom are members of the N.I.M.H. Practical information about herbalism, and the address of your nearest herbalist, can be obtained from the London office.

The *General Council and Register of Consultant Herbalists* and the *British Herbalists Union* are two professional associations run from one headquarters – Abbots Barton in Winchester. They run courses in natural therapeutics: herbalism (general and advanced), homeopathy, dietetics and naturopathy, psychotherapy and hypnotherapy. The courses are shorter and cheaper, more accessible to the layman who wants to learn, and not so rigorous and demanding as the N.I.M.H.'s course in herbalism.

Bach Centre

On the bend of a narrow country lane in the Buckinghamshire village of Sotwell stands Mount Vernon; a redbrick cottage of simple design whose garden overflows with the scents and aromas of rambling flowers. It was here that the late Dr Edward Bach, discoverer of the Bach remedies, spent his last three years. Inside the cottage is some of the furniture that he made with his own hands, to occupy his conscious mind while the subconscious process of intuition was evolving inside him. Few would dream that this was the home and work-place of a once eminent Harley Street doctor and homeopath, but Dr Bach was a man who changed himself totally in order to uncover the simple yet very secret principles of flower-remedy. In her *Medical Discoveries,* Nora Weeks, who knew Dr Bach personally, describes him as someone who rejected the artificial and complex system of allopathy, and sought to discover a simple means which everyone could use, and which would treat what he believed to be the root cause of illness – the negative state of mind. He gave up a successful practice and moved out into the country, becoming a recluse and mystic, and feeling strongly within himself the power of a spiritual universe. He relinquished his reliance on the intellect as the sole means of finding out knowledge, and developed a highly sensitive intuition. It seems that in the course of his relationship with nature and God he took on each of the negative states of mind, experiencing both mental and often physical states of pain and disharmony. The state would remain with him, sometimes for days, until he would be led intuitively to the flower growing in the wild which would cancel out and cure that negative state. By this method in the space of seven years he discovered the Thirty-eight Remedies, one for each of the thirty-eight negative states of mind common to mankind, and these states he divided into seven groups under the following headings: fear, uncertainty, insufficient interest in present circumstances, loneliness, over-sensitivity to influences and ideas, despondency or despair, and overcare for the welfare of others.

The remedies are prepared from summer flowers by floating them in a bowl of clear stream water exposed to sunlight for three hours. It is very important that this is carried out with great love and care, for it is a subtle force that is being transferred from the flower to the water. There is, of course, no demonstrable chemical change in the water. But it is claimed that the sun releases the vital *astral* force of the flower, which corresponds to the *astral* energy of the human being. The astral represents the emotional body of man, where, Dr Bach believed, our illnesses have their origin. It is therefore right that a subtle force must be used to cure a subtle cause.

The Bach remedies can be given to plants, animals, babies and adults, for all living things have an emotional system. A tree that has been replanted in new ground needs to be treated for shock, say followers of Bach, just as an adult who has seen a terrible accident. They produce no harmful side-effects, even if you take the wrong remedy, and can be used in conjunction with other forms of treatment. This will not affect them, because the remedies operate at a subtler level. The final quantity of the remedy that enters the mouth is a dilution of five times the original Essence. The principle here is the same as in homeopathy (which actually employs many of the Bach remedies): the smaller the dose the higher the power to heal.

Mount Vernon is the sole centre for the preparation and dispensation of the remedies, which range from £4.50 to over £16.00 for a complete set. They also dispense a Rescue Remedy, a combination of five of the remedies, which can be given as a general first-aid treatment in times of shock, panic, fear or distress. This comes in liquid form or as ointment in a homeopathic base. Treatment is also given at Mount Vernon, but this is by appointment only. They issue a quarterly newsletter on the Bach remedies, and also give lectures to other groups and societies.

Most plants have a hidden use for man: this was the basis of herbalism in earlier times; a completely natural form of cure accessible to everyone who knew and lived with nature. But whereas herbalism today uses dried plants, the Bach remedies require live flowers and on-the-spot preparation. The emphasis is not on the flowers themselves, but on the subtle force released from them. Dr Bach produced only two books: *The Twelve Healers and Other Remedies*, the essential, practical booklet, and *Heal Thyself*, which sets down his spiritual philosophy. Both books can be purchased direct from Mount Vernon and from some London bookshops, and both are well worth reading and trying out.

Nature Cure Clinic

Health farms and nature cure centres are now fairly commonplace, although there are some which in the name of health and happiness charge exorbitant sums – carrot juice at £1 a glass! *The Nature Cure Clinic* in London, on the other hand, has an honourable record to boast. It was founded late in the 1920s by Miss Nina Hosali, and was at that time quite revolutionary. Her aim was to find fully qualified doctors who were at the same time exponents of vegetarianism, anti-vivisectionism and a naturopathic way of life. Difficult as this may have been at the time, she achieved her aim. Dr Bertrand Allinson, son of the famous nature cure doctor and manufacturer of stone-ground flour, was the first doctor at the Clinic, which has run continuously for forty-five years. In that time it is estimated that over twenty thousand patients have passed through their hands, and over two hundred thousand treatments have been given.

Miss Hosali's motive was to establish a clinic run on strictly humanitarian lines – no drugs prepared with animal serum, no form of treatment which involved the suffering or exploitation of animals, all naturopathic methods of healing which are in harmony with man and nature, and a diet of vegetarian food. The principle behind all this is that 'people reap in their bodies what they sow in their lives'. The law of karmic balance is nowhere more evident than in the scales of health and disease. It is the underlying philosophy of the Clinic that 'man can find real health and happiness only in the observance of spiritual law, of which compassion and pure living are essential aspects'. Illness begins with an absence of inner harmony and works its way out into the physical body. So the Nature Cure Clinic does not offer treatment in the conventional sense, but a way of living that is more in tune with inner spiritual requirements. This includes fresh whole vegetarian food, no destructive habits like smoking or drinking, regular sleep, meals, breathing and exercise, a good posture, and a positive approach to life. Thus Nature Cure is a way of enlightening people about their way of life, of helping them to put their own house in order and to heal themselves.

If this sounds remote and unpractical, there is also plenty of concrete assistance. In addition to dietary changes, homeopathy, osteopathy, physiotherapy, water cure, relaxation, and psychotherapy are some of the methods of treatment employed. The Clinic is a charity, designed to help those who cannot afford to pay the high prices of private health treatment. The first visit costs about £2.50 and after that you pay what you can. They ask you to be as generous as possible, because they are always short of funds, but add that a 'temporary financial embarrassment should deter no one from seeking advice and treatment'. Nobody has ever been turned away because they could not afford treatment.

In the near future the Clinic will be moving a little up the road, where in new premises they hope to offer a bigger and better service. It will also have a lecture hall where they can develop the important aspect of health education. This will include lectures and demonstrations on such subjects as diet and food preparation in the hope of enlightening not only the ordinary person but also orthodox doctors about the value of the naturopathic way of life.

Tyringham

Situated halfway between London and Birmingham, and just four miles from the M1, stands the elegant and spacious Georgian mansion of Tyringham, set in thirty acres of landscaped gardens. It is the home of *Tyringham Naturopathic Clinic*, where each year some fifteen hundred chronically sick patients are treated by natural therapeutic methods.

The overall space of the one hundred-roomed mansion house undoubtedly helps patients unwind, and the relaxed atmosphere is enhanced by the friendly attitude of the clinic staff. Each one of the staff is regarded as equally important, for the Clinic is an organic whole where each person has their part to play. In this respect, Tyringham is more like a community than a clinic, where staff and patients work together in an atmosphere of mutual understanding. It is this, the social and spiritual aspect, that the Director hopes will develop even further. For in the correct mental and spiritual environment, where there are people who give love, understanding and encouragement, patients can gain inspiration and increase their desire to get well.

It was along the lines of the continental spa, where solely naturopathic methods are used, that the Director, Mr Sidney Rose-Neil, decided to try to set up a clinic in Britain. Having found sufficient benefactors and the right environment, Tyringham was opened to the public in 1967. It was established as a non-profit-making charity to allow as many people as possible of a low income to receive treatment. Many of the seventy-nine beds are in the low-range bracket, although one can have one's own luxury room for £50 to £60 a week. The low-price rooms range between £25 and £30 which is all-inclusive of meals and treatment. For those who cannot afford this, the Clinic runs a special reduction scheme to help subsidise costs. No one in the whole of its seven-year history has ever been turned away because they could not afford the fees. The Clinic loses thousands of pounds each year and yet it continues to grow. It is estimated that the kind of intensive treatment received would cost eight to ten times as much if it were delivered privately under the state medical system.

Tyringham is also a registered nursing home, and thus has to comply with the standards of health and hygiene as laid down by the government. It has a notably large range of treatments – osteopathy, massage, physiotherapy, acupuncture, yoga, meditation, homeopathy, herbalism, sitz baths, saunas; seaweed baths and wax baths for rheumatism, oatmeal baths for skin complaints, peat, sulphur and brine baths. There is a naturopathic treatment for almost every kind of illness – chronic bronchitis, asthma, high blood pressure, depression, ulcers and stomach conditions, and so on, as well as a great number of nameless debilitating illnesses. The only people refused by the Clinic are terminal or infectious cases. Normally young children are not admitted because of the nursing problems involved.

As in Nature Cure, diet plays an important part on the path to health-recovery, and much of the vegetarian diet is grown organically in the Clinic's own nursery garden. However one may not at first be able to enjoy this wholesome food, because fasting is often prescribed to patients to help cleanse out the impurities from the body, in an attempt to reset it in its own patterns of natural harmony. No matter how much the mind rebels against the thought of such forms of treatment, it is one of the rules of the Clinic that everyone must accept what is given to them.

Many of the patients come to the Clinic in a state of depression. Mr Rose-Neil sees their illness as part of the general state of life, rather than the original cause of their unhappiness. We are sick because we have allowed ourselves to become alienated, sad, and lonely. Even if we live in a negative environment, we still have to have negative reactions before we feel unhappy or sick. So we are the authors of our own happiness and misery. We are responsible for our health, also. This is quite a subtle principle, and may be difficult to accept for patients who do not think their illness has begun with them, but that an enemy is attacking them from without. But it is an integral part of Mr Rose-Neil's approach to his patients and, in fact, part of the whole philosophy of naturopathy, that we as individuals must take responsibility for our own health and health-problems. Naturopathy is therefore not just a form of treatment, but a way of life which extends to the whole of our being. The principles of the Clinic – whole-food vegetarian diet, relaxation, meditation, exercise, positive social and spiritual values – need to be carried out into the whole of the patients' lives.

Acupuncture Association

Acupuncture is the ancient oriental science of piercing the body with needles in specific places to produce a cure in a sick person. One version of its origin says that many thousands of years ago it was noted in China that soldiers wounded by arrows sometimes recovered from illnesses which had been troubling them for a long time. From these observations evolved the principle that by penetrating the skin at certain points many diseases were apparently cured.

At first, pointed wooden sticks were used, then thorns and later bronze and iron needles. The use of gold and silver needles was then developed, for it was thought that gold produced a stimulating and silver a sedative effect, and that different diseases needed different kinds of treatment.

The theory behind acupuncture is that there exists in the body dual flows of energy called Yin and Yang, united within an overall conception of energy called the Ch'i or Life-Force. Everything has its complementary opposite: day and night, hot and cold, positive and negative, joy and suffering. The whole universe is maintained in a subtle balance by the dual forces of Yin and Yang, the latter being the stimulating, expanding, positive principle, while the former tends to sedate and contract and is the negative principle.

Likewise the health of a human being is dependent on the correct equilibrium of Yin and Yang. The Chinese discovered that our vital energy circulates along certain lines known as 'meridians' and similar to the blood, nerve and lymphatic circuits. The flow along these paths of energy can be detected in the living body by electronic and other means, and it is significant that these paths disappear at death. There are twenty-six circuits or meridians, each associated with a different body function or organ. The condition of Yin and Yang and the various systems in the body can be assessed before any symptoms become apparent. Thus illness can be 'predicted' and treatment given before it develops. In fact, it was traditional in China that the doctor was only paid a fee when the patient was well. Thus the role of acupuncture in forecasting illness was very important.

The body balances the Yin and Yang forces by dispelling surplus energy via the skin surface at certain points on the meridians. These are the nodes into which the specialist will stick the needle. It also shifts energy to deficient areas of the organism. Traditionally there are about eight hundred acupuncture points, but new ones are continuously being discovered. In diseased conditions there is a breakdown of these balancing processes, and Yin and Yang do not flow in harmony with each other. In order to treat the illness, it is necessary to rectify the imbalance, and this is done by piercing the skin at specific points to stimulate or sedate the energy flow, and thus restore the functioning equilibrium of the organism. In China today there are over half a million doctors who practise acupuncture; in Japan there are thirty thousand, and throughout the East the total approaches eight hundred thousand. In France and Germany acupuncture is used in many hospitals and can be obtained under the National Health scheme, while in Russia it is taught in several universities.

Heading the advance of acupuncture in this country is the *Acupuncture Association*. This was founded as a result of Mr Rose-Neil, Director of Tyringham, and a colleague visiting Germany in the late 1950s to study acupuncture. They established the Association in 1960, and Mr Rose-Neil is the present Chairman. Very soon, in 1963, the *Acupuncture College* was to follow, its aim being to train and award diplomas in acupuncture. The College trains students on a post-graduate level by a rigorous three-year part-time course. Before admittance, the student must already hold a degree or diploma in one of the medical arts, which include registered doctors, naturopaths, osteopaths, physiotherapists, state registered nurses, herbalists and homeopaths.

Linked to the College and the Association is the *Acupuncture Research Association*, which was founded in 1963 by a group of students who had studied under a French acupuncture specialist. The aim of the Association, which is only open to qualified acupuncturists, is to raise and develop their technical expertise and to take part in advanced courses in the philosophy and theory of Chinese medicine.

In Britain there are roughly 120 acupuncture specialists who are members of the Acupuncture Association. Treatment per session costs between £4–£7, and the Association's London office will be only too glad to give you details, or send you a directory of British acupuncturists. Although small in number at the moment the Association is sure that 'in the next decade acupuncture will become one of the most important diagnostic methods in medicine'.

Veganism

In contrast to vegetarians, Vegans base their diet solely on food derived from the plant kingdom. The *Vegan Society* began tentatively in 1944 with about twenty-five members, and has grown in thirty years to about one thousand or so in twenty-six countries. To many if not most people, veganism may seem awkward and even downright cranky, but to the Vegan it is society that is at fault. The reasons for their unusual diet are threefold: ethical, economic and nutritional. The underlying philosophy of veganism is a humane one, based on a reverence of all life-forms, from the insect to the animal worlds, and a profound respect for the eco-systems of Mother Earth.

Many Vegans come to what is in fact a way of life rather than just a dietary changeover through their natural love of animals, and a reaction of disgust and abhorrence at the way the meat and fish industries have degenerated into ruthless money-making enterprises. The argument of the Vegan is that this kind of food-production does not serve society, for it is more economical to grow crops than rear cattle. If you love animals and hate suffering, your only logical recourse is to stop eating meat and all dairy products. Nevertheless, even if animals were reared humanely, Vegans would still refuse to eat meat, the reason being one of ethical law. Because of their belief in *Ahimsa* – a Sanskrit word meaning non-killing, non-injuring, and dynamic harmlessness – Vegans are naturally inclined towards pacifism, opposing all kinds of violent and aggressive activities, although the Society has no connection with any political party or ideology. Likewise, although individual Vegans may be deeply religious, veganism does not embrace any one faith in particular, but holds as its fundamental principle the humanitarian instinct.

Veganism is also a way of looking at nature, gardening or farming without exploitation of the land. Veganic gardening, it is claimed, can produce fruits and vegetables as large and tasty (if not more so) as artificially-grown food.

The *Ahimsa* principle covers not only the food Vegans eat but also a long accompaniment of household items – woollen and leather clothing, furs, commercial soaps and cosmetics, hair and wool rugs and carpets, blankets and brushes. Sports such as hunting or shooting, and amusements like circuses and zoos, also carry with them, they believe, the karma of animal slaughter or exploitation.

Even if you go along with Vegan principles this far, you may still wonder how it is possible to have a sufficiently nutritious diet without milk. eggs or cheese. The Vegans claim there is no problem. They even have plant milk, which is similar in composition to cow's milk, and their diet is as rich and varied as an omnivore's. Membership of the Society will give you a quarterly journal, and plenty of advice and ideas, as well as regular meetings, a Vegan garden party and a young Vegans' weekend. They wish to show that even in our present society veganism is practicable, and for those who are trying to live a pacifist or spiritual way of life, it offers a way of eating and living which reduces the amount of suffering and exploitation in the world.

Vegetarianism

If the path of veganism seems a little too hard to adopt, then perhaps vegetarianism can house you. The first Vegetarian Society was formed at Manchester in 1847, with the London Vegetarian Society reaching independence in 1888. The two were reunited under one banner, *The Vegetarian Society of the U.K.*, in 1969.

Vegetarians differ from Vegans in that they do not advocate total abstention from animal products. 'After generations of flesh-eating,' they suggest, 'the break with animal by-products should not be drastic. We advocate the continued use of dairy products, milk, butter, cheese and free-range eggs until our bodies accustom themselves to the new regimen. By this system there is absolutely no likelihood of a vitamin B_{12} deficiency, which sometimes occurs if veganism is embraced too quickly.'

The principles behind vegetarianism are very similar to veganism. Vegetarianism can be justified ethically, medically, and economically. To a Vegan, however, vegetarianism does not go far enough in its ethical reasoning, for although dairy products do not involve direct killing, they do incur suffering. Cows, for example, have to be subjected to yearly pregnancies to produce enough milk for the consumer, and the calf is usually suckled for only three days at the most.

Nevertheless, vegetarianism can claim very spiritual roots: Brahminism, Jainism and Buddhism, and many of the early Christians, all adopted it as part of their philosophy of non-violence and reverence-for-all-life. Pythagoras, Plato, Plutarch, Leonardo da Vinci, Newton and Bernard Shaw (to name but a few) have advocated vegetarianism. And the Society is quick to prove the fitness point by listing some of the famous athletes and sportsmen who have been vegetarians. The extra energy that is required for the digestion of meat, they say, is available to the vegetarian.

Practical changes in diet are similar to veganism: avoid devitalised foods like white bread, white flour and white rice, and eat the whole brown counterpart; avoid foods with large amounts of chemical additives; get your protein from milk, cheese and eggs, as well as soya and nuts; eat food raw wherever possible, as cooking destroys much of the inherent goodness.

The Vegetarian Society estimate there are eighty thousand vegetarians in Britain today, and to those who are already there, as well as to those who are on their way, the Society can offer a range of facilities for a small subscription. These include a regular periodical, a vegetarian yearbook which tells you about facilities at home and abroad, and an information service and reference library. There are branches all over the country, and a Youth Section for the under-thirties. The Society has its administrative headquarters in Cheshire, while its Vegetarian Centre and Publicity Office is situated in London.

Psychic Diagnosis

Naturopathy does not claim to use the intuitive or psychic powers of man in its process of healing. Basically it claims to tap the natural resources of the physical body to effect a cure, and has no mystical or supernatural philosophy behind it. But some naturopathic methods do actually utilise intuition and what is called 'dowsing' as a supplementary aid to their basic science. Homeopathy, for instance, requires such precise diagnosis and treatment that it would take an enormous amount of time to do this by normal rational methods of selection. So many fringe homeopaths resort to using the 'dowsing sense' – a combination of sense, reason and extra-sensory power – to find the right cause and cure.

Some healers have developed their extra-sensory perception to such a degree that it can be used as a central part of their healing method. Practices like this are dowsing, radionics, psionics and the less familiar art of 'somatography'. These all have in common the principle that healing can be conducted not primarily through the physical body but through one of the subtler levels of man – the etheric or astral – where, it is thought, illness or disharmony has its roots. We are here coming much closer to the idea of 'psychic medicine'. Groups employing this are further into the fringe of medicine than naturopathic groups, using methods and theories which the standard medical profession find very hard to stomach.

The *British Society of Dowsers* has been quietly developing for over forty years, and its membership has expanded rapidly in the last ten years to 850. It has not been their policy to invite publicity, and they have concentrated upon gathering level-headed members and concrete examples of their art. Dowsing, of course, can be used not only in healing, but also for archaeological, geological, and agricultural purposes, and to trace all manner of things. The aim of the Society is the development of the E.S.P. faculty, to spread information about its possibilities, and to keep a register of competent dowsers. There are no official 'courses' in dowsing, but individual members do help train others, and there are link-ups with other groups – the Radionic Association and Psionic Medical Society – who use the dowsing faculty in their work.

The apparatus of a dowser is the rod, pendulum or the hands themselves. These are the instruments through which certain subtle signals can be received. There is apparently no universal code in dowsing – you develop your own kind of language and ways of interpreting the movements of your instrument. Dowsing can be carried out over a map or the actual place itself, either close to or distant from the area.

Major-General Scott-Elliot, President of the Society, argues from his years of experience that 'somewhere about 10 per cent of the population could be good dowsers, while 10 per cent have not got a hope, because their sensitivity is too atrophied. Of the remaining 80 per cent I am sure many could be reasonable dowsers if they wanted and if they found a use they could practice and train upon'. To join the B.S.D. there is an entrance fee of £1 and an annual subscription of about £4. For this you receive a quarterly journal, and are eligible to attend monthly lectures, various weekend conferences and to share the Society's own library of books on dowsing and radiesthesia. Further information can be obtained from the Secretary.

Radionics

The practice of dowsing develops the E.S.P. faculty, which can then be applied to all kinds of situations where you wish to find out something. Radionics uses this faculty to a particular end: to diagnose and cure disease in any living form – man, animal, or plant, or soil. Basic to radionic theory and practice is the concept that every object emanates an electro-magnetic field, which, if distorted sufficiently, will ultimately result in disease of the physical organism. Disease, therefore, occurs first in a pre-physical or energy state; it is a vibration or frequency, and therefore every disease must have its own special frequency. In radionic practice the particular energy patterns which relate to the different systems and organs of the physical body are given numerical values, known as 'rates', for use on the dials of the famous radionic box. The 'Black Box', as it has been called, is a device which is used to tune into the vibration emitted by an object. This may be a blood sample or a lock of hair, and from it the operator will detect or diagnose actual or potential illness in the donor. One of the advantages of a radionic analysis, therefore, is that it claims to discover potentially serious conditions at an early stage, before they develop into a clinically identifiable disease. Once analysis has been carried out, treatment is made by selecting those rates which will harmonise the energy imbalances in the patient and transmitting the appropriate frequencies by means of another special box.

Those who practise radionics claim to be handling subtle energies which are not subject to our normal space-time dimensions. Thus treatment can be broadcast as effectively to someone in Australia as to someone in England. While some practitioners prefer to have at least an initial consultation with each patient, it is normally all right to give treatment using only a sample from the person, which acts as a tuning link between practitioner and patient.

The man who started it all was Dr Albert Abrams over sixty years ago. He discovered 'by accident' that matter had radiations, and in particular diseased areas of the body. He thought these radiations were electronic and thus named this phenomenon 'E.R.A.' – the Electronic Radiations of Abrams. Although he was the first to realise these radiations could be converted into electrical measurements, radionics theory now holds that the radiations are not electronic in the strict sense, but are of a subtler nature. It was Dr Abrams who first devised the 'Black Box' for calibrating radiations.

His work was picked up and sophisticated in the 1930s by a remarkable woman called Ruth Drown. She was highly intuitive and reportedly developed a special form of etheric photography which gave impressions of the etheric energy patterns of different parts of the body. From these photographs she was able to diagnose, in quite an unorthodox way, those illnesses which more standard methods would not have been able to detect. She was also the first to 'discover' that a disorder could be both diagnosed *and* treated at a distance. Both she and Abrams were given a rough passage by doctors and scientists, and Ruth Drown was actually sent to gaol on a charge of fraud and medical quackery. She was broken by the ordeal, and emerged from prison only to die a few months later.

It was in the early 1940s that radionics was brought to Britain as an organised practice. Formerly named the Radionic Magnetic Centre

Organisation, *Delawarr Laboratories* was set up by George and Marjorie de la Warr on a sizable estate on the outskirts of Oxford. Originally established as a research centre, it was not long before Mrs de la Warr began a radionic practice for patients in 1943. Delawarr Laboratories also started to design and manufacture original radionic instruments, and this practice, research and manufacture of instruments have become the principle concerns of the Laboratories.

The radionic practice, run by Mrs de la Warr, is an efficient and meticulous system treating up to two hundred patients at a time, including pets and other animals as well as humans. After each diagnosis a medical report is written up, containing detailed clinical information on the patient's illness. The Laboratories treat patients abroad as well as at home, although a personal interview, wherever possible, is preferred before treatment is begun using the normal radiational link – a blood specimen or hair.

For treatment, first write to the Laboratories or visit by appointment. The fee for the U.K. is about £10 for analysis, and about £15 per month for treatment. Although Mrs de la Warr is a highly experienced practitioner in radionics, she never claims to give a cure. If necessary, she may give supportive treatment in the form of colour therapy, vibration therapy or magnetic therapy, or you may be recommended to change your diet, have manipulation treatment, or even undergo an operation.

Although Delawarr Laboratories do take on students and instruct them in radionic practice, it is the larger body, the *Radionic Association*, that runs a full-scale teaching programme. Expanding from fifty members in 1956 to about 450 members in 1974, the Association grew directly as an offshoot of the Delawarrs' activities and in 1960 was incorporated as an independent company.

The Association's official literature gives basically the same theory of radionics put forward by the de la Warrs. To promote the interests of this 'new profession', the Association plays two roles. Its members include qualified practitioners on the one hand, and lay-people who are simply interested in the subject, on the other. Thus it tries to keep a balance of interests so that both types of members find satisfaction. Membership for an unqualified person, costing £5 a year, entitles one annually to a weekend conference, four or five meetings in London, a quarterly journal, various brochures, a large lending library, a list of practising members, and so on. It is an active and well-organised group, and as the 'premier world body' in radionics keeps in touch with other groups and also recent scientific developments.

Should you wish to become a qualified practitioner, training is provided by the School of Radionics which is under the management of the Radionic Trust, an incorporated body set up by the Association in 1962. The course, which may last up to two years, depending on your learning rate, is rigorous and ensures that nobody qualifies who is not competent to be a practitioner. There are introductory courses held six times a year at Burford in Oxfordshire, where you can discover whether you have an aptitude. The basic training consists of developing your dowsing intuitive faculty and then allocating you to an instructor, who is a qualified and experienced practitioner. It is not a course which can be taken by correspondence. A lot of regular practical work is essential, and when you are up to the appropriate standard your instructor will advise you to attend a seminar, where you will be asked to submit an analysis of a patient's condition. This leads on to the Advanced Course, where you study in greater depth the theory and different types of instruments. Finally, if you have been successful up to this point, you will be examined, *viva voce*, on two of your patients' cases.

To ensure that a black-market in radionics boxes does not occur, and the practice does not get misused, the Association only hires equipment out to students. After qualifying, you can purchase your own equipment from them. To make sure you have at least a minimal medical knowledge, you need O-level Human Biology in order to qualify. On average the course costs over £150, but if you are under thirty and low in funds the Association does have a bursary to the tune of £75 to help you in your training.

In 1967, on the initiative of the Radionic Association, the *Keys Trust* was set up, with an emphasis on the religious aspect of healing. It is a charity which aims to promote not just radionics but the whole spectrum of alternative medicine. Like the P.P.C.N.T. it is an attempt at national integration which tries to avoid antagonising the orthodoxy. This has now been merged into the *Healing Research Trust*.

In practical terms, the Trust provides a network of information for all healing practices to use, and welcomes donations to help train new healers, set up new centres of healing, and develop much needed research projects. Bursaries may be given to other individuals, groups and organisations, to help with their work.

Psionic Medicine

Psionic Medicine has been developed by Dr George Laurence, who has been a qualified doctor since the turn of this century. Like Hahnemann, the founder of homeopathy, Laurence felt a need to treat the patient and not just the disease, to put illness right not only by eradicating symptoms, but also by discovering the root cause of the illness. While maintaining a standard practice, Laurence gradually developed his concept of psionic medicine, and in 1968, fourteen years after his retirement, gathered together a group of doctors and dental surgeons to form the *Psionic Medical Society*.

Putting it simply, psionic medicine is a combination of the dowsing faculty with homeopathy, the Bach remedies and colour analysis. The Society is proud of the fact that all its practitioners – about thirty in the U.K. – are qualified doctors or dentists. It sees its role as forming a bridge between allopathy and the state health system, and the more way-out fringe practices. They claim to use the 'radiesthesic' or dowsing faculty to a very fine degree, and this is why they believe psionic medical practitioners should be qualified under law, so that, with an extensive *clinical* knowledge of human disease, very specific and exact questions can be asked of the intuitive faculty.

Like radionics, psionic medical theory upholds the idea that illness begins in a pre-physical energy state, and it employs the terms first introduced by Hahnemann ('miasms' and 'toxins') to refer to the derangement of energy-patterns in the etheric body of a human being. Thus treatment need not be done at hand, for although there are only a few psionic doctors in the country, it can be 'transmitted' on an energy-plane.

The Society welcomes qualified doctors who are interested in a psionic medicine training, and consideration is also being given to the training of assistants who will be registered by the Society, and will work under medical or dental supervision as auxiliaries.

Somatography

If you have ever thought of having your aura massaged then you should go to Mr Bryn Jones, a consultant somatographer and founder of the Company of Somatographers. This unusual form of healing is just part of his total programme involving 'both hard and soft tissue massage, exercise and natural remedy'. 'Somatography' is derived from the Greek, and literally means 'the mapping-out of the soul'.

Originally a successful business-man, Bryn Jones imbibed a rich Welsh folklore as a child. In the late 1960s he turned his energy to meditation and an ascetic way of life, and just as he was becoming interested in healing, he received a series of visionary experiences. These instructed him in an understanding of how to heal through the subtle bodies, and this was the beginning of somatography.

His approach is very friendly and relaxed, and if you want treatment, he invites you to 'come and see him for tea and a chat'. This approach is deliberate, for Mr Jones wishes to break down the existing barriers between healer and healed. With his more sensitive 'patients' particularly, he tries to make them more aware of themselves and of how their reactions affect their energy levels. For instance, he claims, traumatic experiences from the distant past linger in our subtle bodies and obstruct our future growth. This is why Mr Jones massages your aura, because that is where the black-spot is to be found.

Bryn Jones works not only with the more mentally derived illnesses –

depression, loss of vitality, disorientation – but also with physical complaints. To give him a schematic picture of a person's subtle states, he has introduced into his work a type of radionic equipment designed by an American called Mark Gallot. Treatment may further consist of dietary changes, exercise, other natural remedies, and also meditation. A session lasting an hour and a half costs £7.

Bryn Jones's long-term plan is to open a super-health centre community in the country, where people can come and live in a different atmosphere for a period of time, and where a spirit of harmony can exist between one person and another, between work and leisure, and so on. Meanwhile, healing is being carried on in Bryn Jones's centre in Nottingham Place.

Spiritual Healing

An act of spiritual healing is a transmission of energy from the healer to the healed, an energy which is thought to come from a divine source within, and for which the healer acts as a kind of channel. By comparison with most other forms of healing, spiritual healing is extremely simple. It is not a complex rational science requiring observation and deduction, nor does it rely upon a developed intuitive sense. The 'healing touch' is perhaps the most universal healing ability that man has, and is probably latent in many people.

It is perhaps the universality of this method that gives the *National Federation of Spiritual Healers* their outstanding popularity. They have four thousand members in the U.K. and fifteen hundred elsewhere, and are represented in sixty-four countries throughout the world. In Britain fifteen hundred hospitals are open to the Federation, and their work with the state health system is well known. Founded in 1954 with a mere 140 members, it has grown through public demonstration and personal recommendation. Today the Citizen's Advice Bureau or your local library should have information on how to contact the Federation.

The Federation defines spiritual healing as 'healing of the sick in mind or spirit, by means of the laying-on of hands, or by either prayer or meditation, whether or not in the actual presence of the patient'. Thus an exorcism of negative spiritual influences is as much part of spiritual healing as soothing a rheumatic back. The Federation sees its purpose as the protection of the interests of its healers and patients, raising the standard of healing, and getting further recognition for the qualified healer in the community. Although its headquarters are in Loughton, the Federation is in fact sub-divided into regional associations of healers.

The primary work of the Federation is, of course, healing itself, for which no fees are asked and only voluntary donations are accepted. The Federation is a charity and depends for its financial support solely upon these donations and the various fund-raising activities it undertakes. But

211

in addition to being a political and administrative body, the Federation has created an active healers' society, with an annual summer-school, a spring teach-in and various weekend conferences.

There are three types of membership: full membership for qualified healers, probationary membership for those learning the art, and associate membership open to anyone who wishes to support the spiritual healing movement. If you want to develop the gift of healing in yourself, the Federation does provide tuition, leading from an introductory set of classes to a probationary period working with qualified healers. There is no practical or written exam by which you qualify, but you and other healers will sense when you are ready to heal on your own. You will then be asked to take the Hippocratic oath of service, and be issued with a full membership card and a diploma. It is hoped that your abilities as a healer will be further developed after qualifying through contact with other healers and by the various member-activities of the Federation.

If you have any enquiries about spiritual healing, either as a patient or prospective healer, then the Federation's headquarters at Loughton will be glad to supply you with the necessary information.

Burrswood

'People don't know whether they are living in a cosmos or a chaos,' says Dr Aubert, warden and resident physician of *Burrswood Clinic*. Orthodox psychiatry does not provide spiritual answers. It grants man a subconscious and an unconscious, but the superconscious, man's higher spiritual nature, is left to religion and mysticism. Sickness, believes Dr Aubert, involves the whole psyche of a person, and in many cases is the result of a serious disorientation in life away from man's need for inner harmony. It is with this philosophy in mind that Burrswood Clinic attempts a marriage between religion and conventional medicine, by providing facilities to 'heal the sick, comfort the sorrowing and give faith to the faithless'.

Burrswood has a miraculous history attached to it, which the doctors, therapists and workers there regard with reverence. On 17 February 1912 a young woman was lying desperately ill, suffering from tubercular meningitis and peritonitis. A total of twenty-eight doctors had treated her in the course of her illnesses, and now the last one proclaimed her to have little chance of living much longer. The next day saw a miracle. In a deep state of ill health the young woman received a divine vision of great spiritual beauty in which she was healed. On that same day, she got out of bed, although she had not walked for five years, and went downstairs. There she ate a meal of solid food, which was the first she had been able to digest for years. To the utter amazement of her mother and friends, her body, which had been no more than a skeleton the previous day, had grown plump and healthy overnight. A doctor who came to see her that day pronounced her perfectly well. The name of the young girl was Dorothy Kerin.

As she had been healed through the spirit, so Dorothy Kerin understood that she in turn now had to heal others. She set up a chapel and healing centre in which small numbers could come and receive treatment along with spiritual sustenance. Over the years her work spread considerably, and in 1948 she managed to buy Burrswood, near Tunbridge Wells.

Burrswood has a magnificent setting. A large country house and a beautiful church, it was built in only eleven months, and overlooks the Medway valley through the 230 acres of its grounds. It is not a hotel, however, nor a health farm, but a home where healing is carried out in a spiritual atmosphere by state-qualified doctors. There are thirty beds for resident patients who come for a variety of reasons. Some suffer from medically incurable diseases, some with mental illness, and some come prior to, or convalescing from, an operation. Although fees range from £40 to £75 per week, no-one is ever turned away, as financial help is given through a generous bursary scheme. There is a special children's ward, where mothers can stay with children who have come to be healed. Mixing, listening and learning from others is also seen as an important part of the whole experience at Burrswood. Recovering from a disease is of course desirable, but the method of treatment also aims to make a person take more positive values in life, and understand the inner nature and cause of illness.

In the tranquil and beautifully decorated Church of Christ the Healer, which flanks the main house, healing services are held three times a week. The service is very simple and has a universal appeal beyond normal Christian ritual. It consists of the laying on of hands for those present who are sick or who wish to pray for others, and also of absent healing for those unable to attend. The resident chaplain visits all the patients, and counselling can be obtained from him or Dr Aubert at any time by appointment.

Churches' Council for Health and Healing

Although Burrswood is a remarkable example of co-operation between medicine and religion in the treatment of illness, in the country as a whole there is a lack of close understanding between doctors and clergy of their complementary roles in the treatment of sick people. To further this end, the *Churches' Council for Health and Healing* was set up in 1944. The body includes Burrswood as a constituent member, as well as representatives of the British Medical Council, the Royal College of Nursing and other medical associations. One of its principal functions is to promote co-operation between doctors and clergy in their respective roles in the work of healing. The basis for the work of the Council is the belief on which Dorothy Kerin founded her life and work, namely, that all healing proceeds from God, and that all means to that end, including the skill of doctors and nurses, are His tools.

The revival of the healing ministry in the Church began in 1904 with the Guild of Health, followed by the Divine Healing Mission in 1905, and the Guild of St Raphael in 1915. Their common aim was 'the revival of the healing ministry as it has been practised from the first days of the Church'. Today this means in practical terms counselling – listening to people's confessions and giving guidance – the laying on of hands, absent healing, and the encouragement of prayer and meditation.

The Council for Health and Healing was founded in 1944 by Archbishop William Temple with the purpose of uniting all the member churches of the British Council of Churches with the existing Guilds of Healing. The Churches' Council sees this as an important opening whereby the work of the Christian Church may gain a new breath of life. The word 'salvation' is interpreted now in a much broader sense: it is salvation not only of man's soul but also of his mind and body. Thus the Churches' Council has taken up a modern standpoint in the field of healing. It does not offer an abstract theology to a sick person, but certain psycho-religious techniques whereby the subconscious can be freed of its crippling problems. With the increasing recognition that such illness is psychosomatic, that its roots begin in the subconscious mind, the emphasis is on finding a whole way of living free from stress and other negative forces.

World Healing Crusade

Interdenominational and international, as its literature proudly declares, the *World Healing Crusade* is a well-known and well-established organisation that promotes healing on a broad base through a Christian framework. Its founder and organiser is Brother Mandus, a man of enormous drive and charisma. He has produced a large number of books, magazines and tapes on many aspects of health and happiness, and he travels round the country lecturing and giving healing demonstrations. The main method of healing is by prayer, not only group prayer in the Healing Sanctuary in their Blackpool headquarters, but world-wide prayer between all the members of the Crusade. The free magazine *Crusader*, for example, was first brought out over twenty-two years ago, and today millions of copies are sent out to about 130 countries.

Brother Mandus is a practical man, and his cassette tapes on healing and counselling cover a vast range of 'health-and-happiness problems' – personal sickness, worry, fear and nervous disorders, relationship problems, problems of career and finance, marriage problems, and so on. He has also produced an 'Immaculate Meditations' series on tape 'for healing in depth'. Brother Mandus invites everyone to send him their

214

problems, to turn to God for their healing and happiness, and to become part of his ever-growing world-wide network of prayer and meditation.

Foundation for the Wholeness of Man

'My upbringing was not poised towards religion nor was I conditioned for belief,' writes the Rev. Michael Wynne Parker, the man responsible for the *Foundation for the Wholeness of Man*. 'Yet at the age of sixteen I had a distinctly supernatural experience which ultimately caused me to be ordained and later on two more such "happenings", each of which was instrumental in leading me towards vital decisions.' These 'vital decisions' were to enter into the field of Christian healing as a minister of the Church.

With his illumined experiences, and awareness that he possessed the 'inward and spiritual energy' of healing power, Michael Wynne Parker established the Foundation for the Wholeness of Man to help bring back the original Christ-principle of healing. This principle, he believes, is a sure and visible sign of 'God's involvement in His creation'.

The main aim of the Foundation is the promotion of its literature – books and pamphlets by Michael Wynne Parker – although it does have also sponsored conferences and lectures. Mr Parker held a parish for five years during which time he conducted a weekly service of healing and evolved his own counselling clinic. When his work with healing the sick became well known and demands for individual help presented him with the challenge to leave parish work, he decided to specialise in this vital area of need. He has travelled widely, lecturing in the U.S.A., U.K. and much of Europe.

Health for the New Age

From their pleasant West Kensington house Marika and Marcus Mc-Causland run their international link-organisation *Health For The New Age*. Although membership is small, the McCauslands' work is extensive, and has already had a strong affect on unconventional medicine. They have organised conferences, run their own courses, and worked with researchers of the Philippine psychic healers. They have also established a strong Anglo-American co-ordination, and two of the trustees of Health For The New Age are American scientists. Other trustees include the Rev. Michael Wynne Parker, founder of the Foundation for the Wholeness of Man.

The McCauslands believe the world is entering a breakthrough period into a higher and more holistic knowledge of man and nature. Their motto – 'there is nothing so powerful as an idea that has reached its time' – bears witness to their efforts to bring together all the fragments of our present medical sciences, conventional and unconventional, and to build a network of healers and practices in which all parts interrelate and develop with each other. 'A single system of medical health care is required,' they write, 'which combines relevant medical, scientific and religious knowledge, both conventional and unconventional, into one medicine which treats the whole being.'

Like many fringe practitioners, the McCauslands hold the view that 'each of us is a whole being consisting of physical, emotional, mental and spiritual levels . . . Health is a normal human condition which exists when all our energy is balanced within us and we are balanced within our environment.' Besides trying to build a unified system of medicine between healing groups, Health For The New Age aims to encourage the formation of international research teams 'to break the bonds of dogma and self-interest and assist human evolution and progress'. It also hopes 'to encourage research into the principles of psycho-energetics, and into devices and techniques for measuring and using the energies involved', and to communicate its ideas and findings to whoever will listen. The McCauslands hope eventually to set up their own healing centre which will be the embodiment of their principles, where all kinds of healing practices can be successfully integrated.

Membership of Health For The New Age is open to everyone who wishes to support or participate in the goals and activities of the organisation. Associate membership costs £5 a year (£2 for students) for which you will receive the quarterly news-sheet and advance notification of all materials and publications by the organisation. Participating membership at £10 a year grants you the extra privilege of access to all material used in research projects, books, T.V. programmes, etc.

Hygeia Studios

Brook House, a picturesque Cotswold dwelling near the Gloucester village of Avening, is the home of Theo Gimbel and his brain-child, *Hygeia Studios*. It is here, in an atmosphere of tranquillity, that you can go either on a weekend tuition course, or to be healed, using the subtle principles of sound, form, colour and movement.

Taken prisoner by the Russians in 1945 and forced to work under severe conditions in the Ural, it was here that Theo Gimbel claims he received 'further education' from spiritual sources, and began to develop his own subtle powers of consciousness. He became a naturalised Briton in 1954, and for nineteen years taught art to children and young people in the Bristol area. During this time he became deeply interested in the way his pupils, particularly the handicapped and E.S.N., were influenced by colour, sound, form and movement. Eventually he left teaching (in 1968) to found Hygeia Studios and to apply his discoveries in the field of healing.

All Mr Gimbel's therapeutic methods are concerned with the healing and liberation of people from mental diseases. One example is his eight-foot-square colour wall for people in a state of deep shock. It works on a very simple alternation of red to blue and blue to red, in certain pre-regulated proportions. The theory is that when we receive a deep shock we often hold the tension within us subconsciously instead of releasing it, and so the red-blue pattern is like spiritual breathing – red (inhale and contract) followed by blue (exhale and relax). Theo Gimbel is keen not to be known as 'someone who dabbles in things he doesn't understand' and wishes to maintain his good relations with the B.M.A. Therefore he only takes patients who specifically ask for treatment.

Hygeia Studios also runs as part of its yearly programme several day, weekend or longer period courses on the more subtle and esoteric aspects of colour, sound, form and movement. Courses for 1975, as well as covering these aspects, deal with other subjects such as bio-architecture, space-energy, platonic solids, and how business executives can deal with their stress problems. Prices range from £15 upwards, including board and lodging, for a weekend course, and meals are vegetarian.

7 Development Groups

Many of the groups discussed in this book have adopted, in whole or part, an approach to spirituality based on Eastern mysticism. In recent years, however, a number of people have begun to develop techniques of transformation which are essentially Western in outlook and method. Such groups – which we have labelled for convenience 'growth and personality groups' – have in many cases developed totally new concepts, while others have adopted and adapted more traditional methods to the needs of modern man living in a technological society. It follows, therefore, that such groups may not appear to have a spiritual emphasis in the generally accepted use of the word. Some take very 'down-to-earth', almost scientific approaches, and give only minimal emphasis to spiritual aspects. But fundamentally they are all concerned, each in their particular way, with the search for greater self-awareness and self-development.

Most of these groups and their techniques are relatively young. Their philosophical and technical roots lie mainly in the psycho-analysis originating in the early decades of this century probably with Jung, and expanded by Reich, Perls and many others since.

Encounter groups first came to the public notice in the late sixties when the name of the Esalen Institute in California attained a certain notoriety because of connotations linking it with the hippy movement and free love. The first groups appeared in Britain at the end of the sixties and beginning of the seventies, and are growing each year. Much has changed since then, and many of the groups have become respectable. Their techniques are now being used in prisons, by the Civil Service and the clergy.

Generally speaking, the techniques offered can be split into four categories. The 'body' groups concentrate mainly on relaxation, massage, movement, posture and breathing exercises as a way of releasing emotional blocks and stress, besides their elementary purpose of keeping the body fit. Those stressing mental clarity and emotional release tend to go together. They often combine more specialised techniques like cybernetics, transactional analysis and *gestalt* which are explained elsewhere. Groups designed specifically to give enlightenment and increased spirituality, use mainly meditation, chanting and yoga techniques.

Although some groups demand a certain intellectual capacity, most are suitable for all. It is widely accepted, however, that people with severe emotional and mental problems are likely to impose excessive demands and should seek more conventional treatment.

Many group sessions have a similar format and atmosphere. Numbers are not usually less than ten or more than twenty people, whose age could be anything from sixteen to sixty. While the group feeling is invariably friendly and constructive, it is rarely cosy, and can become hostile. Success is dependent on how much individuals are willing to bare their souls and avoid being vindictive to others. The atmosphere can become too intense and force participants to bale out.

The encounter format is designed for people to confront and openly express their feelings, from personal problems to others' faults. The intention is to absolve all guilt feelings, whether they are fears, frustrations or anxieties, caused by repressive conditioning.

Gestalt is a widely used technique dealing with people on a more individual basis to help them understand what affects them at that precise moment. It points out that all aspects of the personality and even physical gestures have to be considered in order to understand the individual's 'here and now' situation. People are encouraged to explore out loud their fears, loves, hates, problems, and their relationship with and observations on other group members.

The purpose of bio-energetics is to release built-up mental and emotional stress by first releasing body tension. This is based on the belief that every mental block creates a physical equivalent, and the relaxation of one automatically affects the other. This body 'armouring' is said to begin in earliest childhood when we tense our bodies against environmental pressures. These physical and mental defences stay rigid in our bodies, and the purpose of bio-energetic work is to locate these physical blocks and purge them, which can mean actually re-experiencing the original emotions that caused them. Thus the body's life (bio) energy is released, permitting more natural movement, greater relaxation and self-awareness. It makes use of deep breathing – from the diaphragm rather than the throat – and corrects unnatural or distorted postures, either by exaggerating them or through massage.

Psychodrama is the enactment of an imaginary situation to discover the roles people play and their effect on others. One person will play himself, while another group member takes the part of someone close to him. Certain emotions like anger and fear may be exaggerated, but the aim will be to recreate a likely situation where problems can be clarified and dealt with.

A typical 'drop-in' introductory group consists of complete newcomers and some regulars who have been attending for a few months, although those who wish to continue the work normally join the 'ongoing' weekly groups. They usually involve a mixture of different techniques. In a bare carpeted room, with cushions on the floor, the atmosphere is at first awkward. But then everyone introduces themselves and talks about how they feel as they sit in a circle on the floor. A few warming up exercises might follow to make people feel more at ease, and to allow them to develop trust and get to know one another. They would probably be asked to take a partner at random and get to know them more intimately by touch.

The ways in which inhibitions constrict body movement might then be explored. When the body is felt to be more at ease, the group will concentrate on emotions. Gradually the group becomes more of a unit and people start responding to each other. It splits into smaller groups and tries to release more of people's mental and emotional blocks. When a closer contact has been established, people begin to express their personal feelings about one another. The atmosphere becomes more intense, normally focusing on the people who react to the situation.

Someone might burst into tears or express anger over a personal problem brought to the surface. When this happens, the group is encouraged to merge again and share its feelings, particularly empathising with the most distressed person. This whole process is designed at best to confront and release people's problems, fears, and inhibitions in the belief that it is the best way of solving them. At worst it can turn into a slanging match. But hostilities are usually resolved and after the normal appreciation session, involving friendly hugs and comments on what has been gained, everyone departs.

Arica

The Arica Institute combines Eastern mystical traditions of meditation and movement with Western techniques of psychology through a series of intense exercises. It aims to increase physical vitality, reduce emotional tension and anxiety, increase mental clarity, and create a permanent higher level of consciousness by 'developing and unifying' the three fundamental centres of the body – physical, emotional and intellectual.

Much of Arica's philosophy is a restatement of ancient teachings stripped of all cultural trappings. They are combined with modern theories of personality, motivation and consciousness. It is termed as a system of 'scientific mysticism' because, despite its spiritual teachings, it requires no faith. Each exercise should be approached experimentally, as a hypothesis to be tested. The ultimate goal is unity within the individual, between persons and in society as a whole.

Arica was founded by Oscar Ichazo in 1970, after he had spent many years with various teachers in South America and the Orient, studying the many different techniques designed to give enlightenment. After a ten-month training programme with fifty Americans under his direction in the remote Chilean town of Arica, he set off with the forty-four who had completed the course to establish the Arica Institute in New York in 1971, so that his teachings could be made generally available.

Arica training is seen by its adherents 'as the communication of technical information. The responsibility of the trainer is to pass that information clearly, precisely and without personal interpretation. The responsibility of the trainee is to participate in the training process with an open, alert and curious attitude.' The work, only five per cent of which is theory, is practised in large and small groups and individually, with importance laid on working as a group. 'The process of learning and the depth of experience are greatly accelerated in a situation where people give and accept support readily, where the group is a reflector and monitor of each individual's progress.'

The first function of Arica training is to get the body in good shape so that the trainee can fully experience 'all higher levels of consciousness'. This is achieved through a series of breathing, relaxation and movement exercises, a mixture of gymnastics and hatha yoga called psychocalisthenics, which is aimed at increasing 'energy, alertness and co-ordination'. Its specific aim is to co-ordinate mind and body through breath, the middle point between the psyche and the physical being. Most exercises are accompanied by music, to develop awareness of rhythm and of the natural movement of the body. Techniques of meditation and mantram include use of breath, listening to sounds within and outside the body, visualisations, movement, and chanting and singing to help 'focus consciousness and eliminate unwanted mental activity'.

In the more intensive courses, trainees explore their own ego patterns in greater depth, examining the nature of their own subjectivity, seeing how the ego works and developing detachment from it, thus allowing the emergence of their 'essential selves'. Other training methods used are African dance, theatre, music-making and the study of the level and states of consciousness.

Arica recommends a high protein diet, which is low in fats and carbohydrates. 'Protein provides the sustained energy necessary during the training', and they recommend fresh fruit and vegetables for essential minerals and vitamins, fish, cheese, eggs, nuts and dried fruit, and the avoidance of bread, alcohol and dark meat.

Arica's London teaching house was formed in April 1973 and now has a fully trained teaching staff of thirty. The programme is constantly revised as they discard certain practices and adopt new ones. They run a very energetic and stimulating free 'Open House' introductory programme of 'work, music and relaxation', at their London centre on Wednesday evenings at 8.00. There is a 'Psychocalisthenics series' and a 'Meditation and Mantram series' of four evening classes. Also organised are Open Path weekends, 'a twelve-hour survey of the Arica Training, including techniques of physical exercise, movement and equilibrium, essential contact, breathing, relaxation and meditation'. Five-day and nine-day courses offer 'deeper, more extensive experiences of the Arica Training programme'.

The most important Arica training is the forty-day intensive or extended 'basic training for life' programme, 'for developing consciousness so that high states of awareness become permanently available'. The programme culminates in advanced meditation techniques and social yoga, 'the practical transmission of love from one to another'. This is prepared for by a few days of isolation and silence to help the group become one body so that 'the mystical states occur normally'. Use is made of 'psycho-alchemy', a Taoist-type technique that transmutes possibly wasted or dissipated life energy, like the sexual drive, by transforming it into consciousness. The forty-day intensive includes 320 hours and over 400 individual and group exercises, six days a week for six weeks. Hours are 9 a.m. to 6 p.m., Monday to Friday, Saturday free, and Sunday 2 p.m. to 6 p.m. At times during the training the group meets for evening sessions, and individual evening work is regularly scheduled. Participants are generally discouraged from maintaining outside commitments for the six weeks. Accommodation is not provided, nor is food, except for a period towards the end of the training when a special diet is prepared at a small extra cost.

[Note: Arica closed its London centre after this went to press. The organisation is still active in the United States and in France. A contact address is given in Part II.]

Quaesitor

Quaesitor is the largest growth centre in the country, and possibly Europe, and offers a wide ranging programme including encounter, *gestalt*, bio-energetics, yoga, massage and meditation. 'Quaesitor' is Latin for 'the seeker', and the centre is designed for people wishing to develop their emotional, physical, spiritual and intellectual awareness – 'Each group offered is not an answer, it's a tool!' It is not, however, a therapeutic community capable of catering for people with severe mental and emotional problems.

The groups are designed for complete newcomers through to experienced trainers, and are held in the ten-roomed house run by director David Blagden and a small staff. He acts as administrator, organising the programme and other events, and although he has some growth work experience, including completion of a six-month intensive course, he steers clear of any direct involvement in group work. Quaesitor established its roots in England over six years ago, and now has about forty different leaders running the various groups. Over 2,000 people passed through the centre in 1974.

Besides appealing to all types of individuals, they have also run groups in polytechnics, and for social workers, probation officers, prison service psychologists, university and college staff, the clergy, doctors and nursing staff, Weight-watchers, Alcoholics Anonymous and one-parent families.

The Quaesitor introductory 'drop-in' is held every Thursday and Sunday at 7.30 p.m. and costs £1.10 and 55p for students. There are fairly regular twelve-hour newcomers' groups held on Sundays for about £7, and special one-day introductory groups in specialised subjects such as movement, the Feldenkrais method (*see* Franklin School), transactional analysis, psycho-synthesis and psychodrama, all costing about £5. The on-going groups for people who want more contact and involvement meet once weekly for a four-week commitment, usually in encounter and movement, and are held mainly on Mondays and Thursdays at a cost of about £10.

The weekend workshops offer the widest range of activities. These include twenty-four-hour and forty-eight-hour encounter marathons and a twelve-hour newcomers' workshop 'for people that are new and reluctant to join a group where others are already familiar with the group "mystique"'. These use a variety of growth techniques. A three-day 'Enlightenment Intensive' residential course in the country offers 'structured meditation using a strict format combining aspects of Zen meditation with communication techniques'. There are also massage groups mainly for friendly twosomes. 'Massage is one of the most direct ways of being in touch with somebody else, and of tuning in to the flow of the good life inside us'. Relationships and Tai-Do (*see* Community), *gestalt* and Feldenkrais techniques, and work with psychodrama, bio-energetics and movement are also part of the programme. Certain groups are held during the daytime, including a three-day 'House Church Process' group for clerical and lay people 'who seek renewal for themselves and for the religious system of which they are a part', within the framework of the Human Potential movement. There have also been reciprocal counselling and Tai-Chi-Chuan courses.

For people with some experience of different types of groups who wish to have a deeper personal experience of the work, there are long-term, summer, residential and intensive groups. They require a 'deep commitment', and each group is led by a co-ordinator who is 'guide and mentor' of the group, and is available for personal counselling. The one-month intensives have included personal training by Dr Moshe Feldenkrais, and there are regular three-month intensives in encounter and Tai-Do, six-month intensives and nine-month groups. These can cost between £100 and £400.

Quaesitor organises its own Thursday lectures most weeks on diverse subjects related to personal growth. There are advanced and training groups for people with considerable group experience or involved in the helping professions, which are run over a period of three or four days.

Community

The *Community* growth centre uses group therapy to help the individual explore himself and his relationship with others. Its various groups use many different types of 'therapy' aimed at releasing a person from his emotional, sensual and mental shells.

Community is a direct descendant of the original People Not Psychiatry network and Kaleidoscope, which moved from helping people unable to cope by giving them warmth and sympathy in others' homes, to the present group-help framework.

The emphasis of the groups, which take between six and eighteen people, is on experience and action rather than talk and analysis. For some people participating in the group could be seen as therapy, but for others it is 'simply assisting the development of people into fuller, more complete and richer human beings'.

In his book *People Not Psychiatry*, Michael Barnett, the first director of Community, gives a personal explanation of encounter: 'In encounter groups people tell each other what they see in each other, as openly, directly and honestly as they can . . . Before long most false moves and phoney presentations are spied by someone. This way everyone becomes more real. Lies, masks, roles, pretences, drop away'.

A small group of about eight people actually form the Community commune at a Highbury house, but over thirty leaders with wide and varying experience take the drop-in introductory, weekend, one day, on-going, seminar and intensive groups.

For newcomers Community runs two drop-in introductory groups on Tuesdays and Fridays, using techniques like 'sensory awareness, *gestalt*, bio-energetics, body expression and one-to-one communication'. They cost over £1 (half price for students), and start at 7.30 p.m.

People who decide to continue with Community might then like to join the on-going groups. 'A continuous experience with the same group of people creates an environment of strong support and increasing trust,' where you can 'experience yourself as others see you,' helping you to change and grow. People are encouraged to meet each other outside the groups, which include 'Newcomers' Encounter', yoga, and coming to terms with 'Homosexual and Bisexual Experience'. These are held once a week over a period of four to six weeks, mainly in the evening, although some include weekends, and cost from £6.60 to £28.20.

The weekend workshops and special one-day groups have by far the widest range of activities, offering people the chance to spend a long period, from twelve to forty-eight hours, on a particular aspect of group therapy. A single, long, intensive period gives people the chance to create a heightened group atmosphere, and the chance to probe deeper within themselves.

These groups have included a twenty-four-hour 'encounter, *gestalt*, and fantasy' workshop, a one-day introduction to personal growth, and a day-long mixed group of 'male/female consciousness raising', to try and 'discover how we oppress each other by sticking to stereotyped sexual roles'. There is also a 'relationship weekend' for people with or without relationships 'to explore their sexuality – both hang-ups and pleasures – based on the premise that people need people'. An advanced healing training group weekend and follow-up for people with experience in 'sensitive massage' is staged to learn ways of 'contacting our deeper selves, channelling energy and developing intuitive ability'.

Various encounter day or weekend groups are run using *gestalt*, Reichian and bio-energetic approaches. There is a teenage day workshop for people between twelve and nineteen, massage workshops, *gestalt* weekends, and co-counselling, Arica and transactional analysis trainings. Tai-Chi-Chuan sessions are combined with meditation and massage to help integrate mind, body and spirit. There is also a 'Tai-Do-The Way of the Body' workshop employing 'methods of meditative movement integrating aspects of yoga, Tai-Chi-Chuan, aikido and dance' with everyday life.

For those who have gained some experience in the growth movement, Community offers a 'Three-Month Intensive' involving detailed work on the various methods for 'people committed to self-exploration and the belief that they must find their own way'. It is tailor-made for those who plan a greater involvement in the work of the centre, especially those who wish to become group leaders. Consisting of five weekend sessions and two evenings a week, it costs about £150.

There is a series of seminars 'of special interest to group leaders, therapists, people in training, as well as anyone interested in growth processes', covering diverse aspects of growth. Reductions are offered in all activities for those genuinely unable to pay. A communal meal is held at Community each Thursday at 6.30 p.m. – this is open to all.

Bristol Centre

The *Bristol Encounter Centre* is the largest of its kind in the south-west of England, and offers a wide range of development techniques. Approaches employed include encounter, *gestalt* therapy, psychodrama, guided fantasy workshops, creativity groups and Zen meditation. Two weekend workshops – 'Play Space' and 'Creative Awareness' – use creative and artistic processes to obtain greater awareness. Encounter workshops employ both structured and unstructured techniques, and a special drop-in conversational encounter is staged for individuals who are lonely or somewhat confused about people and relationships. The atmospere at these is very informal.

For people who have already gained some experience of working with organised groups, 'do-it-yourself' leaderless groups are arranged. There is encounter for couples who want to break free from the 'ruts of verbal and emotional reaction', and individual counselling offering confidential help and support.

Among its more ambitious projects, the Bristol Centre organises a 'searching the heart Zen intensive residential weekend', which employs a variety of Zen meditation techniques in a monastic, 'retreat' atmosphere. These weekends are held in a remote farmstead in central Wales. They usually involve about ten people, and living conditions are rough and primitive. The aim is to lead a pure weekend away from all external distractions, and much of the time is devoted to sitting in 'zazen' meditation, involving 'active observation of on-going mental activity'. You are also encouraged to take quiet walks in the hills for reflection and relaxation. Work periods, in which the various practical tasks are carried out, are done with maximum awareness on the part of those involved, and silence is generally observed except at designated periods. There is time for general discussion and personal consultation.

The Centre is also involved in a project known as the 'Joint Mini-Society Venture', which is an experiment in getting people from different areas of society to live together in a positive group environment. The experiment is held at a youth centre, caters for sixty people and lasts for nine days. Initially various social groups – family units, young people, etc. – are placed with people from a similar environment so that they can clarify their problems by living together as much as possible. They must find ways of co-operating with other groups in the community, on whom they depend for various aspects of community life. During the first two or three days, a special programme of activities is organised – various meetings and sessions involving the whole community, etc. – to help get things off the ground. An important aspect of the experiment is 'research', and various developments within the community, sub-groups or individuals are recorded as a means of helping the community to understand itself better.

Atma

'Atma' is a Sanskrit word for the 'Self' present within the mind and body. The *Atma Growth Centre* aims to help people discover and treat this as a 'functioning unity' so as to develop outer perception coupled with inner awareness. Their techniques are directed towards spiritual growth and are designed for an on-going process of personal growth.

A variety of ancient and modern techniques are incorporated into groups. For example, humanistic astrology is a group work exercise where the individual is taught to draw up his own elementary birth chart. With the emphasis on self-improvement, members of the group are taught to perceive their projected image by observing the chart and personality characteristics that it points out.

226

Sufi techniques used include breathing exercises practised in conjunction with movement and co-ordination, and relaxation and centring exercises. Psychosynthesis, as developed by Robert Assagioli, incorporates the use of music, art and clay with astrology, *gestalt* and encounter, and is specifically used for inner and outer awareness. There are also training groups for mediums, with sessions in parapsychology and bio-feedback. The groups, which are open and attended by all types and age groups, are intended for people who 'wish to see things more clearly'.

Atma is the largest group of its kind in Birmingham and it hopes to extend its work to state institutions where it has already held communication groups. Groups are limited to fourteen people and are normally held at the Shantasea Centre, 8–10 Albert Street (just off the High Street), Birmingham 4. For newcomers there is a group on Tuesdays between 7.30 and 10.30 p.m. which costs 80p and 50p for students.

There are weekly evening on-going groups for 50p a session, and these require a basic commitment of four weeks. They include meditation (various methods are discussed and practised), hatha yoga, relaxation (to learn increased control of the body as a means to physical and mental relaxation), deep tissue massage ('to explore ways of awakening sensitivity, reducing tension and contacting feelings'), and a *gestalt* training group with a basic commitment of twelve weeks. Weekend workshops include one-day introductory encounter groups and Friday-evening-plus-all-day-Saturday-and-Sunday groups that include basic encounter, meditation, massage, Tai-Chi, music and stillness, yoga, *gestalt*, and sensitivity training.

Individual appointments can be made for counselling. There are occasional six-month intensives and weekends in the country, and fairly regular films and lectures at 50p each on different aspects of growth, awareness and spirituality.

Centre House

Centre Community and the *Centre Community Association* is a free fellowship where people interested in spiritual development are offered training in yoga, meditation, awareness, sensitivity development and related subjects. It was founded in 1966 by Christopher Hills, a former American businessman who has written a series of books including *Nuclear Evolution* which explains the basic philosophy behind Centre.

Centre serves a social and educational purpose aimed at a 'conscious evolution towards a society based on love and peace'. It runs a programme of weekly classes and regular seminars by members and visiting speakers.

Based at Centre House is the community of twelve residents who live semi-communally and are responsible for running Centre House activities. They share the Centre's expenses and lead most of the various ses-

227

sions besides working full-time, several of them as yoga teachers. They choose to live in the community for the advancement of their own growth and development and 'the evolution of man towards his ultimate perfection'. They have their own regular morning group meditation sessions and embrace a spectrum of methods and disciplines including astrology, Tarot, the I-Ching, personality testing by colour, Tai Chi, and palmistry, all of which are integrated into the various groups.

A diverse group of people attend groups which include different level yoga classes held every weekday evening, and occasionally during the day. As well as the practice of recognised yoga asanas, each week there are in-depth studies of a particular area of consciousness. They teach yoga 'for the whole being' and include philosophy, mind concentration and meditation techniques as well as physical postures. The 'Awareness and Self-Development' course provides light encounter sessions using sensitivity 'games' aimed at awakening a person's spiritual aspects. The sessions 'provide feedback and challenges, giving encouragement towards self-realisation and self expression', and are based on the book *Conduct Your Own Awareness Sessions* by Christopher Hills and Robert B. Stone.

A series of evenings called 'Mind Games' has been organised to attempt to undercover and develop the 'subconscious and super-conscious minds'. The group examines 'the outer limits and inner reaches of our imagination and physical world, so that we can experience altered states of consciousness that can help us to tap the vast potential that lies within us'.

The Centre offers an 'Inward Bound' course that combines meditation and different forms of yoga with mountaineering. Its purpose is to 'discover and experience in depth the harmony between individuals and the cosmos by development of the relationship between mind, body and Nature'. Introductory sessions on rope and rock practice are held, and instruction is given as required prior to the weekend and longer sessions of camping or staying in bunkhouse accommodation in mountainous areas during expeditions.

There are also special meetings and seminars on the entire range of esoteric study including alchemy, Buddhism, healing, human cybernetics, and philosophy. No set charge is made for meetings and courses, but a minimum of 35p for evening meetings and £2 per day for seminars is suggested 'in order for the charity to function and meetings to be made available'.

Sempervivum Trust

The aims and objectives of *The Sempervivum Trust* are to promote the health and wholeness of the individual by conducting studies and promoting interest in various group activities. These include encounter and sensitivity training, the analytical and religious aspects of psychotherapy, meditation, the religious and medical aspects of parapsychology, the works of modern theological and mystical writers, and co-operation with other groups devoted to 'promoting the development of the individual'. It also works to promote the integration of knowledge from formal disciplines such as theology, anthropology, sociology, psychology and others 'pertinent to the development and maintenance of human relations'. The Trust publicises the results of its work and studies through publications, conferences, lectures and group meetings.

The name 'Sempervivum' derives from a family of succulent garden plants, commonly called the house-leek, which the Trust hopes to emulate. Beginning as a single rosette formed like a lotus, the plant throws off daughter rosettes often found at a distance. After flowering, the central rosette dies, but the continuity of the plant is assured through the daughters. In favourable conditions there are many groups formed in proximity to the original parent.

The Trust's various groups are run in and around Edinburgh, and there is also a centre in Glasgow. There are analytical and dream groups, unstructured therapeutic groups, a group for mothers of young children, encounter, painting, a search for God group (Edgar Cayce), and an E.S.P. group. There have also been some drop-in encounter sessions at a cost of 30p.

The Sempervivum Trust encounter groups aim to 'provide an opportunity for people to get to know themselves and others at a deeper level by focusing on the immediate experience of what is happening in the group, rather than on ideas or past experience'. The group may explore in a number of non-verbal ways such as music and movement, collage, sensory awareness exercises and painting, as well as ordinary words and gestures. There are follow-up groups that may have a more specific focus or emphasise one method. These have included creative play groups and non-verbal workshops, and planned groups in *gestalt*. There also is a Sempervivum co-leaders' group that sets out to explore what skills leaders need to develop if they are to become 'creative facilitators' for others in groups.

The Trust organises Easter and autumn schools, and is associated with the Teilhard Group, the Beshara movement, the Rajneesh Meditation Centre and the Netherbow Church of Scotland Centre.

Centre for Group Work

The *Centre for Group Work and Sensitivity Training* is run by Hans Lobstein, an adult educationalist who adapts his teaching methods for training groups. The group work is mainly geared to 'educated' people and includes exercises in communication, counselling, massage and movement. 'Sensitivity training' is a general term for exercises designed to help people become more aware of their senses.

Lobstein stresses that his groups are for learning rather than therapy. This means allowing people to come to terms with whatever anger is within them and live in a fuller, more loving, more intelligent way. Other exercises used in the group work are hypnotherapy, dream analysis, fantasy, psychodrama, *gestalt*, the use of colour and clay, inter-group work for learning about conflict and co-operation between groups, besides exercises in honesty and alternative behaviour, communication without words, mutual peer counselling and Ida Rolf and Wilhelm Reich-type massage and body awareness.

Hypnotherapy is a method of delving into a person's past through deep relaxation methods such as breathing and yoga, and differs from hypnosis in that it depends on full awareness. It aims to help individuals understand and come to terms with their past besides helping to improve their memory.

Dream analysis is designed to help people discover the meaning of their dreams. It is done in a group in which one person recalls a dream, going over it again and again while others point out any disparities. This is to help people recount a dream accurately and identify closely with it and the personalities in it, so that they can understand the feelings that were expressed.

Clay and colour work involves the depiction of feelings and problems through art to facilitate self-discovery. A person with the inability to scream would be urged to make a clay form of all the things that prevent him from doing so. The act of kneading the clay into an identifiable object of repression would be the means for the person to discover himself. The exercise would be successful if he were able to scream after making representations of all his inner barriers without having uttered any noise in the learning process.

Use is made of other growth techniques explained elsewhere, as well as a method of inter-group work which quickly exposes the conflict and aggression created by 'us and them' group loyalties.

A monthly series of four on-going sessions are held for about £15, and there are special groups like leadership training, massage and hypnotherapy, and art groups held at weekends from about £2 for one day to £5 for two.

Walks and picnics combined with group work are arranged for many weekends and most holidays throughout the year from a cottage in the Derbyshire Peaks. These cost about £6 for a weekend and £12 for four or five days. Living is communal and food is extra. A discount for all groups can be offered to people with low incomes and regular students.

Entropy

'Entropy' means energy which is locked up and untapped. *Entropy* is a mild encounter group to help 'competent' people broaden their awareness and gain confidence in themselves and their day-to-day experience. The group situations are intended to give support and friendship to like-minded people striving for sincere relationships.

Groups are led by Ronald Ullman, a lecturer in accountancy, from his Hampstead flat. He gained experience attending encounter groups in the States, where he ran a transactional analysis group at Esalen for a short while, and he has run sensitivity training groups for British senior Civil Servants.

The groups are open to the type of person able to hold a job and relate fairly openly and intellectually to others. But the groups are not therapy, nor are they for 'lame-ducks, weirdos or misfits' with serious problems and in very depressed mental and emotional states.

'No pressure will be brought to bear on any participant', comments Ullman. 'Growth comes from inner compulsion not outward pressure'. People are encouraged to approach the group with honesty, a willingness to be vulnerable, and with an openness to change. They are urged to interrupt others engaged in futile chat or discussion within the group. The use of 'creative aggression' is encouraged to help release tension. This 'clean fighting airs resentments and purges them', and is thought necessary before warmth and intimacy can be achieved. Various sessions are run with not more than twelve people in each group. The 'Basic Encounter' group encompasses a variety of techniques used in the other groups including psychodrama, 'the acting out of personal relationships', and guided fantasy.

Gestalt, 'the acting out of inner conflicts', is combined with transactional analysis which 'aims at revealing to the individual his unconscious behaviour patterns and changing them if the individual so decides'. The experimental 'Pairing' group looks at how people hide their real feelings when forming relationships, and gives advice on how to cope. The 'Couples' group concentrates on creative aggression and is aimed at helping couples enjoy intimacy which is the 'foundation of growth'. There is also a group called 'Encounter – the sexual world', to help 'toward the freedom and enjoyment of the sexual side of our nature'.

Introductory groups costing about £1 are run on Sunday evenings from 7–10. There is an on-going group of five sessions costing £10 at time of writing. All-day Saturday groups cost about £5 and weekends £8. People should phone before attending. A deposit of fifty per cent is required and reductions are available to students and others unable to afford the full price.

London School of Bodymind Health

The most important therapy offered at *The London School of Bodymind Health* involves reversion to traumatic events in the past. This includes re-living experiences, many of which the patient is not even conscious of,

231

by 'profound regressive discharge', a state equivalent to abreaction and primal scream.

Run by Dr Glyn Seaborn Jones, a psychotherapist, and his assistant Ruth Harrison, the School uses a variety of approaches in its 'Intensive Therapeutic Re-Education' courses. These include psychodrama, bio-energetics, dream analysis and here-and-now relationships. They stress that the 'most rapid, sure and profound' way of achieving 'self-integration' is to begin with a three-week period of isolation from all habitual activities. The purpose of this is to achieve the breakthrough of experiencing past trauma. After this first phase, 'the progress towards bodymind (mind and body) health is more rapid and at a deeper level'.

The second phase, which lasts about twelve months, consists of integrated and group sessions which can be fitted into normal working life. These sessions try to come to terms with the material released by the breakthrough, in a growth environment. In the third phase, the patient is encouraged to phase out sessions, to become more independent, and is encouraged to establish at least one reliable relationship outside the therapy to help 'continue the process of self-liberation and integration'. In the final phase, the person should no longer be in need of professional skill, and is encouraged to explore and develop using a type of peer counselling.

Dr Seaborn Jones believes that successful psychotherapy is the step-by-step release of conscious and unconscious fear. Conscious fears such as phobias, compulsions and avoidances, and unconscious fears built into the body in the form of tension, lead to various psychosomatic illnesses. A successful therapy deals with the whole body, as it is necessary not only to deal with thoughts and words but also body tensions. As fear reduces, the fear of experiencing fear is reduced, tension can be discharged and anger or grief can be experienced more easily.

He claims that most of the people who come to him are having to exercise tight control over themselves: 'People have a vague sense of holding in to avoid disaster, others come cracking up. That is quite a good sign. If you can allow yourself to crack up it can be a tremendous relief'. During the three-week period the patient is isolated from all habitual activities, distractions and drugs. At least two hours a day are spent with the therapist. The patient lives in accommodation near the therapist's home, and is not allowed contact with anybody else. In this way it is assumed that all his reactions will stem from past internal influences still affecting him, rather than from everyday situations. At the start of the period the patient recalls his original family situation. The feelings he has for his parents are transferred to the male and female therapists who now represent them.

The methods used during this period are deep relaxation, the intention being to put compulsive thinking out of action, and release relaxation which is aimed at verbally helping the organism to relax and narrow its awareness within a shorter space of time. At first the patient is encouraged to forget about the past or the future, and be concerned only with the next twenty minutes. This provides a framework in which the patient can feel in a position of relative security. And as the period shrinks more and more, so he can feel more in the here and now. The organism then begins to allow impulses from within to be expressed as other impulses evaporate. And so there is an automatic reversion to traumatic events. The breakthrough is said to be only the starting point for the therapy. After that, people need to relate to others and learn to use this therapy as a safety valve rather than a way of life.

After the three-week period, the patient is introduced to a group in a similar situation. The therapists and the group, who become his brothers and sisters in the family representation, work together with him. It is here that the 'reciport' method is introduced whereby two patients familiar with techniques of release give each other reciprocal support. There is then at least one individual and one group session each week for twelve months or longer before the individual sessions are phased out. After all the treatment, only the group and 'reciport' remain. This process could go on for twenty years years according to Dr Seaborn Jones.

People who wish to take part in this type of therapy on a less committed level can have membership of an intensive on-going group with or without occasional individual sessions. These groups have about ten people in each. Dr Seaborn Jones and his assistant are probably the only people in Britain to practise such an intensive breakthrough therapy. But Dr Seaborn Jones does not believe in sticking to one particular therapeutic technique. He feels people should find their own therapeutic rhythm that allows them to live in a balanced way, and he wants them to do his therapy in their own way.

The people who take part in the groups tend to have professional jobs. If you want to attempt the full intensive it will cost about £1,000 and obviously needs a firm commitment. The three-week period costs £480, but can vary according to hardship, and since there can only be one person at a time on the three-week intensive, the number of people having this therapy is very limited. The fee for groups is £30 for a three-month minimum period.

Centre for Human Communication

The *Centre for Human Communication* offers a course combining participatory lectures, discussion groups, experimental groups and communication growth games to encourage the practice of human communications. A series of extensive courses in yoga is also organised. Emphasis is laid on human communications as the 'supreme art', because it is believed to be 'the basis of Society and the creator of community. Through deep human communication comes the most positive of man's experience: co-operation, sharing, harmony, peace and love. All particles and forms are created and maintained by energy which is shared. Communication means "sharing together" '.

The Centre was founded in 1972 by Kevin and Venika Kingsland who had both studied yoga and related subjects extensively. The Human Communications course consists of five units, said to tackle the most fundamental and neglected areas of the subject. 'The nature of the person' and 'personal growth' involve at first the discussion of various aspects of the nature of the personality: ego, security, motivation, needs, loves and hates and status. Also examined is consciousness and unconsciousness, the growth and change of the ego through learning, memory, attention and perception, and how to get beyond it.

Analysis of the 'psychology of the environment', 'media' and 'communication breakdown' involves discussion on how people experience time and space. A colour test is taken in which a person chooses one of the seven colours of the spectrum, which will correspond fairly accurately to his personality. The identification of the whole person in terms of these categories is a familiar part of yogic philosophy. Each colour is related to an aspect of the personality, ranging from red, the lowest gross physical level, to violet, the level of imagination and creativity.

There are exercises in body language, examining gestures and posture; and verbal language, examining words, sentences and reasoning. This includes symbolism in dreams and the imagination, and parapsychological communication and sensory extensions. Communication breakdown deals with pathological aspects like psychosomatic illness and includes humour and what there is beyond communication. Each session costs £1 and there are forty in the entire course.

The yoga courses include an introductory hatha yoga course, 'organised according to modern psychological understanding of the way we learn'. The twenty sessions, each lasting about one and a half hours, cost a total of over £10. Beginners and advanced intensive courses in 'yoga living' are 'aimed at giving the individual a firm basis in the traditional yoga techniques, theory and philosophy. Full reference to modern scientific knowledge will be given in simple language. The course will be run on a personal basis and each individual will have ample opportunity for personal advice and counselling throughout'. The entire course lasts sixty weeks.

Courses in integral yoga for people with some experience place greater emphasis on relaxation, concentration, and meditation. There is a six-day intensive for teachers of hatha yoga, and hatha yoga for children, raj yoga on-going groups, and hatha yoga and relaxation for businessmen and women.

Students can enrol by writing to the course secretary. Those unable to pay may be exempted. Facilities at the Centre for use by course participants include a colour and sound laboratory, library, psychological consultancy, natural beauty consultancy and an arts and crafts workshop. Personal callers are encouraged between 10.30 a.m. and 5 p.m. Those attending courses from outside the area will find a wide range of accommodation nearby.

Psychosynthesis

Psychosynthesis, as developed by the contemporary Italian psychiatrist Roberto Assagioli, is 'a comprehensive psychological and educational approach to the development of the whole person'. It is being developed in Britain by *The Institute of Psychosynthesis*, which has been established to disseminate information and provide training.

It represents a synthesis of many traditions, and views man as a whole, according each aspect its due importance. Psychosynthesis balances Eastern approaches that have tended to emphasise the 'spiritual' side of being and Western approaches that have usually focused on the 'personality' level. 'It recognises in man a trans-personal essence and at the same time holds that his purpose in life is to manifest this essence or self, as fully as possible in the world of everyday living'.

In an individual session, a weekend group or an evening introduction to psychosynthesis, there are a variety of methods to meet the different situation and the individual needs. They are designed to fit in with the person's present situation and his own goals and path of development. Guided imagery or *gestalt* is used to determine some of the reasons that prevent people from functioning effectively in relations with others. Creativity and meditation are used to show people they have a far greater potential in life than they previously realised. The self-identification exercise aims to help people to begin to develop a greater understanding of who they are and the importance of the correct quality of life.

The Institute is interested in making psychosynthesis available to all sections of society and hopes to make contact with a large number of communities throughout Britain so it can introduce these ideas, concepts and practical techniques for use in daily living. It offers weekend workshops and groups that give an introductory presentation of the psychosynthesis process and the techniques used. There is an on-going group programme for those who want to develop a greater understanding of the concepts and put them into use in their daily lives, and also individual psychosynthesis sessions and training programmes for professionals. Lectures are given to any interested groups or institutions. There is an information service providing scientific papers, reading lists, books and publications from other centres in Italy, U.S.A., Canada and Holland.

Hallam Centre

Transactional analysis is a system based on the cognitive understanding of oneself by becoming aware of one's 'programmed life plan' – the past impressions that condition behaviour. These are corrected so that a person can 'write the script he wants'. It sets out to give increased autonomy, spontaneity of emotion and the ability to achieve deep and satisfying relationships and internal awareness. Basically a system of growth and reorientation, the courses are not intended as primary treatment for emotional disorders, although a therapeutic reaction may occur as part of the training experience.

The Principal of the *Hallam Centre*, Dr Alan Byron, is a medical practitioner, a visiting prison psychotherapist and a consultant in human relations to industry.

Transactional analysis is based on the works of Eric Berne, author of *Games People Play* and other books on psychotherapy. His theory is that a child's ideas and feelings about his worth – how he should act for his benefit and what his future will be – emerge in a distinct pattern from the continual stream of messages he receives from his parents. These ideas become fixated and remain with the child the rest of his life 'to form his life position, the games he plays and the script he has', preventing the adult from acting in a natural manner.

Initial training in T.A. focuses on the five main sub-personalities derived from the parent, adult and child ego states which programme a person's ideas. These are the 'Prejudicial Parent', the prejudiced and negative messages received from the parent; the 'Nurturing Parent', who is permission giving, and is sympathetic, protective, loving and enriching; and the 'Mature Parent', who makes firm, realistic decisions and refuses to accept things at their face value. The 'Child' category is split into two major divisions. The 'Natural Child' is free, spontaneous and expressive, and does not possess any parental decisions; the 'Adapted Child', by learning to react to verbal and non-verbal parental demands, is neurotic and manipulative, has inhibitions and prohibitions and is the source of problems.

The aim of T.A. therapy is to get the separate sub-personalities integrated and working harmoniously together. It uses a simple terminology to illustrate emotional and mental activities. 'Re-Parenting' is an important part of T.A. therapy that aims to rid people of the 'Prejudicial Parent'. It involves regressing the person to his childhood and re-feeding the parental message as clear, positive instructions which are continually repeated. By telling a person to be straightforward or successful enough times, the parental impression can be erased and replaced. 'Script-redecision' involves altering the absolute decision a child sometimes makes (such as 'I'll never trust anybody again'), which might remain with him throughout his life, and helping him to become ready to make a new decision.

Much of the training given through the Hallam Centre is on-going, giving participants an opportunity to develop their T.A. skills over a period of time. A professional system being applied in industry, it is recognised by both the International and British Transactional Analysis Associations. The courses prepare individuals for regular and advanced membership of the I.T.A.A. For those not familiar with the technique of T.A., basic training courses are available. For more advanced work, individuals should hold a recognised post involving support, counselling health or organisation development. They should also have attended a basic training course in T.A. or *gestalt* or be able to demonstrate a sound basic knowledge of the material.

The Hallam Centre arranges introductory and advanced workshops throughout the British Isles on request; there is also a two-day course in T.A. principles for those who are not in the helping professions and a training marathon for those who would like to use T.A. in their work. There is an intensive basic training weekend using audio-visual aids and discussion, and an opportunity to do supervised practice for people who wish to make professional use of T.A. Successful completion of this course plus a written open book exam entitles one to regular membership of the I.T.A.A. There is a regular study group for those who have completed this weekend and a series of on-going evening workshops for people wishing to apply for advanced membership of the I.T.A.A.

Transactional Analysis

The *Institute of Transactional Analysis* is a training establishment mainly for those in the helping professions. It integrates transactional analysis, described as an 'analytic mode of enquiry to illuminate human behaviour', with techniques that include *gestalt*, role-playing and psychodrama. A fuller description of T.A. theory is outlined in The Hallam Centre section, but Dr Michael Reddy, one of the Institute's five practitioners and a trained clinical psychologist, says the theiry covers ever aspect of human behaviour, employing language accessible to the average person. It stresses the need for self-responsibility to enable a person to bring about a 're-decision' in his life.

The work is mainly done in groups of ten, and at the beginning of a session each person establishes a 'contract' specifying what part of his personality and attitudes he would like to come to terms with or see altered – it might be a particular relationship or an unfulfilled ambition. The session will only be concerned with fulfilling the one contract for each person.

The leader explores with each person within the group environment how his present problems are related to the 'life-script' that originated in

237

his childhood. This stems from the view that adults still react to many circumstances the same way they did as children, and that the child personality can live autonomously with a person throughout his life. By recognising and getting in touch with imposed childhood feelings such as timidity, guilt, favourite bad feelings and personal myths, a person should be able to get rid of many of his present problems. When the group leader has helped the person fully experience the child-feeling level, he will then help bring that understanding to an adult level of comprehension.

The groups are mainly on-going and a session normally lasts for two and a half hours. The workshops are recognised by the International Transactional Analysis Association.

Human Cybernetics

Human cybernetics is an educational system of behavioural psychology devised to give people 'greater control, complete governance and deeper guidance of the mental mechanism'. The system was evolved by Dr George Hall, a consultant psychologist and a leading member of the International New Thought Alliance.

Applied human cybernetics is a method of programming the brain to improve the nature of mental activity, and Dr Hall believes that all problems can be solved by correcting the thought processes using this method. The system is set out in a fourteen-part discussion workshop or home study course. Each student's studies in the workshop course are guided by a workshop director. He leads discussions, directs exchanges of views, and assists in the exercises and questions of each student. In the home study course students study prepared lessons at home and have weekly written communications with a tutor for home studies, who deals with each student on an individual basis. The courses are suitable for people of 'normal intelligence' and aim to improve and reveal a person's potential by a 'reorganisation of concept' that 'clarifies a person's understanding of himself, establishes a better self-image and a positive attitude'. This is achieved by increasing the positive balance rather than eliminating negativity. It aims to give peace and contentment, freedom from tension, and greater work proficiency.

The core of the system is planning. By planning the behavioural foundations and attitudes 'which control, govern and guide all phases of human activity and relationships, there can only come good relationships, better behaviour and greater sensitivity'.

The theory is that the mental mechanism is made up two parts – the mind and the brain. The mind is the thinking part and data-gathering area. The brain is the area of human control where data is stored – it is 'the channel of contact with intuition', and can be accurately programmed with data to establish the basis of all action and expression. The

238

control of all the input into the brain makes it possible also to control all action or 'output' and expression, and this should be 'positive'.

One of the basic principles is that each human can develop a 'brain filter' which makes it impossible to record or be affected by negative impulses that are 'destructive to success and stifling to happiness'. Negative feedback 'ensures each person keeps to and expresses only what has been input and reacts only to external impulses that are positive in nature – this creates an extraordinary human being capable of motivating and communicating only the highest, positive, intuitional impulses or thoughts' with complete self-confidence. All feeling and love can also be programmed and transmitted by correct thought, and as such needs to be properly channelled. According to Dr Hall, 'feeling is an emotional fool'.

The application of the system also includes establishing a creative capacity using a Western system of meditation and relaxation and directing imagination in a constructive, positive manner. People are taught a planning formula that provides for the behaviour pattern and attitude structure to be clearly determined in advance, and then programmed and input. It also provides a system of short and long-term goal planning.

There are regular introductory demonstration workshops where people are shown how human cybernetics is applied. People are asked to take part in a personality profile questionnaire to show them how negative or positive their thoughts and attitudes are. The discussion workshop meets for a two-and-a-half hour session once a week in the day or evening. The fee for this and the home study course was £85. There are also six-session seminars and an eight-session Total Personality Development course 'for sales-people, supervisors, personnel managers, teachers and anyone who must contact the public in their work', cost £40, but is probably more now. For all course enquiries contact the Lecture and Seminar Secretary of the *Human Cybernetic Organisation*.

Centre for Therapeutic Communication

The major aim of *The Centre for Therapeutic Communications* is 'to present different types of training to enhance the professional skills of those who work with people'. Most of its work is now centred around its Family Training Institute which operates between July and August. This is designed for those who work with families and want to become trained family therapists, and also for families that need guidance.

The Centre aims to strike a balance between mysticism and body techniques, and believes that people need to be in charge of their learning. Basically it is an educational institute for professionals and students who will not be able to find such a progressive course in establishment institutes, and feel that a more humanistic approach needs to be taken, as opposed to 'unimaginative and sterile' conventional methods.

'The Institute's training course is designed to integrate theory and practical experience based on direct work with families', mainly utilising Virginia Satir's model of family therapy. One of the staff has been trained by her and the rest have gained their experience in various therapeutic communities.

The Family Therapy course for professionals takes eight weeks. Headed by a supervisor and assigned a number of families, it begins with a three-day encounter workshop, 'which has the dual purpose of helping participants to get to know each other, as well as providing a number of techniques which will be useful in working with families'. It includes weekly theoretical seminars, a body awareness workshop and a theory workshop where 'role-playing (to practise theory in a closed setting and to experience the feelings of both therapist and family) is used, as well as a demonstration family'. Video tapes are employed to 'enable both the group and the individual trainee to examine their practical implementation of treatment skills more clearly', with a film and voice workshop 'designed to enable the trainee to become more aware of the potential influence of his voice and the effect it has on the family'. The Family Therapy course used to cost £340 plus V.A.T. (£170 plus V.A.T. for students), and grants can be obtained from some authorities – but better to find out what it costs now!

The course is related to the Conjoint Family Therapy course, which involves using an entire 'problem' family as an educational model for the therapists. The family is usually sent to them by a child guidance clinic because of a child's trouble at school. The therapy involves questioning people about what they do, what they get out of their actions, and how they would like things to change. The family finds itself shaken up in the attempt to make communication between members more direct and honest, and in the effort to help them relate on a more physical and emotional level.

The Centre, which has groups in the U.S., also runs courses in reality therapy which 'stresses the need for a warm structured relationship between client and therapist'. Its aim is to help people find out what their real desires are and to help them on the way to realising them, particularly in the family situation. It claims to be a common-sense growth model for people to develop closer relationships, stressing that individuals are responsible for themselves and that such things as 'mental illness' do not really exist.

Courses are also held in applied group treatment to give people a taste of the different kinds of course work. It is a cross between encounter and conventional teachings, designed mainly for social workers. Making use of group structuring, which emphasises the need for planning therapy, it stresses that a leader dealing with a patient should know what to ask at any given moment. This includes understanding what is being done, where everything is leading to, and why it is being done. The treatment also makes use of communication exercises, games, psychodrama and programme media which are games and exercises in groups where people can loosen up, learn how to relate and allow themselves to fall into different patterns of behaviour. They also use action techniques similar to encounter methods.

Franklin School

The *Franklin School of Contemporary Studies* is a private college which aims to provide an 'informal, intimate and comfortable environment where one can learn more about the issues and subjects that are important to today's society . . . through discussion groups and seminars'. The School's activities are split into several departments each with its own head. The 'Bio-feedback and Self-Development' department is led by C. Maxwell Cade who runs courses in psychocybernetics, psychotechnics, hypnopsychedelics, and higher states of consciousness.

Psychocybernetics – self-fulfilment through self-control – encourages the use of the unconscious mind, and involves meditation, auto-hypnosis, creative thinking, and memory development. It makes use of bio-feedback instruments such as brainwave monitors and skin resistance meters which show instantly the changes produced by each new experience. These machines measure mental or physical, and thus emotional, levels of relaxation or tension by the electrical activity of the brain or the amount of perspiration through the pores.

Psychotechnics is described as a 'very broad practical psychology', and the course aims to facilitate the 'teaching of superior mental skills'. The hypnopsychedelics course is of general interest, but is especially for students of parapsychology or psychical research. It covers different aspects of parapsychology and altered states of consciousness including hypnosis and dreams.

The higher states of consciousness course is mainly aimed at psychologists, experienced meditators, psychotherapists, and students of mysticism and religious experience. It covers such facets of mysticism as trance states, mantras and mandalas, Eastern mysticism, and Zen.

There are one-hour sessions in bio-feedback training, and also courses in yoga, meditation, and awareness. Groups in the 'Mind and Body Co-ordination' department include the 'Feldenkrais method of body-mind awareness', which uses the simple physical exercises developed by Dr Moshe Feldenkrais to help people direct their awareness into 'releasing energy held in fixed patterns in the body, mind, emotions and spirit'.

The 'Tai-Do and Tai-Chi, meditation in movement' course is designed to help people become aware of how they interfere with the natural functioning of their body and mind. There are also groups using growth games for the development of sensory awareness; creative movement groups for regeneration and the release of tension, making use of basic and relaxing exercises; and a centring group that follows a series of exercises in 'seeing, listening, sensing and use of breath', to develop a balance of body, mind and emotions.

There are dialogue groups to help people break down barriers of shyness or role-playing through talking in depth with another individual and later discussing it in a group. Other groups employ psychodrama and music therapy, while others are particularly for divorced, separated and widowed people and for 'resolving the mid-life crisis'.

The transactional analysis courses run at the Franklin School are directed by Shulamit Peck, a clinical member of the International Transactional Analysis Association. They offer an official one-day introductory course in T.A., with examination of the theory and some practical work covering ego states, analysis of transactions, game analysis and script analysis. Those who have completed this course are eligible for the Training Programme for Transactional Analysis, providing the opportunity to complete the necessary training and requirements for clinical membership of the I.T.A.A. The five weekends and a one day on-going session last over a period of six months. Besides taking part in the training sessions, the participant also works as a therapist or co-therapist, and finally takes a written and oral examination.

The 'Mystical and Psychic Research' department involves courses like ritual and ceremony in magic and mysticism, Tarot, and Atlantis. The 'new Approaches to Health' department has groups using relaxation techniques, meditation, prayer, healing, nature cure, and sound and colour healing.

The 'Aids to Psychology' department includes courses in graphology, astrology, palmistry, and numerology. 'Art and Music' has courses in sculpture, painting restoration, applications of mirror and glass, a quick method of learning to play a musical instrument, and novel ways of making musical instruments. There are also general courses such as natural childbirth, gambling and gaming, jazz, philosophy, politics and sociology, theatre and writing.

Most of the courses (except T.A.) are ten sessions long and cost £15. The School has autumn, winter and spring terms, and all applicants must register for courses, most of which have an upper limit of twenty people. There is a preview week just before each term where many of the instructors are available for a discussion, and sometimes introductory sessions are held. There is a discount of ten per cent for students registered for two or more courses. Classes generally last for one-and-a-half hours, and the bulk of them are scheduled for evenings, although many are also available during the day.

Organisational Research

Organisational Research and Development works with management organisations and individuals in a variety of settings to initiate self-directed learning programmes and personal growth work. It was set up in 1969 by Eve Godfrey, a consultant in management and organisational development. Her work in this field incorporates the use of non-verbal communication, power and authority games, transactional analysis, group fantasy and encouraging the use of leisure time for self-development. She works with the Civil Service and large organisations where stress and its associated physical illnesses affect health, job satisfaction and performance.

O.R.D. is also involved in more personal growth work in free and supportive community environments. It has an annual month-long summer school scheme held in a different country each year that involves using educational learning materials and a wide range of group, dance and movement work. It aims to create a self-directed learning environment where people provide their own learning situations by deciding and then acting on what they want to do. The summer schools use many growth techniques including individual therapy and co-counselling, also using the experience of living as a community on their 'personal journey of discovery'.

Dean Cottage is the base for O.R.D.'s activities in England and is its research centre and training ground in the area of ecological skills, particularly horticulture and animal care.

Churchill Centre

Many of those involved in professional work in the psychiatric and therapeutic fields might look upon the new 'human psychology' groups as little more than a bunch of quacks. It was in an effort to bridge the gap to such people that Dr Ken Holmes set up the *Churchill Centre* which, working within the growth movement, would offer training courses for doctors, psychiatrists, social workers etc., as well as offering individual and group therapy sessions. Dr Holmes studied clinical psychology and psychiatry at university and has worked in hospitals, gathering most of his experience in group dynamics and psychotherapy from travelling in Europe and the U.S. He now acts mainly as an administrator.

The Centre offers occasional programmes in *gestalt*, Reichian therapy, psychodrama and encounter, and has also tried in the past to include a wide range of activities from elsewhere in the movement – primal re-education, yoga, healing, etc. The atmosphere at the Centre is somewhat more formal than similar groups. In addition to the regular group of trainers it tries to get as wide a range of guest therapists and speakers as possible.

Occasional evening lectures are held on a wide range of mainly intellectually oriented subjects, which sometimes include demonstrations in areas such as yoga and *gestalt* counselling. Dr Charlotte Bach has lectured on

243

Jung, Reich, Tao, alchemy and on the subject of human ethology, described as a 'study of the total behaviour of the individual'. More irregular groups run by guests, many of them from the United States, include further adaptations of various basic methods.

A seven-session course called 'Getting together the family within' is designed to help members improve their capacities to engage in more satisfying social transactions'. Attention is given to 'non-verbal communication and body language and audio and visual feedback is used in helping members to become aware of self-defeating patterns of communication and behaviour'. These have been run by Dr John Staude, who studied *gestalt* therapy at Esalen with Dr Fritz Perls, the founder of *gestalt* therapy. There are also basic training courses in *gestalt* therapy, which, similar to some other courses, award certificates to those who have completed the training. Grants are sometimes available through local authorities. About one hundred people a week pass through the Centre and Dr Holmes would now like to see more work involving couples and families.

The Churchill Centre is now increasingly orientated towards becoming a training centre for those who have already established basic therapeutic skills, but would like to develop them further. It is concentrating on *gestalt* work, with some special courses in Holmes's industrial work. The *gestalt* courses are modular, involving training sessions followed by periods of application in the field. The course is integrated with counselling and psychotherapy, with one or three-month courses run at weekends or a combination of evenings and weekends.

The Centre recently extended its work to include the Centre for Bio-Energy, to which they are now devoting a large amount of their attention. This concentrates on the work of Dr Gerda Boysen, who helps to run her specialised therapy derived mainly from Reich. A trained psychotherapist, she gives individual and group training during a six-month course aimed at releasing 'body armour'. This intensive psycho-therapeutic programme takes place one evening a week and one weekend a month with additional lectures added from time to time. With sixteen people on each course at present, there are plans to set up a one-year course and eventually a three-year course. Dr Boysen's bio-energy work is concerned with neurosis and psychosomatic conditions, and also with helping people to generally develop themselves and become less inhibited. 'I have found people hold emotions back, but the body has a way to dissolve nervous tension', she claims.

The Centre has provided sessions for individuals, couples and groups, and has run workshops in bio-energy and Boysen's tension release massage.

Human Potential Research

The *Human Potential Research Project* is fundamentally a research body concerned with investigating three areas. 'Conceptual research' is aimed at clarifying our understanding of the human condition. 'Experimental research' examines personal and inter-personal development, including personality change, both in theory and practice. 'Action research' uses the 'intervention method' where a consultant works with a small group or larger organisation, seeking to clarify through action 'the relation between individual needs and corporate needs'.

The methods developed by the Project can be put into practice in many fields to enable organisations to 'introduce changes which enable people to realise a wider range of their potential'. This involves setting up and studying the workings of a number of experimental social structures. Since it began operation in 1970, the Project has worked with a wide range of varying organisations, including the police, fire brigade, hospitals, banks and educational institutions. They aim to help professional people, such as managers, social workers and teachers, who encounter problems with 'attitude, communication, decision-making and human relations'. Group interaction methods are employed to 'open up communication and increase understanding between different sections of the community.'

In addition to their 'professional' work, the Project has in the past operated training laboratories for the public, through the Adult Education Centre, and have also run re-evaluation counselling classes as part of the adult education programme at Surrey University.

For anyone who seeks to further his self-awareness and social sensitivity in a small group of persons with similar aspirations, there is a programme of human relations laboratories or self-actualisation workshops, and also work in the fields of parapsychological and transcendental experience.

Groups with research workers 'explore group problem-solving techniques', and work with teachers and lecturers aims 'to encourage the cultivation of emotional and interpersonal competence at all levels of the educational system'.

The framework in which all the separate projects are carried out is reciprocal counselling. This is a two-way growth process where two people take it in turns to be both client and counsellor, each assisting the other person's growth with his attention and support. The counsellor's interventions are in the form of suggestions as to what the client may say or do, based on a tentative mental hypothesis about what is going on in the client. The client is engaged in a process of human flourishing, basically aiding him to understand and come to terms with mental and emotional forces acting on him. He then develops from this new under-

245

standing. An important aspect of reciprocal counselling is the cathartic release of tensions and distress using 'insight, action-planning, creative thinking, and expansion of awareness'.

The programme of courses and workshops – both residential and one-day – held in the past has covered topics such as family interaction, group interaction, and experimental techniques in higher education. These courses are usually intended for people working in the relevant areas, including professionals like doctors, teachers, social workers, etc. If you would like further information on any particular area of the Project's work, write or phone and ask for more written material. Exploratory discussions with the Project director may be arranged on an informal basis.

Humanistic Psychology

The Association for Humanistic Psychology serves as a co-ordinating body within the humanistic psychology growth movement to draw the different groups together and to find out how they can be of use to each other. It acts as an information centre of the movement for educational establishments, psychologists, sociologists and interested groups and individuals. It supplies detailed information on a range of growth centres, encounter groups and special therapies, aiming to bring together people 'interested in psychology as a means of developing awareness and sensitivity and making psychological theory in these areas more widely known', in order to, 'build a society in which people are valued as creative self-realising persons'.

The Association publishes a monthly magazine, *Self and Society*, and sends speakers and group leaders on invitation to universities and other centres to give an intellectual and experimental introduction to the whole area of humanistic psychology. It encourages research and sets up occasional educational meetings and workshops to work on specific subjects such as education, work in industry, bio-feedback, and *gestalt*.

Meetings are held at regular intervals and membership is about £6 per annum, and £4 for full-time students.

Part Two
Making Contact

(a) The Principal Societies

To make it easier to keep them up to date, the addresses and phone numbers of all the societies described in Part One have been gathered together. Also, you will find here short listings of other national organisations for which there was insufficient space in Part One. Please help us by sending changes of addresses or suggestions for short listings to the editor, Stephen Annett, c/o Turnstone Books.

CHRISTIAN

Children of God (pp.12–15)
P.O. Box 31, London WC2E 7LX
01 458 1766

Lonesome Stone (pp.15–16)
56 Beulah Hill, Upper Norwood,
London SE19
01 771 9642

Jesus Liberation Front (pp.17–18)
Sunnyhill, Hemel Hempstead,
Herts HP1 1SZ
0442 59817

Musical Gospel Outreach (pp.19–20)
10 Seaforth Avenue, New Malden,
Surrey KT3 6JP
01 942 8847

The Unified Church (pp.20–3)
Rowlane Farmhouse, Reading,
Berkshire
0734 472299

Assemblies of God (pp.23–6)
108–14 Talbot Street,
Nottingham NG1 5GH
There are assemblies in most major towns.

Contact: Nottingham for information
0602 44525/6

Society of Friends (pp.26–9)
Friends' House, Euston Road,
London NW1 2BJ
01 387 3601
There are meetings in most larger towns.
Contact: Friends' House, London, for information

Christian Community (pp.29–30)
34 Glenilla Road, London NW3
See also: East Grinstead, King's Langley, Bristol, Stroud, Stourbridge, Manchester, Leeds, Danby, Keswick, Edinburgh and Aberdeen
01 722 3587

Mormons' Church of Jesus Christ of Latter-Day Saints (pp.30–5)
64–8 Princes Gate, London SW7 2PA
01 584 8867

Christian Science Church (pp.35–8)
Committee on Publication,
108 Palace Gardens, London W8
01 221 5650
There are some 300 Christian Science churches in Britain

Unity School of Christianity
(pp.38–40)
Unity House, Blind Lane,
Bourne End, Bucks SL8 5LG
06285 22001

Science of Mind Centre (pp.40–1)
3 Alumdale Road, Westbourne,
Bournemouth
Meetings: Friends' Meeting House,
Wharncliffe Road, Boscombe,
Bournemouth

Association for Promoting Retreats
(pp.41–3)
Church House, Newton Road,
London W2 5LS
01 727 7924

New Church Enquiry Centre
(pp.43–5)
20 Bloomsbury Way,
London WC1A 2TH
01 242 8574

New Church House (pp.43–5)
34 John Dalton Street,
Manchester M2 6LE

Swedenborg Society (pp.43–5)
20 Bloomsbury Way,
London WC1A 2TH
01 405 8574

**Churches' Fellowship for Psychical
and Spiritual Studies**
5 Denison House, 296 Vauxhall
Bridge Road, London SW1
Influential and exclusive group
including orthodox churchmen,
anxious to restore to the Church
a true mystical perspective

Friends' Fellowship of Healing
Room 23, Friends' House, Euston
Road, London NW1
01 387 3601
About 44 groups around the U.K.

**Fellowship of Christian Healing
Trust**
21 Devonshire Place,
London W1N 1PD

Seekers' Trust
The Close, Addington Park,
West Malling, Kent
0732 843589
Over 5000 members linked in prayer
circles

Guild of Pastoral Psychology
Mrs Nina Farndon,
41 Redcliffe Gardens, London
SW10
01 352 6963
Jungian based

**Holy Spirit Association for
Unification of World Christianity**
28 Liverpool Road, Thornton Heath,
Surrey

Christian Telephone Ministry
Methodist Healing Fellowship.
Telephone: Wilfrid Brown
0243 84525

City Temple Psychological Clinic
City Temple, Holborn Viaduct,
London EC1
01 583 5532
Staffed by Methodist and
Congregational clergy, and by
psychiatrists

**Church of England Information
Office**
Church House, Dean's Yard,
Westminster, London SW1P
3NZ
01 222 9011

EASTERN

Hindu Centre (pp.48–9)
Dr S. S. Sharma,
39 Grafton Road, London NW5
01 485 8200

Sai-Hindu Centre (pp.49–50)
25 Hoop Lane, Golders Green,
London NW11
01 458 3813

Swaminarayan Hindu Mission
(pp.50–1)
Mr P. Patel,
Swaminarayan Hindu Temple,
77 Elmore Street, London N1

Krishna Consciousness Movement
(pp.51–3)
Bhaktivedanta Manor, Letchmore
Heath, Watford, Herts
Radlett 7244/5

Divine Light Mission (pp.53–6)
131 Clapham High Street,
London SE4
01 622 9261/3

Sai Baba Devotees (pp.56–8)
c/o Sitaram, 80 Cuckoo Hill Road,
Pinner, Middlesex
01 866 6493

Sri Chinmoy Centre (pp.58–60)
31 Niagara Avenue, Ealing,
London W5
01 579 0160

Rajneesh Meditation Centre
(pp.60–2)
82 Bell Street, London NW1
01 262 0991

**Spiritual Regeneration Movement
(T.M.)** (pp.62–4)
32 Cranbourn Street,
London WC2H 7EY
01 240 3103

18 Buccleuch Place,
Edinburgh EH8 9LN
031 667 6933
66 Eccles Street, Dublin 7, Eire
0001 306 204

The School of Meditation (p.64)
158 Holland Park Avenue,
London W11 4UH
01 603 6116

Meher Baba Association (p.67)
3a Eccleston Square,
London SW1V 1NP
01 834 4212

Sri Aurobindo Society (pp.67–70)
82 Bell Street, London NW1
01 722 8194

Self-Realisation Fellowship
(pp.70–2)
c/o Mrs G. White,
33 Warrington Crescent, London W9
01 286 1524
or write direct to:
3880 San Rafael Avenue,
Los Angeles, California 90065,
U.S.A.

Ramakrishna Vedanta Centre
(pp.73–4)
54 Holland Park, London W11
01 724 4010

Sikh Cultural Society (pp.75–6)
88 Mollison Way, Edgware,
Middlesex HA8 5QW
01 592 1215

Sikh Missionary Society (p.76)
c/o Mr Sidhu,
20 Peacock Street, Gravesend, Kent
0474 62017

251

3HO Foundation (pp.76–8)
Guru Ram Das Ashram,
22 All Saints Road, London W11
01 727 8487

Subud (pp.78–81)
342 Cricklewood Lane,
London NW2 2QH
01 455 0136/7
There are Subud groups in most of
the larger cities in Britain

**National Spiritual Assembly of the
Baha'is of the U.K.** (p.83)
27 Rutland Gate, London SW7
01 584 2566

Beshara (pp.84–6)
Local centres: London, Canterbury,
Bristol, Brighton, Oxford,
Cambridge, Leeds, Leicester
Other centres:
1 Swyre Farm, Aldsworth,
Cirencester, Glos.
045184 377
2 Chisholme House, Roberton,
Hawick
045088 248
3 The Warren Farmhouse,
Rhos-y-Meirch, Knighton, Powys
05472 612

Sufi Order (pp.86–8)
Sufi House, 6 Parkwood Road,
London SW19
01 947 2626

**Sufi Cultural Centre (and Sufi
Movement)** (pp.88–9)
53 West Ham Lane, Stratford,
London E15 4PH
01 534 6539

Khankah Abadan Abad (p.89)
Four Winds, Temple Hill,
Dockenfield, Farnham, Surrey
025125 2440

Sufi Society (p.90)
Dr Sufi Aziz Balouch,
41 Pembridge Road, London W11
01 727 9356

Idres Shah
c/o A. P. Watt & Son,
26 Bedford Row,
London WC1R 4HL

BKS Iyengar Yoga Group (pp.91–2)
c/o Bharatiya Vidya Bhavan,
37a New Oxford Street, London
WC1

Wheel of Yoga (pp.91–3)
c/o Acacia House, Centre Avenue,
Acton, London W3 7JX
Enclose s.a.e. for details

**International Tai Chi Chuan
Association** (pp.93–4)
38 Thirlmere Gardens, Wembley,
Middlesex
01 904 2682

Gerda Geddes and Beverley Milne
c/o Stephen Annett, Turnstone
Books,
37 Upper Addison Gardens,
London W14

The Liu Academy
Renshuden Judo Building,
William Road, London NW1
01 387 8611

School of Intensive Esoteric Studies
The Secretary, (p.86)
74e Eccleston Square, London
SW1

Aikikai of Great Britain (p.95)
c/o Greater London Sports Club,
1a Airedale Avenue, London W4
01 994 2182

Sati Society (pp.95–6)
John Garrie,
16 Crestview, Dartmouth Park Hill,
London NW5 1JB
01 485 6419

Sati Journal
Editor: Eve Godfrey, Dean Cottage,
Water End, Ashdon, Saffron Walden,
Essex

BUDDHIST

Buddhist Society (pp.99–100)
58 Eccleston Square, London SW1V
1PH
01 828 1313

Friends of the Western Buddhist Order (pp.100–1)
1a Balmore Street, London N19
01 263 2339

Aryatara Buddhist Community (p.101)
3 Plough Lane, Purley, Surrey
CR2 3QB
01 660 2542

British Mahabodhi Society (pp.101–2)
London Buddhist Vihara,
5 Heathfield Gardens, London W4
01 995 9493

Buddhapadipa Temple (pp.102–3)
99 Christchurch Road, London SW14
01 876 9188

London Zen Studies (pp.103–4)
7 Antrim Mansions, Antrim Road,
London NW3

British Buddhist Association (p.104)
c/o 8 Hatton Garden, London ECI

Indian Buddhist Society of the U.K.
c/o 42 Broxholm Road, London SE27

Samye-Ling Tibetan Centre (pp.104–5)
Eskdalemuir, Langholm,
Dumfriesshire DG13 0QL
05416 232

Kham Tibetan House (pp.105–6)
Rectory Lane, Ashdon, Saffron
Walden, Essex VB10 2HM
079 984 415

Throssel Hole Priory (pp.106–7)
Carr Shield, Hexham,
Northumberland
04589 204

Hakurenji (p.107)
40 Deansway, London N2

Mushindo Karate Do Association (p.109)
4a Edge Hill, London SW15

Ugyen Cho Ling, see p. 264

ESOTERIC

Theosophical Society (pp.110–12)
50 Gloucester Place, London
W1H 3HJ
01 935 9261
Write here for information about the
90 other branches in the U.K.

The Theosophical Bookshop (p.112)
68 Great Russell Street, London
WC1B 3BU

Anthroposophical Society (p.115)
Rudolph Steiner House, 35 Park
Road, London NW1 6XT
01 723 4400
See regions for 37 local centres
Other related addresses:

Bio-Dynamic Agricultural Association
Secretary: John Soper, Broome
Farm, Clent, Stourbridge, Worcs.
Gives practical, horticultural
advice

Goethean Science Foundation
Clent Grove, Clent, Stourbridge,
Worcs.
Spiritual principles in science

British Weleda Co.
Littlehurst, East Grinstead, Sussex
Sells medicaments and toiletries

Lucis Trust (pp.116–19)
(World Goodwill, Triangles, The
Arcane School and Lucis Press) 253
Finchley Road, Hampstead, London
NW3
01 794 5788

Universal World Harmony
(pp.119–21)
1 St George's Square,
St Annes-on-sea, Lancs. FY8 2NY

Gurdjieff Society (p.123)
B.M. 4752, London WC1V 6XX

The Dicker (p. 123–4)
The Secretary, The Dicker, Upper
Dicker, Hailsham, Sussex BN27 3QH

**Institute for the Comparative Study
of History, Philosophy & the
Sciences and International Academy
for Continuous Education**
(pp.124–5)
Sherborne House, Sherborne, Glos.
GL54 3DZ
045 184 448

**Teilhard Centre for the Future of
Man** (p.127–8)
St Mark's Chambers, Kennington
Park Road, London SE11 4PW
01 582 9510

Grail Foundation of Great Britain
(p.129)
10 Dryden Chambers, 119 Oxford
Street, London W1R IPA
01 437 5338

**Movement of Spiritual Inner
Awareness** (pp.130–1)
4 Athena Court, St John's Wood,
London NW8
01 586 4125
or
P.O. Box 3935, Los Angeles,
California 90051, U.S.A.

Findhorn Foundation (pp.131–4)
The Park, Findhorn Bay, Forres,
Moray IV36 QTY
03093 311

Church of Scientology (pp.134–7)
Saint Hill Manor, East Grinstead,
Sussex
0342 24571
See also: London and Edinburgh

Order of the Pyramid and the Sphinx
(pp.138–9)
The House of Maat, Queen Anne's
Gardens, Bedford Park, London W4

Order of the Cross (pp.139–41)
10 De Vere Gardens, London W8
5AE

Esoteric Society (p.141)
40 Buckingham Gate, London SW1
01 828 2702 or 01 222 4683

Avatar (p.142)
52 Victoria Road, London W8

The Emin (pp.142–4)
St Martin's Church Hall,
Vicar's Road, Gospel Oak,
London NW5

Axminster Light Centre (pp.144–5)
Clinton House, Castle Hill,
Axminster, Devon EX13 5RL

Dartington Solar Quest (pp.145–7)
Apple Green Court, Dartington,
Totnes, Devon TQ9 6NU
080426 630

Aetherius Society (pp.147–50)
757 Fulham Road, London SW6
5UU
01 736 4187 or 01 731 1094

Viewpoint Aquarius (pp.150–1)
c/o Fish Tanks Ltd, 49 Blandford
Street, London W1
01 935 3719

The Atlanteans (pp.151–3)
42 St George's Street, Cheltenham
GL50 4AF
See also: London, Slough, Bristol

The Institute of Pyramidology
(pp.153–4)
31 Station Road, Harpenden, Herts.
AL5 4XB

The Druid Order (pp.154–6)
77 Carlton Avenue, London SE21
01 693 4748

Order of Bards, Ovates and Druids
(pp.156–7)
42 Gledstanes Road, London W14
9HU

Torc (p.158)
3 Jacobs Close, Windmill Hill,
Glastonbury, Somerset

**Society for the Preservation of the
Glastonbury Zodiac** (pp.158–9)
Rollo Maughfling, Dove Cottage,
Mill Road, Barton St David,
Somerset

Holonomics Group (p.162)
c/o Alan Mayne, 63a Muswell
Avenue, London N1O 2EH
01 883 7703

World Congress of Faiths (p.163)
Younghusband House, 23 Norfolk
Square, London W2 1RU
01 723 9820

Acacia House
Centre Avenue, The Vale, Acton,
London W3
01 743 1463

School of Economic Science
90 Queensgate, London SW7 5AB
01 373 1984
An esoteric school based on
Ouspensky's and Gurdjieff's
teachings

GENERAL

Wrekin Trust (pp.159–60)
Bowers House, Bowers Lane,
Bridstow, Ross-on-Wye,
Herefordshire HR9 6QQ
0989 4853

Human Development Trust
(pp.161–2)
16a Hallowell Road, Northwood,
Middlesex HA6 1DW
Secretary: Emily Skillen

**U.K. Advisory Council for Human
Development** (p.162)
Hon. Secretary: Sir John Sinclair Bt.,
16 Great Ormond Street, London
WC1N 3RB

The Soil Association
Walnut Tree Manor, Haughley,
Stowmarket, Suffolk
044970 235

Speakers International Agency Ltd
77 New Bond Street, London
W1
01 493 3321
Publishes directory of New Age
speakers available for lectures.
Contact: Marie-Louise Lacy

Science of Thought Review
Bosham House, Chichester,
Sussex
PO18 8PJ
Officially a monthly magazine
devoted to the teaching of Henry
Thomas Hamblin, it has a very wide
catalystic influence. Editor: Claire
Cameron

ASTROLOGY

**Astrological Lodge of the
Theosophical Society** (p.166)
50 Gloucester Place, London W1
01 935 9261

Faculty of Astrological Studies
(pp.166–7)
Hook Cottage, Vines Cross,
Heathfield, Sussex

Astrological Association (pp.167–8)
36 Tweedy Road, Bromley, Kent
01 464 3853
For information about local groups,
contact Bob Tully, 56 Fielding Way,
Brentwood, Essex CM13 WN
0277 266194

Mayo School of Astrology (p.168)
Piper's Wood, Slackhead, Beetham,
Milmthorpe, Westmorland

John Iwan (pp.168–9)
B.C.M. Aquarius, London WC1
01 242 2320

White Eagle Lodge (p.169)
New Lands, Rake, Liss, Hants.
London Headquarters: 9 St Mary
Abbot's Place, London W8
01 603 7914

Federation of British Astrologers
c/o Y.M.C.A., 16 Great Russell
Street, London WC1

Astroscope (p.169)
23 Abingdon Road, London W8
01 937 0102

Bhagawan Soaham (pp.169–70)
90 Alma Road, London SW18
01 870 3602

PSYCHIC AND SPIRITUALIST

Society for Psychical Research
(pp.172–4)
1 Adam & Eve Mews, Kensington,
London W8 6UQ
01 937 8984

College of Psychic Studies (pp.174–6)
16 Queensberry Place, South
Kensington, London SW7 2EB
01 589 3292

**Spiritualist Association of Great
Britain** (pp.178–80)
33 Belgrave Square, London SW1
01 235 3351

Spiritualists' National Union
(pp.180–2)
Britten House, Stanstead Hall,
Stanstead, Essex CM24 8UD
0279 812705

Arthur Findlay College (p.182)
Stanstead Hall, Standstead
Mountfichet, Essex CM24 8UD
0279 813636

White Eagle Lodge (pp.184–7)
New Lands, Rake, Liss, Hampshire
GU33 7HY
073082 3300
or
9 St Mary Abbot's Place, Kensington,
London W8
01 603 7914

Psychic Press Ltd (pp.187–8)
23 Great Queen Street, London
WC2B 5BB
01 405 2914/5

Confraternity of Faithists
(pp.188–9)
Kosmon Press, BM/KCKP, London
WCIV 6XX
01 405 1420

World Healing Crusade (pp.214–15)
476 Lytham Road, Blackpool FF1
JF. Bro. Kennett (U.K.) Bro. Hardus
(World)

**Greater World Christian
Spirtualists' League** (pp.182–4)
3 Lansdowne Road, Holland Park,
London W11
01 727 7264

The Christian Parapsychologist
Produced on behalf of the
Committee for the Study of Psychic
Phenomena of the Churches'
Fellowship for Psychical and
Spiritual Studies, and published
quarterly. Editor: Leslie Price,
12 Carlton Road, London
W4
01 994 2002

FRINGE MEDICINE

Natural Therapeutics

I.F.P.N.T. and P.P.C.N.T.
(pp.193–4)
Robert J. Bloomfield (Liaison)
21 Bingham Place,
London W1M 3FM
01 935 6933

British Homeopathic Association
(p.195)
27a Devonshire Street, London W1
01 935 2163

Nelson's Homeopathic Dispensary
73 Duke Street, Grosvenor Square,
London W1
01 629 3118

National Institute of Medical Herbalists
(pp.196–7)
68 London Road, Leicester

Society of Herbalists
(p.197)
21 Bruton Street, London W1
01 629 3157

General Council and Register of Consultant Herbalists
(p.197)
Abbots Barton, Worthy Road,
Winchester, Hants.
0962 2156

Bach Centre
(pp.197–9)
Mount Vernon, Sotwell,
Wallingford, Berks.

Nature Cure Clinic
(pp.199–200)
13 Oldbury Place, London W1
01 935 2787

Tyringham Naturopathic Clinic
(pp.200–1)
Newport Pagnell, Bucks.
0908 610450

Acupuncture Association (pp.202–3)
2 Harrowby Court, Seymour Place,
London W1
01 723 4107

Vegan Society
(pp.203–4)
47 Highlands Road, Leatherhead,
Surrey
53 72389

The Vegetarian Society (pp.204–5)
Parkdale, Altrincham, Cheshire or
53 Marloes Road, London W8

E.S.P. Groups

British Society of Dowsers (p.206)
P. B. Smithett (Secretary),
19 High Street, Eydon, Daventry,
Northants.
0327 60525

Delawarr Laboratories
(p.208)
Raleigh Park, Oxford
0865 48572

Radionic Association
(pp.208–9)
J. Wilcox (Secretary),
Field House, Peaslake, Guildford,
Surrey
0306 730080

Keys Trust
(p.209)
Same address as Radionic
Association

Psionic Medical Society (pp.209–10)
Carl Upton (Secretary),
Garden Cottage, Beacon Hills Park,
Hindhead, Surrey

Company of Somatographers
(pp.210–11)
Bryn Jones, 39 Nottingham Place,
London W1
01 935 5964

Spiritual Healing and Christian Groups

National Federation of Spiritual
Healers   (pp.211–12)
Shortacres, Churchill, Loughton,
Essex
01 508 8218

Burrswood Clinic   (pp.212–13)
Groombridge, Tunbridge Wells,
Kent
089 276 353

Churches' Council for Health and
Healing   (pp.213–14)
8–10 Denman Street, London
W1
01 439 3871

World Healing Crusade (pp.214–15)
476 Lytham Road, Blackpool,
Lancs.
0253 43701

Foundation for the Wholeness of
Man   (p.215)
Iona House, 234 Unthank Road,
Norwich
0603 56546

Healing Centres and Organisations

Health for the New Age (pp.215–16)
1a Addison Crescent, London W14
01 603 7751

Hygeia Studios   (pp.216–17)
Brook House, Avening, Tetbury,
Glos.
045 383 2150

Alexander Technique Institute
3 Albert Court, London SW7
01 589 3834

British Society of Dowsers
High Street, Eydon, Daventry,
Northants.
032 76 0525

Chapman, George
St Bride's, 149 Wendover Road,
Aylesbury, Bucks.
Psychic surgery

DEVELOPMENT GROUPS

Arica Institute   (pp.220–2)
57 Marlborough Mansions,
Cannon Hill, London NW6
01 435 6902

Quaesitor   (pp.222–3)
187 Walm Lane, London NW2
01 452 8489

Community   (pp.224–5)
15 Highbury Grange, London N5
01 359 1372

Bristol Encounter Centre (pp.225–6)
28 Drakes Way, Portishead, Bristol
0272 7490

Atma Growth Centre   (pp.226–7)
72a Wake Green Road, Moseley,
Birmingham 13
021449 2947

Centre House   (pp.227–8)
10a Airlie Gardens, London W8 7AL
01 727 3865

Sempervivum Trust (pp.228–9)
c/o Catherine Gillespie,
15 Falkland Gardens,
Edinburgh EH12 6UW
031334 7175

**Centre for Group Work and
Sensitivity Training** (pp.229–30)
Hans Lobstein,
7 Chesham Terrace, Ealing,
London W13
Similar groups, see Pt IIB under
SW2, Hants, W. Yorks, Lancs,
Northumb.
01 579 2411 Ext. 231
Or: 01 579 2424 Ext. 409

Entropy (pp.230–1)
Ronald Ullman,
Flat 8, 11 Lindfield Gardens,
London NW3 6PX
01 435 8427

London School of Bodymind Health
(pp.231–3)
Ruth Harrison,
10 Steeles Mews South, London NW3
01 586 4109

Centre for Human Communication
(pp.233–5)
63 Abbey Road, Torquay, Devon
0803 28802

Institute of Psychosynthesis (p.235)
Highwood Park, Nan Clark's Lane,
Mill Hill, London NW7
01 959 3372

**Hallam Centre for Transactional
Analysis and Related Studies**
(pp.236–7)
Weston House, West Barr Green,
Sheffield SL 2DL
0742 20869

Institute of Transactional Analysis
(pp.237–8)
52 Cranley Gardens, Palmers Green,
London N13 4LS
Contact: Dr Margaret Turpin and
Dr Michael Reddy
01 889 4311

For general **Transactional
Association** activities, contact:
David Porter,
Flat B, 56 Westwood Road,
Southampton SO2 1DP
0703 551335

Human Cybernetics Trust (pp.238–9)
Contact: George Hall,
London W1A 4WL
01 935 6373

**The Centre for Therapeutic
Communications** (pp.239–41)
46 Antrim Mansions, Antrim Road,
London NW3

**Franklin School of Contemporary
Studies** (pp.241–2)
43 Adelaide Road, London NW3
01 722 0562

**Organisation Research and
Development Ltd** (p.243)
Dean Cottage, Water End, Ashdon,
Saffron Walden, Essex
079 984 592

**Churchill Centre and Centre for
Bio-Energy** (pp.243–5)
22 Montague Street, London W1
01 402 9475

Human Potential Research Project
(pp.245–6)
Centre for Adult Education,
University of Surrey, Guildford,
Surrey
Project director: John Heron
0483 71281

**The Association for Humanistic
Psychology** (p.246)
57 Minster Road, London NW2 3RE
01 435 9200

Energy and Character
Abbotsbury Publications,
Abbotsbury, Weymouth, Dorset
Quarterly journal on Reichian
bio-energetics

Creative Action
This training is the result of several years of intensive research, originally sponsored by the Science Research Council, aimed at understanding the nature of creativity, and how it might be quickly developed and released across society. Pilot courses have been given in industry and at universities in the U.K., and abroad over the past few years, and the training is now being launched on a wider scale.

For further information contact:
Ted Matchett, 14 Montrose Avenue, Redland, Bristol BS6 6EO

(b) The Regional Centres

The chief characteristic of the New Age movement is in the coming together and co-operation between diverse groups, especially within a community. The purpose of this section of the book is to list as many regional centres as possible. We are aware that it is incomplete, so please send to the editor, Stephen Annett, c/o Turnstone Books, your suggestions for new information for the next edition. Please refer to the map for the regional breakdown. Where a centre is affiliated to a national society, the page reference to that organisation is given. In London, the order is by postal district; outside London centres are arranged alphabetically by town within the county.

LONDON

Central

Krishna Consciousness Movement
(pp.51–3)
7 Bury Place, WC1
01 405 1463

South Place Ethical Society
Conway Hall Humanist Centre,
Red Lion Square, WC1R 4RL
Advocates ethical humanism.
Secretary: Peter Cadogan
01 242 8032

Homeopathic Hospital
Great Ormond Street, WC2
01 837 3091

Watkins Bookshop
Cecil Court, Charing Cross Road,
WC2
Still the best specialised bookshop
in Britain. Has a branch in Lower
Belgrave Street, SW1

Southwest

Spiritual Regeneration Movement
(T.M.)
(pp.62–4)
Central London Centre,
65 Winchester Street, SW1

Wherley, Casper
(pp.229–30)
15 Chatsworth Avenue, London SW2
Wednesday evenings: drop-in groups,
on similar lines to Hans Lobstein's
Centre for Group Work and
Sensitivity Training
01 540 3521

Holy Trinity Church
Rev. Nicholas Rivett-Carnac,
Brompton Road, SW3

Divine Light Mission
(pp.53–6)
131 Clapham High Street, SW4
01 622 9261

Ananda Marga
c/o Virupaksa and Eomati,
14 Hendrick Avenue, SW12

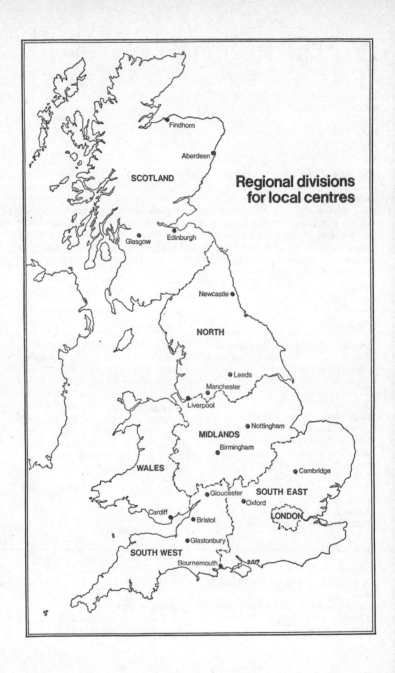

Regional divisions for local centres

Anthroposophical Society (p.115)
Mrs A. Raeside,
3 Park Avenue, East Sheen, SW14

**Theravada School of Buddhism
and Buddhapadipa Temple**
(pp.102–3)
99 Christchurch Road, East Sheen,
SW14
01 876 9188

Sivananda Yoga Centre
175 Finborough Road, SW17
01 970 5374

The Forum
6 Parkwood Road, Wimbledon,
SW19 7AQ
Contact: Joyce Purcell 6–10 am.:
01 947 2626 or
Hilary Ricketts eves: 01 278 6379
Runs courses in Wimbledon, Earl's
Court and South Kensington, in Sufi
dancing, esoteric philosophy,
Christian mysticism and astrology.

Science of Mind Centre
16 The Crescent, SW19

Mystic Forum
114 Kings Road,
Kingston on Thames, Surrey
01 549 2601
Organises lectures on occult subjects,
tours and a quarterly journal.
Secretary: Mrs S. Rouseet

**North Surrey Positive Health and
Growth Centre**
c/o Spelthorne Institute of Further
Education.
Contact: Ron Shepherd, The Flat,
36a Kingston Road, Staines,
Middlesex
81 57372
Organises evening classes,
workshops, etc. in wide variety of
growth techniques incl. encounter,
meditation, psychosynthesis.
Lunch and coffee bar

West

Church of Scientology (pp.134–7)
68 Tottenham Court Road, W1
01 580 3601

British Hypnotherapy Centre
67 Upper Berkeley Street, W1
01 262 8852

United Lodge of the Theosophists
(pp.110–12)
62 Queens Gardens, W2

Society of the Inner Light
3 Queensborough Terrace, W2

Buddhist Vihara (pp.101–2)
5 Heathfield Gardens, Chiswick
Corner, W4
01 995 9493

**Spiritual Regeneration Movement
(T.M.)** (pp.62–4)
West London Centre,
15 Herne Road, W4
01 995 0455

Liu Clinic and School
13 Gunnersbury Avenue, Ealing, W5
01 993 2549

Atlanteans (pp. 151–3)
The Drama Studio,
Cnr. Grange Road and Ealing
Green, W5
01 579 3796
Meetings held first Thursday in every
month at 8 p.m.
Secretary: Betty Wood

Christian Community (pp.29–30)
Temple Lodge,
51 Queen Caroline Street, W6 9QL
01 748 8388

Cosmic Forum
Cosmo Box C.F.,
17 Luxembourg Gardens, Brook
Green, Hammersmith W6

263

Centre House (pp.227–8)
10a Airlie Gardens, W8 7AL
01 727 3865

Truth Forum
57 Biddulph Mansions,
Elgin Avenue, W9
01 286 3891

Cope Trust
15 Acklem Road, W10
Contact: Brian Wade.
01 969 9790
Community-based organisation
aiming to stimulate community
concern and action about mental
problems. Encounter groups,
women's groups, Sunday social

B.I.T. Information Service and Help
Centre
141 Westbourne Park Road, W11
01 229 8219

Gentle Ghost Services
33 Norland Road, W11
Secretary: Hugh Berger.
01 603 8983/2871
A successful community experiment
in helping people to work
responsibly and to explore individual
growth. The jobs are mostly
skilled – decorating, removing,
secretarial, etc. Courses in
alternative medicine, yoga,
psychology, theatre and dance and
many others. Important emphasis on
advice and counselling and on trade
apprenticeships. Restaurant is
popular. A centre with wide impact.

Kundalini Yoga Centre
22 All Saints Road, W11
01 727 8487

Ecumenical Centre
9 Denbigh Road, Notting Hill Gate,
W11
Many different groups meet here.

Meditation Group
Leighton House,
12 Holland Park Road, W11

School of Meditation (p.64)
158 Holland Park Avenue, W11
Transcendental meditation
01 603 6116

**Centre for Group Work and
Sensitivity Training** (pp.229–30)
Hans Lobstein,
7 Chesham Terrace, Ealing, W13
01 579 2411 Ext. 231
01 579 2424 Ext. 409

**Consciousness Training and
Research Group**
Ian Gordon-Brown/B. Somers,
Talgarth Centre,
143 Talgarth Road, W14 9DA
Weekend workshops in
Transpersonal psychology,
relaxation, body awareness, esoteric
psychology and astrology

Northwest

Compendium Books
240 Camden High Street, NW1
Wide range of cheaper books on all
New Age subjects

Nirvana Rajneesh Meditation Centre
82 Bell Street, NW1
01 262 0991

**Islamic Cultural Centre and London
Mosque**
Regents Lodge, 146 Park Road, NW1

Quaesitor (pp.224–5)
187 Walm Lane, NW2
01 452 8489

Ugyen Cho Ling
The centre of Tulku Sogyal Lakar,
Tibetan teacher (Northwest London)
Contact: Dominique Side,
6 St Phillips Road, London, E8

Yoga Centre
13 Hampstead Hill Gardens, NW3
01 794 4119

Entropy (pp.230–1)
Ronald Ullman, 11 Linfield Gardens,
NW3 6PX
01 435 8427

Nicholas Roerich Society
Secretary: Kenneth Archer.
91 Fitzjohn's Avenue, NW3 6NX
01 435 5490
To promote interest in the ideals of
Prof. Roerich, a Russian artist,
lecturer and philosopher

Agni Yoga Workshop
c/o Kenneth Archer, 91 Fitzjohn's
Avenue, NW3 6NX
01 435 5490
A loose association related to the
A.Y. Society Inc. of New York, to
study the esoteric knowledge of the
teaching of the Hierarchy of Light

Christian Community (pp.29–30)
34 Glenilla Road, NW3 4AP
01 722 3587

**Franklin School of Contemporary
Studies** (pp.241–2)
43 Adelaide Road, NW3 30B
01 722 0562

London School of Bodymind Health
(pp.231–3)
Ruth Harrison, 10 Steeles Mews
South, NW3
01 586 4109

B. K. Raja Yoga Centre
98 Tennyson Road, NW6
01 328 2478
A centre of the Raja Yoga University
of Brahma Kumaris in Mt Abu,
India. Regular classes

Arica Institute (pp.220–2)
57 Marlborough Mansions, Cannon
Hill, NW6
01 435 6902

The Terrace
8 Tayler Court, Alexandra Road,
NW8 OSB
01 722 4930
Small group sympathetic with
Findhorn's philosophy. Silent
meetings, discussion groups, music
and ritual dance. Contact: Margery
Hurst

North

Rajneesh Meditation Centre
(pp.60–2)
47 Lonsdale Square, N1
01 607 7848
Bhagwan Rajneesh is a retired
professor of philosophy who lives in
Poona. His methods emphasise the
rediscovery of our natures through
use of physical energy. His
techniques have similarities with
those of Wilhelm Reich. There is a
full programme of daily, weekly and
a fortnight's course in meditation.
Whirling on Hampstead Heath.
Taped lectures of Bhagwan. Gestalt,
Encounter and Bio-energetic
workshops

Hakurenji
40 Deansway, East Finchley, N2
Contact: Mushindokai

Community (pp.224–5)
15 Highbury Grange, N5
01 359 1372

Divine Light Mission (pp.53–6)
Divine Residence, 3 Woodside
Avenue, N6
01 883 5386

Self Health Centre
507 Caledonian Road, N7
Community healing

**Spiritual Regeneration Movement
(T.M.)** (pp.62–4)
North London Centre, 69 Woodland
Rise, London N10
01 883 0832

Beshara (pp.84–6)
31 Raydon Street, N17
01 272 0777

Hindu Cultural Society
82 Saxon Road, Southall, Middlesex

Southeast

Atlanteans (pp.151–3)
St Mary's Church Hall, College
Road, Bromley, Kent

Buddhist Society
Mrs Keegin,
78 Alexandra Court, Bromley, Kent

Miraculous Research Foundation
Effiom Okon Ephraim, Efikon House,
36 Eggerton Drive, West Greenwich

**Spiritual Regeneration Movement
(T.M.)** (pp.62-4)
South London Centre, 2 Gilkes
Crescent, SE21
01 693 5640

Divine Light Mission (pp.53–6)
Palace of Peace, 72 Grove Vale,
SE22
01 693 9511

White Rose Foundation
Monywa, 623 Davidson Road,
Croydon, Surrey
Contact: Leslie Harvey
01 654 6879

Anthroposophical Society (p.115)
Mr & Mrs D. Bromige, 48 Norfolk
Avenue, Sanderstead, S. Croydon
CR2 8BP

SOUTH EAST

Berkshire

Priory Centre
Binfield
Contact: Mrs H. F. Stanley
Small conference and retreat centre
0344 3417

Unification Church
D. Orme, Dorney Cottage, Dorney,
Windsor
734 472299

University Buddhist Society
Miss White, Fine Arts Dept, Reading
University, London Road, Reading

Anthroposophical Society (p.115)
W. Nobes, 40 Howell Road, Sutton
Courtenay

Buckinghamshire

Brotherhood of the Christ Light
Sunbeam Ends, Latimer Road,
Chesham
Retreats, healing community

Wheel of Yoga (pp.91–3)
66 George Street, Chesham
Yoga centre. Courses, retreats,
research

Atlanteans (pp.151–3)
Eric Stannard, 57 Langley Road,
Slough

Cambridgeshire

Beshara (pp.84–6)
80–2 Fitzroy Street, Cambridge
0223 67052

Divine Light Mission (pp.53–6)
14 Pretoria Road, Cambridge

Sufi Group
Mrs Mansower Thomas, Thatched
Cottage, Caxton Road, Cambridge

266

Essex

Anthroposophical Society (p.115)
Mrs W. Elin, Green Island, Adleigh

Essex Healers' Association
E. S. Bredin, 17 Fernwood, Hadleigh, Benfleet

Buddhist Group
Harry Knight, 262 Halling Hill, Harlow
0279 25432

Kham Tibetan House (Inst. for Tibetan Religious & Cultural Studies) (p.105–6)
Rectory Lane, Ashdon, Saffron Walden CR10 2HM
079984 415

Organisation Research and Development Ltd (p.243)
Dean Cottage, Water End, Ashdon, Saffron Walden
079984 592

Hampshire

Buddhist Society (pp.99–100)
Mrs Sue Tucker, Loraine, Hamble River Boatyard, Lower Swanwick

Krishnamurti Educational Centre
Brockwood Park, Bramdean, Alresford

Saltings Caravan Site
Godshill, Fordingbridge SP6 2LN
0425 53401
Contact: Mrs K. Trevelyan.
Retreat community of 6 caravans for families or small groups.
Optional hour's work together; meditation, music, shared meal.
Sympathetic Wrekin Trust, Steiner, Sherborne, etc. An 'open centre'

Merrilyn and Terry
Oatlands Guest House, Copse Lane, Freshwater, Isle of Wight
Group on similar lines to Centre for Group Work and Sensitivity Training

Ramana Health Centre
Ludshott Manor Hospital for Natural Medicine, Bramshott, Liphook GU30 7RD
Dr Chandra Sharma's centre

Buddhist Society (pp.99–100)
39 West Street, Ryde, Isle of Wight

Encounter Groups
Contact: Merrilyn and Terry, Oatlands Guest House, Copse Lane, Freshwater, I.O.W. *See* Hans Lobstein (pp.229–30)

Transactional Association (pp.237–8)
D. Porter, Flat B, 56 Westwood Road, Southampton SO2 1DP
0703 551335

Hertfordshire

Anthroposophical Society (p.115)
Mrs M. Macpherson, 67 Hampstead Road, King's Langley

Christian Community (pp.29–30)
The Priory, King's Langley, WD4 9HH
40 67262

Universal Peace Mission
Purple Heather Farm, Cholesbury, Tring

Shantock Coach House
Bovington, Herts
0442 832339
Contact: Dr John Mason
Principally a work and seminars centre for those connected with Sherborne and the J. G. Bennett groups. Also Sunday p.m. open meditation

Kent

Krishnamurti Foundation
24 Southend Road, Beckenham

Atlanteans (pp.151–3)
St Mary's Church Hall, College
Road, Bromley

Beshara (pp.84–6)
17 New Street, St Dunstan's,
Canterbury
0227 53504

Anthroposophical Society (p.115)
Mr A. Brockman, Perry Court Farm,
Petham, Canterbury

Deva
12 Church Street, Folkestone
0303 53700
Discriminating metaphysical
bookshop and wholefood shop.
Publishes magazine *Towards the
Infinite*

West Kent Natural Healing Centre
Dr C. Tuttle, 30 St John's Hill,
Sevenoaks
0732 54158

Grail Foundation
C. Whitfield Kingdom, 22 Preston
Court, Sidcup

Anthroposophical Society (p.115)
Dr L. Engel, 9 Blatchington Road,
Tunbridge Wells

Meditation Group for the New Age
Sundial House, Nevill Court,
Tunbridge Wells TN4 8NJ
A centre based on the teaching of
Alice Bailey, which runs
well-established courses in
meditation for the New Age

Norfolk

Anthroposophical Society (p.115)
Mrs R. Eedle, 3 Beatty Road, Eaton
Rise, Norwich NR4 6RQ

St Barnabus Counselling Centre
Derby Street, Norwich, NOR 61K

**Foundation for the Wholeness of
Man** (p.215)
Iona House, 234 Unthank Road,
Norwich
0603 56546

**Friends of the Garden Central Seed
Centre**
24 St Margaret's Close, Norstead,
Norwich

Oxon

Swanlands
Ingrid Lind, Top Hill Lane, Chinnor,
Oxford OX9 4BH
0844 51405
Small conference and meditation
centre. By previous arrangement only

Beshara (pp.84–6)
1 Moreton Road, Oxford
0865 54456

Living Art
Michael Exchange, 39 Holywell
Street, Oxford

New Age Education Group
Mrs E. Horne, 99 Banbury Road,
0X2 61X
Cassette-taped readings of a number
of books available on free loan

Buddhist Society (pp.99–100)
Mrs Flint, 50 Park Town, Oxford

Sufi Group
C. Clark, The Square,
Stow-on-the-Wold

Surrey

Viewpoint Aquarius
Fish Tanks Ltd, 49 Blandford Street,
London W1
Regular meetings held in Camberley
on U.F.Os, Yoga, healing, theosophy;
study groups on esoteric
mathematics; *Viewpoint* published
monthly

Science of Mind
Michael Grimes, 63 Nonsuch Walk,
Cheam

Shree Gurudev Ashram
Coxhill, Cobham

Anthroposophical Society (p.115)
Mr A. G. Wills, 75 Fairdene Road,
Coulsdon CR3 1RJ

Human Potential Research Project
Centre for Adult Education,
University of Surrey, Guildford
0483 71281
Project Director: John Heron

Aryatara Buddhist Community
(p.101)
Sarum House, 3 Plough Lane, Purley
01 660 2542

Church Healing Ministry Trust
18 Harefield Avenue, Cheam, Sutton
Contact: Mr J. W. Head

Kosmon Unity
Walton Manor North,
Walton-on-the-Hill, Tadworth

Natural Body Movement Centre
30 Wey Barton, Byfleet, Weybridge
KT14 7EF
Contact: D. Chapman
91 43020

Smith, M.
11 Broadwater Close, Woodham
Lane, Woking GU21 5TW
91 41619
Lectures and demonstrations
highlighting the latent abilities
within man, leading to self awareness
and realisation

**Society for Spreading the Knowledge
of True Prayer**
P.O. Box 29, Woking

Sussex

Rosicrucians
Queensway House, Bognor Regis

Divine Healing Mission
(p.214)
The Old Rectory, Crowhurst,
Battle
A small but important centre

Sufi Group
Norman Gregory, 293 South Coast
Road, Peacehaven, Brighton

Beshara (pp.84–6)
7 Ditchling Rise, Brighton
0273 693775

Anthroposophical Society (p.115)
Mrs H. Jarman, 15 Montpelier
Villas, Brighton

Ruhani Satsang
M. Waterfield, 10 Tott Yew Road,
Lower Willingdon, Eastbourne
03212 3502

Anthroposophical Society (p.115)
Mr J. Cornish, 54 Watts Lane,
Eastbourne

Anthroposophical Society (p.115)
Mr J. Davy, Lindon Cottage,
Ashdown Road, Forest Row

Christian Community (pp.29–30)
The Barn, Wood's Hill Lane, East
Grinstead RH19 3RQ
034282 2054

Anthroposophical Society (p.115)
Mrs T. Larg, 2 Wayside, E. Dean,
Eastbourne

The Dicker (pp.123–4)
The Dicker, Upper Dicker,
Hailsham
BN27 3QH

Rosicrucian Fellowship Centre
W. Horn, 5 Honeysuckle Lane,
Golden Cross, Hailsham

Porter, Mrs Erika
15 Birchen Lane, Haywards Heath
0444 4910
Meditation and discussion group

Christian Healing Fellowship
3 Cokeham Lane, Sompton,
Lancing

New Renascence
Weald, Laughton, Lewes BN8 6AH
Secretary: D. de C. Baker
032183 325
Puts into practice the creative
psychological ideas of Ian Fearn

Sphere Club Spiritual Foundation
Greenacres, 24 Firlie Road, North
Lancing BN15 0N2

Capstick, Dr Norman
22 Arundel Gardens, Rustington,
Worthing BN16 3TH
One or two groups meet once a week
for meditation, lectures and
discussion

WEST

Avon

Bath New Age Centre
16 Old Orchard Street, Bath
Contact: Francis Leonard
0225 77377
or Russ Needham
0225 28728

Anthroposophical Society (p.115)
J. Turner, Daneslea, St Catherine's
Court, Bathwick Hill, Bath

Western Meditation Centre
17 Park Street, Bath
Emphasis on Western traditions of
meditation, mysticism and magic

Divine Light Mission (p.53–6)
103 Belmont Road, St Andrews,
Bristol
0272 48545

Bristol Encounter Centre (p.225–6)
28 Drake's Way, Portishead, Bristol
0272 7490

Anthroposophical Society (p.115)
M. Madge, 12 Cavendish Road,
Westbury-on-Tryn, Bristol BS9 4DZ

Christian Community (pp.29–30)
6 Hillside, Cotham, Bristol
BS6 6JP
0272 36612

Beshara (pp.84–6)
20 Theresa Avenue, Bishopston,
Bristol 7
0272 421913

Atlanteans (pp.151–3)
Oakfield Road Unitarian Church,
Clifton, Bristol 8

Arkle, William
Backwell Hill House, Backwell,
Bristol BS19 3DB
Residential and non-residential
groups on esoteric ideas, painting
and music

Cornwall

**Devon & Cornwall Healers'
Association**
Major M. McDermott, Clifftop,
Upton, Bude, Cornwall
EX23 0LY

Vipassana Growth Centre
Director: V. R. Dhiravamsa
Carn Entral Farm, Beacon,
Camborne TR14 9AJ
020 92 5579

Buddhist Centre
Enprill Farm, Beacon, Camborne
Community of 12 residents, planning
to be self-supporting, living off the
produce of their land

Buddhist Group
W. B. Picard, The Mousehole
Pottery, Mousehole

Divine Light Mission   (pp.53–6)
Paradise Farm, Mullion,
Penzance
032624 366

Khankah Wahdat
Karima Clark, Higher Penals,
St Agnes
087255 2530
Sufi Khankah, following teachings of
Hazrat Inayat-Khan. Affiliated to the
Khankah Abadan-Abad,
Dockenfield, Surrey

St Austell Spiritualist Society
Doublegates, Edgecombe Road,
St Austell

Theosophical Society   (pp.110–12)
Peter Dorey, 38 Falmouth Road,
Truro

Devon

North Devon Movement
107 Pilton Street, Barnstaple
0271 5665
Publishes magazine: *Voices of
North Devon*

Saunders Bookshop
Queen Street, Barnstaple

Ashram
King Street, Combe Martin
Active local centre-courses in
healing, Christian mysticism, yoga,
dream interpretation, self-regulation,
etc. Very simple accommodation. No
fees, only donations. Director: Tony
Crisp

Moongate
Mrs Freda Jenkins, Stoke Hill,
Exeter EX4 9JN
0392 75991
Retreat centre; meditation, healing,
esoteric philosophy – by previous
arrangement only

Valley Meditation Centre
Lynton
05985 2285
Contact: Dinah Day.
Gives low cost meditation courses.
No particular sect, but influenced by
Dhiravamsa's teachings

Lodge of Light and Love
Healing Clinic, British Red Cross
Society, 1 Midvale Road, Paignton
TQ4 5BD
A free healing and helping clinic,
every Wednesday morning.
Contact: Mr H. G. Weston

Sidmouth House
Cotmaton Road, Sidmouth
EX10 8ST
03955 3963
Retreat centre, affiliated to the
Scientific and Medical Network for
research into the paranormal and the
spiritual content of philosophy,
psychology and healing. Available
for group meetings and conferences.
Contact: Mrs E. M. Noakes

Mermaid Bookshop
Sidmouth

Anthroposophical Society   (p.115)
Miss W. Andrews, 93 Forest Road,
Torquay

Centre for Human Communication
(pp.233–5)
63 Abbey Road, Torquay
0803 28802

Dartington Solar Quest   (pp.145–7)
Apple Green Court, Dartington,
Totnes TQ9 6NU
0803 863924
Yoga and healing groups; mass
healing services, weekly lectures.
Contact: Mr D. I. Hunt

Anthroposophical Society   (p.115)
Mrs P. Bearden, Perry Elms,
Woodbury Salterton, Exeter

Dorset

Science of Mind Centre
3 Alumdale Road, Westbourne,
Bournemouth
0202 763554
Contact: Mrs K. M. Green

Church of Religious Science
Rev. N. Boyd, 138 Richmond Park
Road, Bournemouth
BH8 8TW
0202 57908

Gloucestershire

Anthroposophical Society   (p.115)
Mrs Anne Druith, 73 Cainscross
Road, Stroud GL5 4HB

Christian Community   (pp.29–30)
73 Cainscross Road, Stroud
GL5 4HB
04536 4764

Atlanteans   (pp.151–3)
Mrs Lewis, House of Isis, 42 St
George's Street, Cheltenham
GL50 4AF

Universal World Harmony
The Red House, Lansdown Road,
Cheltenham, Glos.
Meditation centre

Beshara   (pp.84–6)
Swyre Farm, Aldsworth, Cirencester
045184 377
Self-supporting Sufi farming
community

Hawkwood College
B. J. Nesfield-Cookson, Wick Street,
Stroud GL6 7QW
04536 4607
An important conference centre
which issues its own programme

Helios Book Service
8 The Square, Toddington,
Cheltenham GL54 5DL
024681 244
A mail-order bookshop specialising
in occult, metaphysics and New Age
books. Produces monthly catalogue

Somerset

Anthroposophical Society   (p.115)
Mrs Mallet, Curry Mallet, Taunton

Aquarian Centre
Mary Cane, Oaklands, Locks Lane,
Butleigh Wooton

Vita Florum Trust
Cats Castle, Lydeard St Lawrence,
Taunton
Contact: Elizabeth Bellhouse
Produces special mixtures and
ointments for healing

Wiltshire

Atlanteans   (pp.151–3)
Pinehurst Common Room, The
Circle, Pinehurst, Swindon
Contact: Wyn Ratcliffe

MIDLANDS

Derby

Anthroposophical Society (p.115)
Dr T. Gladstone, 51 Longfield Lane,
Ilkeston DE7 4DX

Leicester

Beshara (pp.84–6)
156 St Saviour's Road, Leicester
0533 537968

Leicester Yoga Group
37 Overdale Road, Knighton,
Leicester
0533 884955
Hatha yoga, spiritual healing and
lectures

Leicester Growth Centre
Friends' Meeting House, Queens
Road, Leicester
Contact: Dennis Dunn, 37 Overdale
Road, Knighton, Leicester
0533 884955
Meets each Thursday: yoga, healing,
library, discussion groups, outings

Divine Light Mission (pp.53–6)
157 Mere Road, Leicester
0533 24245

Lincoln

Theosophical Society (pp.110–12)
107 Hawthorn Chase, Lincoln
LN2 4RF
Secretary: Terry Hart
Lodge of Theosophical Society.
Meetings first Wednesday of each
month

Northampton

Buddhist Society (pp.99–100)
C. R. Pettitt, 16 Liddington Way,
Northampton

Nottingham

Anthroposophical Society (p.115)
Mrs F. M. Henton, Lammas Close,
Kneeton Road, East Bridgford

Sri Chinmoy Centre (pp.58–60)
J. & D. Gent, Woodmere, 136
Oaktree Lane, Mansfield

Salop

Buddhist Group
Ebbana Blanchard, 3 Market Street,
Shrewsbury

Warwickshire

Peace Centre
18 Moor Street, Ringway,
Birmingham
021 6430996

Krishna Consciousness Movement
(pp.51–3)
25 Hickman Road, Sparbrook,
Birmingham

Divine Light Mission (pp.53–6)
40 Broad Road, Acocks Green,
Birmingham

Heart of England Mini-Wrekin
F. S. Heilbronn, 12 Church Lane,
Lillington, Leamington Spa
CV32 7RG
A local seed organisation to bring
together different groups

Leamington & District Yoga Circle
B. Sidebotham, 46 Malthouse Lane,
Kenilworth
0926 52638
Affiliated to County Education
authority and to Wheel of Yoga.
Holds classes and seminars in several
local centres

The Other Branch Bookshop
Leamington Spa

Atma Growth Centre (pp.226–7)
72a Wake Green Road, Moseley,
Birmingham 13
021 4492847

West Midlands

Divine Unity of Faith
Sananda, 67 Wildmoor Road,
Shirley, Solihull
021 7448254
Yoga, meditation, lectures. Interested
in flying-saucer contacts. Weekly
meetings (Friday)

Worcestershire

Christian Community (pp.29–30)
22 Baylie Street, Stourbridge
03843 5481

Goethean Science Foundation
Clent Grove, Clent, Stourbridge
Study of spiritual principles in
science

Anthroposophical Society (p.115)
David Clement,
Clent Grove, Stourbridge

Anthroposophical Society (p.115)
Joan Jones, 38 Westminster Road,
Malvern Hills
WR14 4ES

Anthroposophical Society (p.115)
Florence Harioch,
30 Grazebrook Road, Dudley

WALES

Williams, Eileen
11 Hunters Park, Tenby, Dyfed
New Age discussion group;
Agni Yoga group

Theosophical Society (pp.110–12)
206 Newport Road, Cardiff
CF2 1DL, Glam.

Krishna Consciousness Movement
(pp.51–3)
43 Ruby Street, Roath, Cardiff,
Glam.

Anthroposophical Society (p.115)
c/o Russell Evans,
4 Glyndur Road, Penarth, Glam.

Centre of Creative Living
39 Edgeware Road, Uplands,
Swansea, Glam.

Medhope Grove
Tintern, Gwent NP6 7NX
09218 253
Vegetarian guest house and New Age
centre. Director: Harold
Wood

Anthroposophical Society (p.115)
c/o Mr and Mrs Mace,
39 St Hilary's Drive, Deganwy,
Gwynedd

Tyn-y-Fron Farm
Rhiw, Pwllheli, Gwynedd
Contact: Roy Marsden.
A residential art school which also
offers inner work based on
J. G. Bennett's
training

Auroville
Crossgates, Llandrindod Wells,
Radnorshire, Powys.
Yoga, Sri Aurobindo centre

Beshara (pp.84–6)
The Warren Farmhouse,
Rhos-y-Meirch, Knighton, Powys
Intensive courses

NORTH

Cumbria

Christian Community (pp.29–30)
Woodford House, The Heads,
Keswick CA12 5ER
0596 72148

Durham

Anthroposophical Society (p.115)
c/o Mr W. N. Illingworth,
47 South Street, Durham

Humber

University Buddhist and Vedanta Society
Students' Union,
Cottingham Road, Hull

Lancashire

Radiant Creative Thought Group
c/o Rev. M. Hitchen,
Friends' Meeting House, Raikes
Parade, Blackpool

Ruhani Satsang
2 Markfield Road, Bootle

University Buddhist Society
c/o Boonchvay Ketutassa,
Dept of Religious Studies,
Cortmell Cottage, Lancs.

Ananda Marga Yoga
8 Ullet Road, Liverpool 8
Meditation and Hatha yoga

Buddhist Group
16 Judges Drive, Liverpool
051 2630448

Anthroposophical Society (p.115)
c/o Mrs McBrien,
23 Lynton Green, Woodview Road,
Woolton, Liverpool 25

Connell, Heather
Nurses Home,
Withington Hospital, West Didsbury,
Manchester 20
Group similar to Hans Lobstein's
Centre for Groupwork and
Sensitivity Training

Christian Community (pp.29–30)
St Michaels, Spath Road, Didsbury,
Manchseter 2D
061 445 4625

Encounter Groups
Contact: Heather Connell,
Nurses' Home, Withington Hospital,
West Didsbury
See Hans Lobstein (pp.229–30)

Anthroposophical Society (p.115)
c/o B. Switzer,
6 West Place, Manchester M19 2NS

New Jerusalem Fellowship
E. Springett,
Moxham, 8 West View, Ormskirk
Produces monthly magazine devoted
to the New Age

Radiant Creative Thought Group
c/o Rev. M. Hitchen,
20 Scarisbrick Street, Southport

Northumberland

Gilbert, Joan
54 Riding Dene, Mickley, Stocksfield
Group on similar lines to Centre for
Group Work and Sensitivity Training
See Hans Lobstein   (pp.229–30)
06615 3407

Throssel Hole Priory
Carr Shield, Hexham, 04985 204

North Yorkshire

Christian Community   (pp.29–30)
Botton Village, Danby
028 76 281

Ananda Marga
c/o Shyama,
23 Holbeck Road, Scarborough

Anthroposophical Society   (p.115)
Miss M. Wilkinson,
10 St Oswald's Road, York YO1 4PT

University Buddha Dharma Society
c/o Ronald Spencer,
263 Beckfield Lane, Acomb, York

West Yorkshire

Walton, Bill
49 Hartley Crescent, Leeds 6
Residential weekend encounter
group.
See Hans Lobstein   (pp.229–30)
0532 443920

Anthroposophical Society   (p.115)
c/o J. Harman,
2 Oaksfield, Methley, Leeds

Beshara   (pp.84–6)
39a St Michael's Road, Leeds 6 or
c/o 13 Norwood Place, Leeds
0532 785236

Christian Community   (pp.29–30)
15 Kelso Road, Leeds 2

South Yorkshire

People in Sheffield
Rose Evison and Richard Horobin,
3 Clarkehouse Road, Sheffield
0742 686371

**Hallam Centre for Transactional
Analysis and Related Studies**
          (pp.236–7)
Weston House, West Bar Green,
Sheffield S12 DL
0742 20869

Anthroposophical Society   (p.115)
M. E. Battersby, Flat 10, Hunter
Court, Hunter House Road, Sheffield
S11 8TY

Mill House
Aysgarth, Wensleydale
Contact: Peter Charlton.
A centre based on the psychological
principles of J. G. Bennett's
Gurdjieff work. Leatherwork and
potting.

SCOTLAND

Aberdeen

Anthroposophical Society   (p.115)
Mrs M. Kirkaldy, 2 Fonthill
Terrace,
Aberdeen AB1 2UR

Christian Community   (pp.29–30)
7 Queen's Terrace, AB1 1XL
0224 20108

Christian Community   (pp.29–30)
Newton Dee Village, Bieldside
0224 48270

Divine Light Mission   (pp.53–6)
2 Marine Place, Aberdeen
0224 53794

Baha'i   (p.83)
68 Polmuir Road, Aberdeen
0224 20968

Argyle

Argyle Hotel
John Walters, Isle of Iona
Mid-September-mid-June operates
as a New Age conference centre
234

Border

Beshara   (pp.84–6)
Chisholme House, Roberton,
Hawick, Roxburghshire
045088 248/252
Self-sufficient community, providing
6 months' residential courses

Ettrick Shaws Open Centre
Bill and Ludi How,
Ettrick Bridge, Selkirk TD7 5HW
0750 5229
Friendly family hotel (May to
September), 150 miles south of
Edinburgh. Rest of year, conference
centre. Regular meditation and
group work. Library

Dundee

Baha'i   (p.83)
4 Tircarra Bank, Barnhill
0382 730228

Dumfriesshire

Samye-Ling Tibetan Centre
          (pp.104–5)
Eskdalemuir, Langholm
05416 232

Edinburgh

Anthroposophical Society   (p.115)
Mrs C. M. Cook,
65 Murrayfield Gardens, EH12 6DL

Christian Community   (pp.29–30)
21 Napier Road, EH10 5AZ
031 2298093

Baha'i   (p.83)
19a Drumdryan Street
031 2294442

Church of Scientology   (pp.134–7)
20 South Bridge, EH1
031 5565074

Divine Light Mission   (pp.53–6)
22 Pilrig Street
031 5549127

Encounter Group   (pp.228–9)
Ann J. Thompson,
153 Dalkeith Road, EH16 5HQ
Affiliated with Sempervivum Trust
031 6672833

**Edinburgh College of
Parapsychology**
2 Melville Street

**Group Relations Training
Association**
Mona MacDonald,
Dept Extra Mural Studies
031 6671011 Ext. 6523

Kingston Clinic
Gilmerton Road
Sunday evening meditation classes

Krishna Consciousness Movement
          (pp.51–3)
Radha Krishna Temple,
14 Forrest Road
031 2254797

Mormon Church   (pp.30–5)
30 Colinton Road
031 3375825

Netherbow Centre
Rev. Gordon Strachan,
High Street, Edinburgh
Church of Scotland Centre with
lively interest in experimental and
creative arts

**Scottish Association of Spiritual
Healers**
2 Melville Street

Sempervivum Trust (pp.228–9)
Catherine Gillespie,
15 Falkland Gardens, EH12 6UW
031 3347175

Society of Friends (pp.26–9)
28 Stafford Street
031 2254825

Spiritual Regeneration Movement
(pp.62–4)
18 Buccleuch Place
031 6676933

Teilhard Centre (pp.127–8)
Tessa Stiven,
154 Craiglea Drive, EH10 5PU

Theosophical Society (pp.110–12)
28 Great King Street
031 5565385

Fife

Wellbank Trust
Westbank, Strathmigle, Fife
Healing and Metaphysical groups
Director: Major Bruce
MacMannaway

Glasgow

Ammadiyya Muslim Mission
152 Nithdale Road, G14
041 4235089

Anthroposophical Society (p.115)
Mrs M. Coia, 1 Kelvinside Terrace
West, N.W. Glasgow

Association of Spiritualists
6 Somerset Place, G3
041 3320435

Baha'i (p.83)
12 Johnstone Drive, Rutherglen
041 6470443

British Homeopathic Society (p.195)
Homeopathic Hospital,
1000 Gt Western Road

Bridges
102 Byres Road, G12
Contact: Max Magee.
041 3343193
Open afternoon and evening for
healing, discussion and meditation.
Experimental work in altered states
of consciousness

Divine Light Mission (pp.53–6)
79 Overdale Drive, Langside
041 6494828

**Centre for Cross Cultural
Communication**
David Mearns, Dept Social
Psychology, Jordanhill College of
Education G13 1PP
041 9591232

Encounter Group
Maria Campbell, 10 Cecil Street,
W2
041 3397887
Affiliated with Sempervivum Trust
(pp.228–9)

Scottish Homeopathic Supplies
203 Buchanan Street

Sri Chinmoy (pp.58–60)
Tom McGrath, The Arts Centre,
342 Sauchiehall Street

Theosophical Society (pp.110–12)
17 Queens Crescent
041 3325160

Inverness

Baha'i (p.83)
22 Swanston Avenue
0463 38629

Findhorn Foundation (pp.131–4)
The Park, Findhorn Bay, Forres,
Moray
IV36 QTY
03093 311

Orkney

Baha'i   (p.83)
Carmel, New Scapa Road, Kirkwall
0856 2911

Stirling

Beshara   (pp.84–6)
Martin McCrae,
46 Culten Hove Road, St Ninians

Divine Light Mission   (pp.53–6)
Enquire at University Union

Spiritualist Church
27 King Street

Index

Rajneesh Meditation Centre, 60–2, 251, 265
Ramakrishna Vedanta Centre, 73–4, 251
Ramana Health Centre, 267
Reich, Wilhelm, 218, 225, 230, 244, 265
Reichian journal, 259
Reichian therapy, 243
retreats, 41–3
Rose-Neil, Sidney, 200, 201, 202
Rosicrucians, 141, 269
Rudhyar, Dane, 165
Ruhani Satsang, 269, 275

Sai Baba, Sathya, 56–8, 251
Sai Baba, Shirdi, 49, 50, 57
Sai-Hindu Centre, 49–50, 251
St Austell Spiritualist Society, 271
St Barnabus Counselling Centre, 268
Saltings Caravan Site, 267
Samye-Ling Tibetan Centre, 104–5, 253
Sangharakshita, Ven., 100–1
Sati Society, 95–6, 252
Saunders Bookshop, 271
School of Economic Science, 255
School of Intensive Esoteric Studies, 86, 252
School of Meditation, 64, 251
Science and Health, 35, 36–7
Science of Creative Intelligence, 62, 64
Science of Mind, 40–1, 250, 263, 268
Science of Thought Review, 255
Scientology, Church of, 134–7, 254, 263, 277
Scottish Association of Spiritual Healers, 277
Seed Group Project, 162
Seekers' Trust, 250
Self and Society, 246
Self Health Centre, 265
Self-Realisation Fellowship, 70–2, 251
self-regulation, 271
sensitives, 175, 178; *see also* mediums
Sempervivum Trust, 228-9, 259, 277
Shah, Idries, 90–1, 252
Shantock Coach House, 267
Sherborne House, 124–5, 254
Shivapuri Baba, 124
Shree Gurudev Ashram, 269
Sidmouth House, 271
Sikh Cultural Society, 75–6, 251
Sikh Missionary Society, 76, 251
Sikhism, 74–6
Sivananda Yoga Centre, 263
Smith, M., 269
Society for Psychical Research, 172–4, 256
Society for the Preservation of Glastonbury Zodiac, 255
Society for Spreading the Knowledge of True Prayer, 269
Society of Friends, 26–9, 249, 278
Society of Herbalists, 197, 257
Society of Osteopaths, 193

Society of the Inner Light, 263
Soil Association, 255
somatography, 205, 210–11
South Place Ethical Society, 261
Speakers International Agency, 255
Sphere Club Spiritual Foundation, 270
Spiritual healing, 37, 147, 153, 182, 186, 192–3, 211–15
Spiritual Regeneration Movement, 64, 251, 261, 263, 265, 266, 278
Spiritual Truth Foundation, 187
spiritualism, 171–2, 176–87
Spiritualist Association, 178–80, 256
Spiritualist Church, 279
Spiritualists' National Union, 180–2, 256
S.R.F., 70–2, 251
Sri Aurobindo, 67–9, 251, 275
Sri Chinmoy, 58–60, 251, 273, 278
Sri Ramakrishna, 72
Steiner, Rudolf, 30, 110, 113–15
Stonehenge, 141, 156–7
Subud, 61, 78–81, 124, 252
Sufi Cultural Centre, 88–9, 252
Sufi dancing, 263
Sufi Group, 267, 268, 269
Sufi methods, influence of, 124
Sufi Movement, 88–9, 252
Sufi Order, 86–8, 252
Sufi Society, 90, 252
Sufism, 83–91
Sunnyhill Fellowship, 17
Swami Bhavyananda, 73
Swaminarayan Hindu Mission, 50–1, 251
Swanlands, 268
Swedenborg, Emmanuel, 43–5
Swedenborg Society, 45, 250
Swyre Farm, 85–6, 252

Tai Chi Chuan, 93–4, 223, 225, 227, 228, 241
Tai-Do, 223, 225, 241
tantric yoga, 62, 77
Tarot, 138, 144, 228, 242
Teilhard Centre, 126–8, 254, 278
Terrace, the, 265
Theosophical Bookshop, 253
Theosophical Society, 110–12, 113, 114, 117, 253, 271, 273, 274, 278
Theravada School of Buddhism, 263
3HO Foundation, 76–8, 252
Throssel Hole Priory, 106–7, 253
Tibetan Meditation Centre, 104–5
T.M., 62–4, 251
Torc, 158, 255
transactional analysis, 223, 225, 236–8, 242
Transactional Association, 237, 242, 259
Transcendental Meditation, 62–4
Trevelyan, Sir George, 159, 160
Triangles, 116, 118, 119, 254
Trungpa, Chogyam, 104
Truth Forum, 264

285

Please send cheque or postal order (no currency), and allow 18p for the first book plus 8p per copy for each additional book ordered up to a maximum charge of 66p in U.K.

Customers in Eire and B.F.P.O. please allow 18p for the first book plus 8p per copy for the next 6 books, thereafter 3p per book.

Overseas customers please allow 20p for the first book and 10p per copy for each additional book.